Aulikki Nahkola
Double Narratives in the Old Testament

Beihefte zur Zeitschrift für die alttestamentliche Wissenschaft

Herausgegeben von
Otto Kaiser

Band 290

Walter de Gruyter · Berlin · New York
2001

Aulikki Nahkola

Double Narratives in the Old Testament

The Foundations of Method in Biblical Criticism

Walter de Gruyter · Berlin · New York
2001

∞ Printed on acid-free paper which falls within the guidelines of the ANSI
to ensure permanence and durability.

Die Deutsche Bibliothek — CIP-Einheitsaufnahme

Nahkola, Aulikki:
Double narratives in the Old Testament : the foundations of method
in biblical criticism / Aulikki Nahkola. — Berlin ; New York :
de Gruyter, 2001
(Beihefte zur Zeitschrift für die alttestamentliche Wissenschaft ;
Bd. 290)
Zugl.: Oxford, Univ., Diss., 1998
ISBN 3-11-016731-X

Printed in Germany
Cover design: Christopher Schneider, Berlin
Printing and binding: Hubert & Co., Göttingen

Äidilleni
Isäni muistolle

Preface

The patterns of duplication and repetition in biblical narrative first caught my attention while researching for a Master's thesis at Kings College, London. Since then I have been fascinated by both the literary patterns themselves and above all their significance to the development of method in biblical scholarship. Having looked at one doublet in my Master's thesis, the "incidents of violence" in Genesis 19 and Judges 19, I felt that what was most essential in them could not be understood by looking at any one example in detail, but perhaps better by attempting to comprehend the phenomenon of double narratives as a whole. Hence the topic for my doctoral dissertation, which I submitted to the University of Oxford in 1998 and which, with only minor revisions, this book represents.

This work is by no means exhaustive – several areas of double narratives still await exploration. However, what this undertaking has impressed me with more than anything else is the importance of understanding the intellectual context in which Old Testament methodology developed: although double narratives themselves have remained in the focus of each successive critical approach to emerge, the *Sitz im Leben* in which they have done so, and the critical assumptions that go with it, have changed. The study of the development of method in Old Testament scholarship is perhaps as much the study of the context of the scholarship as it is of the biblical traditions that it debates. My hope for the future, therefore, is to see increasing engagement between biblical studies and disciplines with which it shares its intellectual roots, such as folkloristics and genre criticism, and to see the advances in these disciplines utilised to the benefit of biblical studies.

At the end of a long project such as this I have many people to thank for their help and support. First and foremost, I am deeply grateful to Professor John Barton, who supervised my work on doctoral level and whose generous and astute counsel has been readily available also during the preparation of this book. I would also like to thank Dr. Ernest Nicholson, who started me on this project and Rev. Richard Coggins, with whom some of the original storming of ideas took place. My thanks also goes to Wolfson College, Oxford, which has provided me with an excellent academic and social habitat, both while a doctoral student and now as a member of the College, and to Newbold College, Bracknell, for a study leave, which instigated this research, and a sabbatical during which it was completed. Finally, I particularly also wish to express my gratitude to Professor Otto Kaiser, who accepted this work for publication in BZAW.

The support of family and friends over the many years that this research has taken place has been invaluable. My deepest gratitude!

January 25, 2001   Aulikki Nahkola

Abbreviations

AEASH	*Acta Ethnographica Academiae Scientiarum Hungaricae*
BWANT	Beiträge zur Wissenschaft vom Alten und Neuen Testament
BZAW	Beihefte zur Zeitschrift für die Alttestamentliche Wissenschaft
CBQ	*Catholic Biblical Quarterly*
FRLANT	Forschungen zur Religion und Literatur des Alten und Neuen Testaments
HTR	*Harvard Theological Review*
HUCA	*Hebrew Union College Annual*
JBL	*Journal of Biblical Literature*
JDT	Jahrbuch für Deutsche Theologie
JFI	*Journal of the Folklore Institute*
JSOT	*Journal for the Study of the Old Testament*
NLH	*New Literary History*
RB	*Revue biblique*
RHPR	*Revue d'histoire et de philosophie religieuses*
SAT	Die Schriften des Alten Testaments
SEÅ	*Svensk exegetisk årsbok*
SFQ	*Southern Folklore Quarterly*
TBAT	Theologische Bücherei, Altes Testament
UUÅ	Uppsala universitets årsskrift
VT	*Vetus Testamentum*
VTS	*Vetus Testamentum,* Supplement Series
ZAW	*Zeitschrift für die Alttestamentliche Wissenschaft*

Table of Contents

Introduction

Double narratives were first recognised as a potentially important phenomenon for the understanding of biblical composition in the seventeenth century. It was the observation that similar stories (such as David sparing Saul's life in 1 Sam. 24 and 26) were repeated in different books or different parts of the same book, or that there were differing reports of the same event (such as the two Creation accounts) that led early biblical critics, most prominently Spinoza, Simon and Astruc, to question the prevailing view of pentateuchal authorship and to formulate the rudiments of a documentary hypothesis of the Pentateuch. Since then double narratives have played a key role in the formation of every major approach to Old Testament criticism, and many of the minor ones. Double narratives remain as the single most controversial feature of the Old Testament text, yet one which to date has not been studied comprehensively as a phenomenon.

The purpose of this book is to investigate the role double narratives have had in the development of Old Testament criticism, especially in terms of how they have contributed to the formulation of critical methodology. What is of particular importance here is to identify the critical assumptions – mainly relating to how compositional processes are perceived – which have been attached to the doublets in the Old Testament, and to find a conceptual framework and a realm of scholarship within which these assumptions can be explored, even assessed to an extent for their validity. It will also be suggested here that crucial as double narratives have been for Old Testament criticism, the phenomenon remains inadequately defined, and therefore, I will argue, only partially understood. Establishing ways of comprehending the extent and complexity of the double narrative phenomenon is thus a priority for this present research.

These issues will be addressed in four chapters. Chapter 1 traces the role of double narratives in the rise and development of Old Testament criticism. As the nature and extent of the double narrative phenomenon in the Old Testament became better understood in the eighteenth and nineteenth centuries, the theory of documents underlying the biblical traditions, first suggested by Astruc, was refined and elaborated on, until finally articulated by Graf and Wellhausen as the Four Document Hypothesis in the 1880's. In the ensuing attempt to establish the exact limits of the pentateuchal sources doublets came under intense scrutiny. This eventually led to a discovery of weakness in the use of duplication as a criterion for source division, stemming, at least with hindsight, from the lack of definition for the phenomenon: the more meticulously the criterion of duplication was enforced, the more the integrity of the four pentateuchal documents was undermined.

Partly because of the methodological crisis that followed – one that biblical criticism still has not totally resolved – but also because of the changing intellectual climate in which biblical scholarship was pursued, a new way of understanding double narratives arose and was formulated by Gunkel at the turn of the twentieth century as the form-critical and tradition-historical hypothesis of the oral origin and transmission of the early Israelite traditions. Without apparent conflict most Old Testament scholars now seemed to be able to support two critical premises which, this book will argue, are largely incompatible: namely that, on the one hand, duplication in the biblical narrative indicates the presence of literary documents, on the other oral composition and transmission.

The dominance of the heterogeneous compositional models that had monopolized biblical criticism since its beginnings only finally came under attack in a comprehensive and sustained way in the mid-twentieth century, as literary-critical methods developed in the study of secular literature were applied by scholars, such as Robert Alter, to the biblical narrative and doublets were interpreted as indicators of literary artistry, arguing that biblical compositions were more unified than previously thought. Besides this "new" literary approach to biblical criticism other homogeneous ways for the interpretation of the doublet phenomenon were suggested, if more sporadically, by Umberto Cassuto's "theological-intention" model and Samuel Sandmel's model of inner-biblical midrash.

Although the survey of double narrative scholarship in chapter 1 reveals a basic division between approaches that juxtapose the origins of the double narrative phenomenon as either heterogeneous or homogeneous, it is of some significance that none of the critical approaches in question advocate a totally unified concept of biblical composition, but assume, or admit to, at least some amount of heterogeneity of authorship in relation to the presence of doublets in the biblical record.

Chapter 2 approaches the issue of critical methodology from the point of view of the identification of the conceptual models which are attached to double narratives by the main critical approaches and which underline their compositional hypotheses. Three main models are suggested, namely the "nature" model, the "historian", and the "literary artist", formative for the scholarship of Spinoza, Wellhausen and Alter, respectively. The assessment that is attempted in this chapter will be in terms of evaluating how each of the models reflects its wider intellectual framework and contemporary background: the rationalistic philosophy of Spinoza and the dawning scientific consciousness of the early Enlightenment, the nineteenth-century German historiography and literary critical scholarship of the time of Wellhausen, and the "Bible as literature" approach and modern poetics in the case of Alter and the new literary criticism. An intermediate model, the "archivist-historian", is proposed for the groundbreaking biblical critical work of Simon and Astruc during the heyday of the Enlightenment. What emerges uppermost from this chapter is the indebtedness of biblical criticism in general, and the models for the interpretation of double narratives in particular, to the intellectual context of Old Testament scholarship, and consequently the possibilities offered by, and the need for, interdisciplinary research in the pursuit of a clearer understanding of critical method.

The question of whether – and if so how – it might be possible to evaluate the validity of any of the claims supporting the notion that double narratives are indicators of compositional origins of biblical narrative, will be addressed in Chapter 3. The critical tenet that comes under scrutiny here is that "duplication indicates oral origin and transmission of biblical narrative", central to both form-critical and tradition-historical approaches. I will argue that in his formulation of this thesis Gunkel was indebted to, as well as pioneering in, contemporary folklore research, in which the historical-geographical method was beginning to dominate. As folkloristics has in the past century become a major field of scholarship, the concepts of narrative orality held by Gunkel and many of his contemporaries will be assessed in terms of more recent advances in folklore scholarship. Of particular interest here are the so called "epic laws", which were brought to the attention of Old Testament scholars by Gunkel and which have remained one of the most contentious aspects of form-critical and tradition-historical research, debated most prominently in recent decades by Klaus Koch and John Van Seters. Having traced the roots of these laws and the circumstances in which they originated I will argue for the limited benefit of the use of either the "epic", or other oral or literary, laws in the study of biblical double narratives, not necessarily because of any intrinsic unsoundness in the concept of such laws, but because of the relative paucity of variants in the Old Testament, which undermines any serious application of these laws.

One of the main difficulties in the study of double narratives, whether in terms of methodology or as part of Old Testament literature in need of interpretation, is the lack of adequate terminology to address the phenomenon, or even to comprehend its extent. While the terms "double narrative", "doublet" and "variant" are easily recognizable to anyone in the field of Old Testament scholarship, there are no universal definitions for the terms or even consensus on what actually constitutes the duplication indicated by them: the terms have been used as rather broad and overlapping labels for varying accounts of the presumed same event (Creation), strikingly similar accounts of what are portrayed as separate events (David sparing Saul's life), or the conflation of similar accounts (Flood). The aim of Chapter 4 is to demonstrate the complexity of the double narrative phenomenon in the Old Testament and to find ways of describing it which would do justice to its multifarious nature, without sacrificing continuity with how doublets have been historically dealt with in Old Testament scholarship. I will attempt to do this first of all by proposing a double narrative "chart", which illustrates the wide spectrum of the kinds of duplications that have been perceived as doublets in Old Testament scholarship, and suggests more finely differentiated terminology for the treatment of the phenomenon than has previously been the case.

Another area of particular interest in Chapter 4 is the interface between what have traditionally been categorized as literary, as opposed to textual, variants: that is, the question of what is needed to constitute a variant of one type or the other. This area will be investigated particularly with reference to the textual-critical work of Shemaryahu Talmon, which, this thesis will argue, suggests that there is a previously little studied overlap between what literary critics regard as double narratives and what in textual criticism have been classified as textual variants.

This book is not aiming to propose a new theory for the presence of double narratives in the Old Testament – although it does strongly suggest that a more satisfactory solution to the problem of doublets might be found, not in the exclusion of any of the existing approaches, but in a synthesis of them. The phrase "foundations of method in biblical criticism" in the title underlines the analytical nature of the current research. The purpose of this research is to contribute to the discussion of how biblical methodology is formulated, both by providing what I hope is a deeper understanding of how Old Testament methodology has developed in the past, in particular in relation to one of its central features, the double narratives, but also by promoting new debate in the area of how biblical criticism is indebted to conceptual models and its intellectual context. The positive contribution this work aims to make is thus first of all to suggest possible ways of assessing some of the tenets that have been most formative in the development of biblical methodology, such as that in the biblical narrative "duplication indicates sources", by considering them from the point of view of their intellectual history. In the case of the concept of double narratives as oral variants and the use of epic, or other oral/literary, laws to determine their relative originality, detailed assessment is actually attempted with the help of folkloristics and its development as a discipline.

Perhaps most specifically this book aims to make a contribution by proposing, as a first attempt, a more precise way of identifying the character of the double narrative phenomenon than has so far been the case, by means of a double narrative chart and accompanying terminology, intended to inject some methodological rigour into the discussion of the phenomenon. Similarly the recourse to the work of Talmon aims at calling attention to a previously uninvestigated possibility of widening the remit of double narrative studies: a potential interface between textual and literary criticism.

The phenomenon of double narratives is not confined to the Old Testament alone and variants to Old Testament stories can be found elsewhere in ancient Near Eastern corpora, as well as in later extra-biblical literature. Similarly, it is generally recognized in biblical scholarship that a parallel phenomenon exists in the New Testament in the form of the Synoptic Problem. Furthermore, literatures as diverse as the Homeric or Finno-Ugric epics, Icelandic sagas, Koran and the English novel have at times been seen as "parallel enough" to the Old Testament to be resorted to as models for the understanding of its phenomenon of doublets. While it has not been possible to address these issues within this book, I hope to pursue them in a separate work, thus widening the discussion to take into consideration these wider dimensions of the double narrative question. Similarly, I have tended to avoid examining within the Old Testament the material provided by the synoptic relationship of the books of Samuel, Kings and Chronicles, as this has already been the subject of some considerable research.

Chapter 1: Double Narratives in the Rise and Development of Biblical Criticism

1.1. Early Biblical Criticism

As early in critical literature as Spinoza's *Tractatus Theologico-Politicus*, 1670 (ET 1862), double narratives are observed as a phenomenon significant for the understanding of the composition of the Pentateuch. Spinoza points out how in the Five Books of Moses "one and the same story is often met with again and again, and occasionally with very important differences in the incidents" (117, ET 1862:189). This, together with the fact that narrative is "jumbled together" with precept, without order or regard to time, should lead the reader to the conclusion that "in the Pentateuch we have merely notes and collections to be examined at leisure, materials for history rather than the digested history itself" (Spinoza 117, ET 1862:189). Spinoza goes on to suggest that in "the seven books which remain, down to the destruction of Jerusalem" (Joshua, Judges, Ruth, 1-2 Samuel and 1-2 Kings), the same characteristics appear as in the Pentateuch and the same manner of composition can be assumed (117, ET 1862:189). The two records of Joshua's death and burial (Josh. 24 and Judg. 2:6ff) are examples of double narratives in Joshua and Judges and witness to collation of sources in the historical books. Again in 1 Samuel, Spinoza suggests, the story of David's introduction to Saul's court in chapters 17 and 18 must have been "taken from another record, in which a cause is assigned for David's frequenting the palace of Saul very different" from that mentioned in chapter 16 (117, ET 1862:190). The same can be suspected of the stories where David spares Saul's life in 1 Sam. 24 and 26 (Spinoza 117-8, ET 1862:190).

A work that was to become more influential for subsequent biblical criticism than Spinoza's was published almost a decade later: Richard Simon's *Histoire critique du Vieux Testament*, 1678 (ET 1682). Simon's work appears to be an apology for the authority of Scripture, which he feels

Spinoza had attacked.[1] Interestingly, Simon's concept of how the Pentateuch was put together does not in fact differ that much from Spinoza's. What is different is that Simon justifies variations and discrepancies on the basis that "the Authors...having had the Power of writing Holy Scriptures had also the Power of correcting *(reformer)* them" (Preface * 3, ET Preface a 2).

For the presence of repetitions in the biblical narrative Simon has several explanations. First of all repetitions arose from the fact that the Bible as we have it now is "only an abridgement of the Acts *(des Actes)*" which originally were "preserv'd intire in the Registery of the Republick" (Preface * 6, ET Preface a 4). In the process of abridgement "many repetitions of the same things" may have been preserved as they did not seem to those "who joyn'd together the ancient Records *(Mémoires)*" "altogether superfluous, because they serv'd for explanation" and therefore it was "thought not fit to leave them wholly out" (Preface ** 1, ET Preface a 6). Some repetition is also due to the fact that "the Hebrews were not very polite *(polis)* writers", but usually "transpos'd, or repeated the same thing", and sometimes only began one matter and then "on a sudden" went to another, only later to "reassume their former discourse" (Simon Preface ** 1, ET Preface a 6-7). "A good part" of duplication, on the other hand, Simon contends, may also be attributed to the "Genius of the Hebrew tongue", for Hebrew is "a very plain Language, and repeats often the same thing by different terms" (1:38, ET 1:40).

Simon also comments on the opinion of some Jewish Rabbis that when Ezra collected the Scriptures he made use of some copies that were "faulty", *defectüeux,* this now resulting in the fact that "in some places" in the Bible "the sense remains imperfect, and in others there are repetitions of the same thing" (1:29, ET 1:30). He expresses scepticism concerning this idea and suggests that the blame could be given to Jewish "Transcribers", *Copistes,*[2] instead (1:31, ET 1:32). Finally Simon proposes a more mechanical solution. Repetition, he argues, could have been caused simply by the ancient way of book making: the Bible was written on "little Scrolls or separate sheets that were sow'd together" and the order of these could have been changed (1:38-9, ET 1:40).[3]

---

1   See Preface * 3, ET Preface a 2 (asterisks used as part of pagination). What value such apologies have at a time when novel religious ideas often had severe repercussions, is, of course, debatable. See e.g. Strauss 1973:22-37.

2   The ET also renders this word as "Translators" (Simon 1:29, ET 1:30).

3   Or even "upon little leaves", *sur des petites feuilles,* that were only rolled "upon a little Roller", *petit bâton,* without any sewing at all (Simon Preface * 6-**, ET Preface a 6).

Simon is not very specific as to what he means by repetitions – anything from a simple gloss or variation in wording[4] to extensive duplication in narratives such as the Flood story and the two Creation stories seems to qualify (I:35-40, ET I:37-41). He does, however, make a distinction between repetitions that occur within one chapter and "recapitulation", *recapitulation*,[5] i.e. repetitions that arise "when the same thing is repeated in different places" (I:38, ET I:39-40). The explanation of this second type, Simon observes, is particularly "hard" as these repetitions occur with "some changes, that make one believe they are different things, although for the most part it is one and the same thing differently expressed in several places" (I:38, ET I:40).

Some passages, such as the Flood story, Simon does reflect on in more detail, singling out many repetitious elements, such as the number of animals entering the ark and the destruction of all flesh because of wickedness (1:36, ET 1:37-8). While on the whole Simon argues that pentateuchal repetitions do not stem from Moses, whom he regards as the author of much, but not all, of the work, some of the repetition in the Flood story, particularly concerning commands given to Noah by God, Simon does, however, credit to Moses himself. These repetitions, Simon argues, Moses included "to shew the faithfull execution of the Commandment" he had received from God (Preface ** 1, 1:37-8, ET Preface a 6, 1:39).

Both Spinoza's and Simon's work is reflected in Jean Astruc's *Conjectures*, 1753.[6] But what Spinoza had vaguely called "notes" and "materials" and Simon "ancient acts" or "records", Astruc, limiting his discussion to Genesis and the first two chapters of Exodus, now designates as the "documents", *Mémoires*, which Moses made use of in the composition of these works.[7] That different names of God point to different documents is

---

4   See e.g. Ex. 16:35 (Simon 1:37, ET 1:39).

5   Simon acknowledges his indebtedness to Augustine for the use this term (1:38, ET 1:40).

6   See esp. pp. 439, 452, 453 for Spinoza, whom Astruc attempts to refute, and 7 and 476-77 for Simon. However, Astruc did not seem to be aware of the work of Witter, 1711, which anticipated some of Astruc's conclusions but seems to have been forgotten by biblical criticism until "discovered" in the 1920's (see Bray 240-1; Knight 1975:55-7; O'Doherty 301n13).

7   As suggested by the title of Astruc's book: *Conjecture sur les Mémoires originaux don't il paroit que Moyse s'est servi pour composer le Liver de la Genèse*. See also Astruc 16. Astruc seems to have got the term *Mémoires* from Simon, who uses it rather casually as an alternative to "ancient Actes", *anciens Actes*. In the ET of Simon's work the term is translated as "Records", or simply ignored, when it occurs together with "Acts", *Actes* (see Simon Preface * 6-** 1, ET Preface a 5-a 6).

Astruc's real discovery, that repetition of narratives does so is, as we have seen, already implicit in the works of earlier scholars. It may, however, be noteworthy that Astruc's "first proof", *Premiére preuve*, as he unravels his arguments for Moses' use of documents, is "from repetition", and only the second one "from the names of God" (10).[8]

Astruc devotes two substantial sections of his work to discussing various repetitions and their causes. His list of examples includes the Creation story, various aspects of the Flood story, the alliance of Jacob and Laban, as well as the genealogy of Shem (Astruc 360-5). Details of these duplications are worked out both in the text and in his division of Genesis into four columns, representing two main documents and several minor ones[9] — an undertaking that takes up a major part of the *Conjectures*. However, not all repetitions in Genesis, in Astruc's opinion, can be attributed to Moses' use of documents: some must be accredited to other causes. As such causes Astruc mentions marginal notes, the poverty of the Hebrew language, civil formulas of politeness, and emphasis (10, 366-7).

Eichhorn's *Einleitung ins Alte Testament*, 3 vols, 1780-83,[10] developed and refined Astruc's ideas and incorporated them into the wider contemporary scholarly debate. For Eichhorn, too, repetition in Genesis is a proof that the book has been put together from pieces of two different historical works[11] (II:264). The prime example of such piecing together, or that a story gets "told twice", *doppelt erzählt,* is again the Flood narrative, which then comes under Eichhorn's scrutiny (II:264).

The Flood, however, is not the only example Eichhorn gives of double narratives in Genesis. Lot's flight from Sodom and rescue are also notified twice, in Gen. 19:1-28 and 29-30 (II:270). The appearance of visitors to Abraham, a year before Isaac's birth, is told in ch. 17, then retold in ch. 18, though "mit einem eigenen Ton" (Eichhorn II:270). Traces of double narratives can also be detected in the story of Laban and Jacob, Gen. 31:48-

---

8   Astruc also presents two further "proofs", which arise from comparisons within sections of Genesis indicated by the two different names of God, and from anachronisms and inconsistencies (13, 16).

9   Besides the "Elohim" and "Jehovah" *Mémoires* Astruc also proposes ten or so other documents Moses may have had at his disposal, consisting of passages such as the rape of Dinah, the history of Lot and his daughters, the marriage of Esau, and the triplications in the Flood narrative, but the existence of these, Astruc argues, is far more "conjectural" (308-22).

10   References here are to the 1787 second, enlarged edition.

11   "Aus Stücken zweyer besonderen historischen Werke."

54, while double genealogies are present in Gen. 10 and 11:10ff (Eichhorn II:270).

Repetition of this kind, Eichhorn claims, could not have originated either from chance or inexperience in the art of storytelling (II:267). Sometimes something gets told twice even in history books, Eichhorn contends, but a "hypothesis of chance", *Hypothese eines Zufalls,* could not be suggested for a phenomenon as widespread as what we have in Genesis (Eichhorn II:267). Eichhorn also reflects on the nature of repetitions found in the biblical narrative. One usually finds in repetitions "eine genaue Ordnung, eine gute und natürliche Gedankenfolge"[12] (II:268). Occasionally, in two stories, "ist die Gedankenreihe dieselbe, bisweilen ist sie etwas verändert, oder wohl gar umgekehrt; aber immer ist sie im zweyten Fall nicht bloss möglich, sondern auch eben so gut wie im ersten"[13] (Eichhorn II:268).

Besides the book of Genesis Eichhorn deals quite extensively with the relationship of the books of Samuel to the first book of Chronicles. He points to David's "double biography", *doppelte Lebensbeschreibung,* one in Samuel, the other in Chronicles, and observes how "die letztere schränkt sich bloss auf David als König ein; die erstere geht auch in sein Privatleben zurück"[14] (II:451-2). In this "harmony", *Harmonie,* of biographies, Eichhorn observes, there is not only likeness of content and similarity of framework, but also verbal resemblance (Eichhorn II:452). These similarities and dissimilarities of the Samuel-Chronicles narrative can best be explained on the basis of a common source, *Quelle,* rather than Chronicles' borrowing from the books of Samuel (Eichhorn II:463).

A further contribution to the study of double narratives was made by de Wette's *Lehrbuch der historisch-kritischen Einleitung in die Bibel Alten und Neuen Testamentes,* 2 vols, 1817.[15] Though holding somewhat different views on the composition of the Pentateuch, de Wette acknowledges Eichhorn's work and, on the issue of repetitions, quotes it extensively.

---

12 "A good and natural order of thought."
13 "The sequence of thought is the same, occasionally it is somewhat changed, or almost turned around, but always in the second instance not only possible, but also as good as in the first one."
14 "The latter restricts itself to David as king; the former also encompasses his private life."
15 The edition used here is the 1833 revised and enlarged fourth edition. In 1843 the fifth, revised and enlarged, edition of vol. 1 was translated into English and enlarged, in 2 volumes, by Theodore Parker. This work, however, differs to a substantial degree from de Wette's 1833 edition and is not used here for translation.

De Wette's research in the area of duplications takes two main directions. First of all he expands the discussion on parallels to include all the narrative sections of the Old Testament and, in fact, laws and poetry as well. Utilizing an outline already suggested by Eichhorn, he draws up a comprehensive list of narrative, as well as genealogical, legal, poetic, prophetic etc. parallels in the Old Testament, highlighting in particular the correspondence between 1-2 Samuel and 1-2 Kings, on the one hand, and 1-2 Chronicles, Isaiah, Jeremiah, and Ezra on the other (de Wette I:236-8, Eichhorn I:276-80).[16] In the area of the Pentateuch de Wette, too, arranges E and J passages into parallel columns (I:193ff).

De Wette's work deals with the large outlines of Old Testament parallelism and composition and does not discuss any doublets in great detail. However, he does single out some doublets individually. For instance, regarding 1 Sam. 16-17, David's introduction to Saul's court, de Wette points out how it is obvious that the accounts do not agree with each other, concluding therefore that "das Stück XVII. ist also aus zwei oder mehrern Bestandtheilen zusammengesetzt"[17] (I:227-8). In the stories of David's sparing of Saul's life in 1 Sam. 24 and 26, on the other hand, "dieselbe Begebenheit doppelt, nur verschieden, erzählt zu seyn scheine"[18] (de Wette I:228).

The second contribution de Wette makes is an attempt to find a hermeneutical perspective for duplication. He suggests that the development of narratives in the "theocratical-historical" books,[19] Genesis-Joshua, Chronicles, Ruth, Ezra, Nehemiah and Esther, was a progressive one in which historical events and human motives were gradually transferred to divine and miraculous causes in a shift to "theocratical pragmatism" (I:177ff). Thus some parallel stories would include a "natural" account and a "miraculous" one, the human guidance requested by Moses in Num. 10:29-32 being an example of the former, the divine guidance provided by Yahweh in Num. 9:15-23 of the latter (de Wette I:183-4).

---

16 See also de Wette ET I:506-8.
17 "Chapter 17 is therefore put together from two or more components."
18 "The same incident seems to be told in a double form, but differently each time."
19 "Theokratisch historische Bücher."·

1.2. Source Criticism: Wellhausen

The work of Julius Wellhausen is often seen as the culmination of Old Testament critical scholarship of the previous two centuries. In the realm of double narratives it is certainly true that in his book *Prolegomena zur Geschichte Israels*, 1883[20] (ET 1885), we find the fullest treatment of the topic yet seen.[21] Wellhausen's aim in this book is to discuss whether the law of Moses is "the starting-point for the history of ancient Israel, or not rather for that of Judaism" (1883:1, ET 1). In the endeavour to establish that it is the latter, Wellhausen analyses extensively the strata of narrative traditions. It is almost as a by-product of this narrative analysis that Wellhausen's study of double narratives arises.

Wellhausen starts by comparing the two parallel histories, that of the Chronicles with the books of Samuel and Kings. He contends that the difference of the spirit in the way the two histories "represent the same facts and events" arises mainly "from the influence of the Priestly Code, which came into existence in the interval" (1883:178, ET 171-2). Having established this principle Wellhausen implements it by comparing the way the life of David, and the life of Solomon, are portrayed in the two traditions. Narratives under scrutiny include such episodes as the acquisition of the kingdom by David (1 Chron. 10:1-11:3; 2 Sam. 1-3), the bringing of the ark to Jerusalem (1 Chron. 13:1ff; 2 Sam. 6) and the inheritance of the kingdom by Solomon (1 Chron. 28-9; 1 Kgs 1-2) (1883:178-189, ET 172-82).

In the life of David Wellhausen concludes that the difference between the two histories is, however, the total impression: "See what Chronicles has made out of David! The founder of the kingdom has become the founder of the temple and the public worship, the king and hero at the head of his companions in arms has become the singer and master of ceremonies at the head of a swarm of priests and Levites" (1883:189, ET 182). Wellhausen illustrates this difference in impression in individual narratives and narrative clusters, such as the above-mentioned story of David's ascent to power. He points out how in the Chronicler's narratives God takes the initiative and

---

20 The second, enlarged edition of *Geschichte Israels*, I, first published in 1878, and the basis for the English translation, *Prolegomena to the History of Israel*, 1885.

21 In principle Wellhausen's thesis about the composition of the Pentateuch is already present in his *Die Composition des Hexateuchs*, 1876-7, but in less developed form.

provides solutions: after slaying Saul, God "turned the kingdom unto David" (1883:178, ET 172). In the original Samuel-version the human aspects of David's life as a guerrilla leader and his struggle for power with Abner are prominent, and David obtains the kingdom over a lengthy period of time, involving "cunning, and treachery, and battle, and murder!" (1883:179, ET 173). What we have in Chronicles, then, Wellhausen argues, is "a deliberate and in its motives a very transparent mutilation of the original narrative" as it is found in Samuel (1883:179, ET 173). Further examples would show us that Solomon is treated much like his father – in his case, too, "the old picture is retouched", as the history of Judah is idealized in "the spirit of post-exilian Judaism" (1883:194, ET 187).[22]

After the study of these parallel histories Wellhausen goes on to look at double narratives within the Judges-Samuel-Kings tradition and finally the Hexateuch. The victory of Deborah and Barak in Judg. 4 and 5, and the two introductions of David to Saul's court (1 Sam. 16:14-23; 17), form, among many others, such doublets. In both of these pairs Wellhausen points to the tendency of the later story to dehumanize, to make the narrative more religious. Thus the campaign prepared by human means in Deborah's and Barak's song becomes the delivering act of Yahweh in the narrative of Judg. 4, as "the rich colour of the events as they occurred is bleached out of them by the one universal first cause, Jehovah" (1883:252, ET 241-2). Similarly, David meets Saul, not as one known for his "skill on the harp", but as a shepherd boy who faces Goliath and delivers a speech that approaches the tone of the post-deuteronomic times in its religious language (1883:275ff, ET 263ff).

In the section on the Hexateuch Wellhausen endeavours to disentangle the "double or threefold cord" from which Israel's tradition has been woven (1883:310, ET 295). His aim is to bring the various writings into their proper relationship with one another, and ultimately to establish the priority of the Jehovistic narrative over the Priestly Code (1883:312, ET 296). Many of the narratives that Wellhausen discusses in this section have already been treated by other scholars. Yet he manages to bring in new insights, even in the case of the Creation stories, where he observes the ways the two narratives portray man's relationship to "knowledge" and "nature", and suggests that the simpler and more natural story (Gen. 1) is not necessarily earlier than the following more complicated one, as it would be a mistake to "identify

---

22 Wellhausen points out that, in fact, "the worst discrepancy" in the representation of events by the two parallel histories is to be found in Solomon's installation as king (1883:188, ET 181).

naturalness with originality" (1883:324, ET 307). The list of double narratives Wellhausen looks at from outside Genesis is also impressive, and includes such episodes as the Exodus, the crossing of the Red Sea, Manna and the quails, the sending of the spies and the rebellion of Korah (1883:362-84, ET 342-62). Wellhausen thus marks out much of the territory within which later scholarship is to operate.

Even with the hindsight of a hundred more years of Old Testament scholarship Wellhausen's treatment of double narratives was ground-breaking and suprisingly comprehensive. Yet it is important not to lose sight of the fact that he does not, in fact, address double narratives in their own right, as a phenomenon. Rather for him, as for his predecessors, double narratives and parallel histories are an essential medium in an investigation aimed at understanding how the Pentateuch and, secondarily, the historical books of the Old Testament were composed. In Wellhausen's work the investigation reaches the stage of systematization: the *Prolegomena* sets out to argue for the lateness of the Priestly Code among the documents of the Pentateuch, the existence of which was already assumed by many scholars of the time, and for the validity of the literary clues evident in the biblical material, which point the reader to this conclusion.

The prominence of double narratives in accomplishing this task has to do with three literary assumptions fundamental to Wellhausen's understanding of the biblical narrative and intrinsic to all source-critical analysis after him. Firstly, Wellhausen contends that double narratives exist in the Pentateuch because the work is not a unified literary piece by a single author, but rather made up of several documents written at different stages of Israel's history and combined by a gradual process of redaction, "woven together in a double or threefold cord" (1883:310, ET 295). As the documents relate some of the same material of Israel's narrative and legislative tradition, the duplication of some of the individual stories and incidents becomes inevitable. The assumption underlying this argument is that a unified work by one author would not include such duplication.

Secondly, Wellhausen argues, each document bears the literary trademark of its writer and the time when it was written. J and E date from "the golden age of Hebrew literature", that is, the ninth and eighth centuries B. C., and present the material handed down by tradition "with full sympathy and enjoyment" making no claim for Mosaic authority (1883:7, 9, ET 7, 9). D, on the other hand, was composed at the time of Josiah's reform for which it was made a rule, while P is of post-exilic origin and forms the model by which "the Jews under Ezra ordered their sacred community" (1883:9, ET 8). The outlook of P, Wellhausen points out, compares with its origin: it is rich in formulae, lacks imagination and conceals its true origin for the sake of claims for Mosaic authority (1883:6-7, ET 6-7).

Though Wellhausen fully acknowledges the use of traditional, i.e. oral, material by the authors of the documents[23] he maintains that literary or stylistic characteristics – vocabulary, style, religious, ethical or aesthetic points of view – pertain only to the writer of the document and his time, while any earlier forms of the material are veiled and inaccessible.[24] It is this assertion of the determining literary importance of the author that is fundamental to the whole of Wellhausen's thesis. It is on this basis that documents can be identified and dated and, conversely, once the limits of a document have been set, the literary profiles of individual authors can be determined. And it is naturally in this task of characterization that double narratives have the centre stage, for it is in the variants of the same story that the differences between different authors stand out most clearly.

Thirdly, on the question of the interrelationship of the documents Wellhausen postulates that any agreement between the sources, such as is again most obviously manifested in doublets, is not "a matter of course, but a matter requiring explanation", the only conceivable explanation being the "literary dependence of one source on the other" (1883:311, ET 296). How this relationship of dependence is to be defined is, Wellhausen suggests, "much more pressing" a question "than is commonly assumed", yet, one that beyond the fairly obvious assumption of the dependence of P on JE and E on J,[25] falls outside the agenda of the *Prolegomena* (1883:311, ET 296). Yet Wellhausen thus highlights one of the most difficult and elusive aspects of double narrative research, and for that matter, of the development of biblical tradition as such, determining the dynamics involved in the shaping of the tradition, the contribution of composers and transmitters of the text, trademarks left by individuals and the impact of common inheritance and shared culture.

Though there is no systematic theoretical presentation of these literary principles in Wellhausen's work much of the *Prolegomena* is in fact an application of these literary insights to the biblical narrative. Thus on a certain level and almost inadvertently, the *Prolegomena* is one of the most comprehensive treatments yet written on double narratives and parallel histories.

---

23 See e.g. 1883:311, 245ff, ET 296, 326ff.
24 See e.g. 1883:177, ET 171.
25 Or both J and E on a shared hypothetical common source.

The centrality of double narratives to Wellhausen's thesis is over-whelming. Naturally, then, it is at this point that it is also most vulnerable. Were the basic premise, that doublets indicate documents, to be removed, much of the superstructure would collapse too. The possible cracks in the foundation, so to speak, are threefold. One is the basic premise itself. Maybe duplication does not indicate sources, but something completely different, such as literary artistry, as has more recently been suggested by the new literary critics? Then there is another point of vulnerability, which has to do with Wellhausen's treatment of the premise: Does he apply the criterion of double narratives comprehensively and systematically? That is, even if the pentateuchal doublets do indicate an underlying layer of sources, do they indicate *four* sources? This point has been much debated in subsequent scholarship, as will be seen below. But, finally, there is another question that has so far been all but neglected. Is there any evidence in the scholarship reviewed above that the same criteria should apply equally to all doublets? Could the decisiveness of Wellhausen's results indicate the limited understanding of the double narrative phenomenon, rather than the finality of the criteria?

1.3. Source Criticism After Wellhausen

The publication of Wellhausen's *Prolemonena* generated an enormous amount of interest in the theological world. Within a few decades of its appearance a whole genre of literature, which took the Documentary Hypothesis as its point of departure, evolved and proliferated. On the one hand interest in source-critical investigation itself persisted as the Documentary Hypothesis was refined, applied and eventually even challenged. On the other hand, and even more importantly, the Documentary Hypothesis became the basis for all subsequent Old Testament scholarship. We will look briefly at the role of double narratives in these two develop-ments.

Within source-criticism itself two main trends can be identified within which double narratives are central.[26] These relate to the integrity and extent of the sources, and to their date and interdependence.

---

26 Having originally formed a major part of the foundation on which source criticism was built, it is obvious that doublets have some role in almost all post-Wellhausenian scholarship, if only in terms of being a part of the hypothetical framework. However,

1.3.1. Integrity and Extent of Sources

Immediately after Wellhausen a great deal of scholarly energy was spent on trying to establish the exact limits of the sources and scrutinizing the criteria by which this should be done.[27] Elaborate lists of words and phrases indicative of various sources were devised.[28] An explosion of additions, divisions and subdivisions of the documents ensued. J and E were divided into two or more strands each by Budde and Procksch,[29] Eissfeldt adopted L (laysource = *Laienquelle*) for a narrative source prior to J,[30] Morgenstern postulated K (Kenite) as the "oldest" source,[31] Pfeiffer threw in S (south or Seir)[32] and von Rad used PA and PB for strands in the P source.[33] Eissfeldt, in his final summing up of the sources came close to a game of scrabble, presenting the composition of the Pentateuch as "L,J,E,B,D,H,P" (1965:239).[34]

---

much of the literature in question adds nothing new to the understanding of the double narrative phenomenon itself. We will therefore focus only on the areas where some progress of thought or methodology can be found.

27 See Fohrer 109-13; Eissfeldt 1965:166-170; North 53-9; or most recently Nicholson 1998:11ff for a more extensive summary of the developments of the period.

28 One of the last and most thorough champions of this cause was Simpson, who in *The Early Traditions of Israel*, 1948, drew up lists of more than a hundred "Hebrew words and forms characteristic of documents", the RP and a "Deuteronomic Hand" (403-17). Before him Driver had countered the criticism that the names of God were not a consistent criterion for the separation of P by postulating that "*Elohim* is but *one* out of more than *fifty* phraseological criteria alone" by which P can be distinguished from the rest of the Pentateuch (1913:xxvii).

29 See Budde 1883:455ff for J[1], J[2] and J[3], Procksch 1906:220ff for Eα, Eβ, Eγ (this division, based on the work of Sievers, is particularly interesting as there is a metric element involved in the division criteria used). Many other scholars followed with the same sigla but with important differences in the content of the documents or reasons for their separation. Thus, for instance, Smend, too, utilized J[1] and J[2] but with a meaning quite distinct from Budde's (see Eissfeldt 1965:169).

30 Or *Laienschrift,* or *Laienkodex,* for the "oldest source", *die älteste Quelle,* Eissfeldt 1922:ix-x.

31 Morgenstern 1927:4.

32 See especially Pfeiffer 1930:66-7.

33 Von Rad 1934:11-8.

34 But even that pales in comparison to Baentsch's record-breaking stratification of the priestly source as P, Ps, Ps*, Pss, Ph, Po, Pr, Px, R, Rp, with possible second and third hand and editorial refinements thrown in as Po[1], Po[1s], Po[2], Po[2s], Ph[a], Ph[b], Ph[c], Ph[s], Pr[a], Pr[s], Pr[ss], Rpo, Rpo[1], Rpo[2], Rph, Rp[s]! (Baentsch 1903).

One of the main reasons for this splitting and splicing of sources was the pursuit of the doublet criterion to its logical – or illogical – conclusion and thus the tacit perception of the phenomenon of duplication as more complex than in Wellhausen's presentation.   Mowinckel, for instance, detected duplications as minute as "rain" and "mist" in Gen. 2:5-6 and "Eden" and "East" in Gen. 2:8 (1937:8).   In textual terms the result of this was that narratives were dissected – vivisected? – into bits sometimes as small as half verses, phrases, even single words.[35]   In the methodological realm this led some, like Volz, to conclude that the four-source hypothesis had been pulverized, witnessed to by, for instance, "die kümmerlichen Brocken von Erzählungen"[36] left by Eissfeldt's analysis.[37]   Thus exactly the opposite of what had been intended had been accomplished in the attempt to demonstrate the four-document hypothesis.

Then largely as a reaction to this excessive "atomisation", the pendulum started to swing back.   Volz, for instance, proposed that in Genesis there was only one story-writer, whom he called the Yahwist, with the so-called Elohist being "at most a new editor of the great (Yahwistic) storywork"[38] (Volz 1933:13).[39]   The P-stories Volz by and large redistributed to the Yahwist.[40] Winnett, similarly, denied the existence of a continuous E-source parallel to J, finding instead in Genesis one post-exilic J-author who utilized various oral and written materials (1949:viii; 1965:18-9).   The Pentateuch itself, on the other hand, for Winnett was to be regarded as the final, partly editorial, partly authorial, work of P.[41]   Most recently, Van Seters, who has expended more energy than most on finding a credible alternative to the Documentary Hypothesis,[42] has credited the entire "pre-Priestly corpus of the Pentateuch as

---

35   See e.g. Mowinckel's summary of Gunkel's J/E-source of the Flood-story as: 2:4b-7 9-25 3:1-18 19aβ 23 24aβ 4:25-26 [....] 5:28* *ben* 29 9:20-27 (1937:13).

36   "The pitiful fragments of narratives."

37   Volz is referring here particularly to Eissfeldt's columnisation of documents in his *Hexateuch-Synopse*, 1922 (Volz 1923:390).

38   Wellhausen's JE.

39   Cited in North 57. For a concise synopsis of the development of dissenting views on the E-source, see Blenkinsopp 21-4.

40   Volz regarded P not as a "story-writer", but as "a legislator or an author of religious documents", such as Gen. 1 and 7, and at most a reviser of some J narratives (Volz 1933:13, cited in North 57).

41   Winnett saw the Pentateuch as a creation of P, who had prefixed Genesis to the Mosaic traditions of Exodus and Numbers, all of which he had supplemented, and then added to Deuteronomy, which he had detached from RD's history (1965:18, see also 1949:viii-ix).

a whole" to an authorial, creative, exilic J, a historian, who utilized a variety of Hebrew and foreign materials in "an attempt to present an account of Israel's origins as a 'vulgate' tradition"[43] (1992:328, 332).[44]

The discussion on the number and nature of pentateuchal sources has also involved another double narrative issue that came on the agenda soon after Wellhausen: the question of the extent of the duplication before the sources were brought together and combined. A "consistent parallel source hypothesis" was first proposed by Budde[45] and soon there was much support for the idea that what now appeared as disconnected strands supplementing the pentateuchal narrative had originally been continuous narratives themselves (Eissfeldt 965:181). "The existence side by side...of separate and completely preserved parallel narratives on the one hand, and of combinations of two or more parallel narratives mutilated in the process of combination on the other hand" was, Eissfeldt argued, the best evidence that what had been combined were not mere "parallel narratives which existed as individual pieces of material" but parallel strands (Eissfeldt 1965:187).[46] When Mowinckel asked this same question of the extent of the duplication in relation to the non-P material in Genesis 1-11, he concluded that there had existed "two parallel and in substance identical traditions concerning the first people in the world" (1937:14).

According to the consistent parallel source hypothesis the still existing doublets are evidence of both differences in the documents, and indirectly, the authority ascribed to the documents, as, it seems, nothing of substance could have been omitted. Where there are now no traces of duplication, the narratives, Mowinckel suggested in his study of Genesis 1-11, had been very

---

42 This search started in *Abraham in History and Tradition*, 1975, to be reviewed more thoroughly below, and has continued in three subsequent major works of 1983, 1992 and 1994.

43 That is, to present them "in a manner similar to other comparable works of ancient historiography" (Van Seters 1992:328). Van Seters uses "vulgate" instead of "canonical", because, he argues, the latter implies the recognition of a work's authority and antiquity by a much later group (1992:333n1; see also 34-8).

44 Thus, again, there is no E document as such (1992:4). The material conventionally described to E Van Seters redistributes, some ending up as J's own creation. Neither was there, in Van Seters' estimate, any other redactional layer "Dtr or otherwise, prior to the Priestly Writer" (1992:328).

45 See Mowinckel 1937:8. Mowinckel points out that, according to Budde, there were two Yahwistic sources in the "Urgeschichte", "one with, and the other without, a Flood narrative" (Mowinckel 1937:8; Budde 1883).

46 Eissfeldt suggested that there had been four parallel strands, L, J, E and P, but some other scholars worked in terms of three, even two, such strands (1965:194).

similar, almost the same, a fact that now makes the reconstruction of "hypothetical parallels" possible (1937:40-1).

Scholars reacting to the post-Wellhausenian developments in source criticism, such as Volz, Winnett and Van Seters, have viewed the existence of doublets in various ways,[47] but have generally refrained from postulating theories about the phenomenon as a whole, choosing instead to deal with individual doublets or doublets in a particular part of the tradition. For instance, in the patriarchal narratives Winnett finds three E-stories in Genesis 20-22, which form doublets with the main J-narrative in Genesis. The first two, Abraham and Sarah's visit to Abimelech and the following Flight of Hagar, are there, Winnett argues, "to counteract the unfavourable impression of Abraham created by the J story in ch. 12 (where he lies about his wife) and the J story in ch. 16 (where he callously acquiesces in Sarah's ruthless expulsion of her maid Hagar)" (1965:6). The third doublet, the treaty of Abraham and Abimelech in Beersheba Winnett, in turn, sees as a supplement by E, forming "a response to a demand from Beersheba" that it too be recognized as the "scene of some of the patriarch's activity" (1965:7). These doublets are therefore supplements in the sense of revisions, responding on the one hand to the text's already perceived authority – the text could not simply be changed – and to the "apologetic" need to upgrade Abraham's image on the other.[48]

Van Seters, in turn, in his treatment of the Paradise narrative of Genesis 2:4b-3, rejects the conventional concept that the duplications in the story[49] point either to a conflation of literary sources or a pre-literary tradition history, which has combined different creation and paradise narratives to "produce the present unified story" (1992:107-8, 117). Instead, the literary complexity of doublets and signs of disunity are, in Van Seters' estimate, the result of a late Yahwist historian's use of "variety and diversity of 'traditional' material",[50] as well as of his own creativity (1992:128). For instance, the tree of life is a theme Van Seters's Yahwist takes from

---

47 But never as evidence of three, or even two, more or less parallel narratives.

48 Winnett here echoes Sandmel's haggadic approach, discussed in detail below, which sees in these narratives "a process of neutralization by addition" and a need to "embellish and modify" (Sandmel 1961:120-1; see Winnett 1965:6).

49 Such as the "two special trees" in Gen. 2:9, and again in 2:17. 3:1ff, and 3:22 (Van Seters 1992:107-8).

50 In the case of this narrative, of Ez. 28 and Babylonian creation myths (Van Seters 1992:128).

mythology, the tree of knowledge of good and evil one he composes himself (1992:115, 125-6).[51]

The issues of the integrity and extent of the documents have been extensively debated over the years, as seen above, but without in essence enhancing our understanding of double narratives. Instead, what has become more evident through all the detailed research into sources and the criteria for distinguishing them, is the lack of a comprehensive definition for the repetition-duplication phenomenon that would recognize its multifarious nature. What this research has accomplished, however, is to point out the fragmentation of documents and the lack of scholarly consensus that followed the meticulous application of the traditional source division criteria most eminently championed by Wellhausen. Consequently, what we have in the works of Volz, Winnett and Van Seters, among others, is in fact a return to earlier, pre-Wellhausenian documentary models, such as have been with hindsight labelled the Fragment and the Supplementary Hypotheses.

1.3.2. Date and Interdependence of Sources

Finally, the questions of the date of the documents and their inter-relationship has also been of much interest since the conception of the documentary theory. The age of the documents has taken major swings since Wellhausen, from early to late, and back to somewhat earlier – and later – again. For the purposes of our present study the actual date of the documents is not as important as their relative order, which for most source critics has stood as JEDP (or equivalent), and the change of which would have to result in an almost total rethink of the use of variants in establishing documentary criteria. But for Old Testament scholarship on the whole both "knowing" this order and being able to correlate the documents with certain phases of Israel's history, has been vital.[52] This has tended to be so because much of

---

51 Van Seters is here relying on Kutsch 1977.

52 Above we have mainly focused on the debate on the nature of E and J, only to some extent P. The status of P as the last, post-exilic narrative source has remained far more secure than that of either E or J. However, recently the work of Hurvitz has suggested, mainly on linguistic grounds, an early, pre-exilic date for P (Hurvitz 1974:26, 54-6; 1988; see Blenkinsopp 238 for reaction). However, Hurvitz does not reflect on P's relationship to J (or E), and the mind-boggling implications of an early P with a late J have to remain outside our present discussion. Neither will we be able to discuss the

the research into the pentateuchal source division has not been undertaken as much from literary interest as from a need to reconstruct the religion and history of Israel. For the purpose of utilizing the religious, and other, information embedded in the sources, knowledge of their date, extent and interrelationship has been indispensable.

1.3.3. Documentary Hypothesis and Subsequent Scholarship

It is not our task here to outline all the directions the study of the Old Testament has taken since the articulation of the Documentary Hypothesis, however, it is hardly possible to overestimate its influence on them. Wellhausen's *Prolegomena* itself, followed by a host of other "traditions" and "histories" of Israel is a case in point of how the division and dating of sources has been fundamental to the reconstruction of Israel's history and religion.   But works that may have differed widely from Wellhausen's methodological notions and broken ground in different areas, still took the source-division as their basic premise or, at least, point of departure. For instance, Alt in his "God of the Fathers" took the Elohist version of Yahweh's appearance to Moses in Ex. 3 as its starting point for disentangling the roots of the traditions about the God of Abraham, Isaac and Jacob (10-2, ET 10-2). Similarly, in Noth's *History of Pentateuchal Traditions* the source division provides a fundamental structure for the enquiry into the traditions of Israel.   Westermann, in turn, deals not with the theology of the Old Testament, but with theologies of documents.[53] Again, many commentaries, such as von Rad's *Genesis*, as well as most "introductions" to the Old Testament, are fashioned on the source division – and all this besides the steady supply of works in the "Der Jahwist" vein.[54]

The significance of all this is that were the "doublets indicate sources" premise underlying this exercise to be withdrawn, many of the fundamental

---

nature of D. For a challenge to the conventional characterization of D, and a possible earlier date, see Welch 1924 and 1932, and for more recent evaluation, Nicholson 1967.

53 A good illustration of this is Westermann's reflection on the purpose of the primeval histories of J and P: "If both the Yahwist and the author of the Priestly Code begin their respective works – which aim at the history of Israel (J) and at worship in Israel (P) – with creation and primeval history, then they wish to express that the God of the people of Israel is not limited in his working by the boundaries of that people, but that he is the Lord of universal history and the Lord of the cosmos" (Westermann 87-8).

54 And now, finally and liberatedly, "Die Jahwist[in?]"!, as according to Harold Bloom 1990.

tools of Old Testament criticism and notions of its history would have to be reinvented. Thus, were the implications of, for instance, Van Seters's exilic Yahwist-historian to be fully exploited, much of Israel's history and the attendant religious beliefs would need to be reconsidered.

1.4. Form and Tradition-historical Criticism: Gunkel

A new direction for the study of Old Testament narratives was provided by the publication of Hermann Gunkel's *Genesis übersetzt und erklärt* in 1901.[55, 56] The significance of Gunkel's work in relation to double narratives stems mainly from his insight into the nature of oral tradition and the concept of the oral stage as the formative period for certain types of narratives such as the *Sage* (legend),[57] which he now claimed most of Genesis represented. For the study of double narratives as such his work has had a larger impact than that of any other single scholar before or since.

Gunkel proposed that at the time the Genesis narratives were written down they were "already very old", *uralt,* and had "a long history behind them" (1901:x1, ET 88). This history had been passed in oral transmission of "incredible fidelity", *fast unglaubliche Treue,* as we can see from, for instance, "the two variants of the legend of Rebeccah" (1901:xliv-xlv, ET

---

55   ET of the introduction was published as *The Legends of Genesis* in 1901. The whole work was not translated into English until 1997 (*Genesis*, Mercer University Press, Georgia). References here (ET) are to the 1964 slightly expanded edition of the 1901 English translation.

56   Gunkel's work, like Wellhausen's, did not appear "ex nihilo" but was anticipated by prior scholarship. The thought of an oral stage preceding the Scriptures had already been suggested by scholars such as Astruc (6,9), Eichhorn (II:246), de Wette (I:227) and Kuenen (41, ET 38), with Wellhausen himself acknowledging long, but unreliable, periods of oral transmission for certain narratives (1885:311, 345, 352-7, ET 296, 326-7, 333-7).

   Ideas similar to Gunkel's concerning the importance of the oral stage, on the other hand, were expressed in particular by Ewald (I:22ff, ET I:14ff), who even suggested that variants could result from the frequent repetition of the most popular stories (I:25ff, ET I:16ff). But these comments never amounted to a systemized theory of the role of the oral stage, let alone its variants, in the development of the Old Testament narrative. Gunkel himself had already proposed some of the ideas that *Genesis* became famous for in *Schöpfung und Chaos in Urzeit und Endzeit,* 1895. Among these were the concept that Gen. 1 "nicht die Composition eines Schriftstellers, sondern die Niederschrift einer Tradition ist; und zugleich, dass diese Tradition in hohes Altertum zurückgeht" (Gunkel 1895:14).

57   Also translated as "saga", or later in the scholarship often left untranslated.

98). Yet no matter how faithful the process of transmission had been, the narratives had been subjected to what Gunkel calls "the universal law of change", *der allgemeine Wechsel*,[58] (1901:xlv, ET 98). This "law" stems from the fact that with each new generation "the outward conditions" as well as "the thoughts of men" change, in religious, ethical as well as aesthetic realms, and as these change, "the popular legend (*die volkstümliche Sage)* cannot permanently remain the same" either but has to adapt to these changes (1901:xlv, ET 98-9). So Gunkel postulated that it was in the very nature of "legend as well as oral tradition that it exists in the form of variants (*Varianten)*", reflecting the changes in society (1901:xlv, ET 99). These changes are then best detected by comparing the variants of the same story with each other. Because of this variants provide us with valuable insight into the ideas and ideals of Ancient Israel, as well as key to understanding their own literary interrelationships, and as Gunkel famously remarks, a place where the investigator eager to develop a "keen eye" for the dynamics of the biblical narrative should start (1901:xlv, ET 100).

What exactly the law of change is Gunkel does not state anywhere explicitly. It is clear, however, that it presupposes a concept of an "original" narrative, one that adheres as closely as possible to some kind of "folkloristic pattern",[59] in comparison with which any changes are then detectable. Drawing on various, though scattered, remarks in *Genesis* one forms a picture of what Gunkel regards as a simple, lucid storytelling style becoming richer and more complicated over time with elements such as increased length (1901:1-1i, ET 110-113). "Epic excursiveness", *epische Breite*, or repetition of fascinating features, such as Joseph interpreting the dreams for Egyptian officials, also starts to take place, Gunkel suggests, to keep such scenes in front of the audiences as long as possible (1901:xxxviii, ET 82-3),[60] while the removal of objectionable characteristics from narratives becomes even more indicative of a later version than any of these additions (1901:xlvi, ET 101).

---

58 It may be important from the point of view of our subsequent discussions of epic laws that Gunkel does not actually use the word "law" here, though some kind of organized principle is obviously implied, somewhat more imprecisely, in the original German.

59 That is a pattern, such as was suggested by contemporary folklore studies and outlined most famously by Olrik. Gunkel himself describes this pattern in some detail, but not in as structured a form as Olrik (see Chapter 3, below).

60 Gunkel does not comment on whether he regards these repetitions within the narrative, composed deliberately for the sake of effect, as a category that is different from variants that develop over a period of time as a natural consequence of storytelling. Understanding this distinction becomes, however, essential as we look at some more recent approaches to patterns of repetition in biblical narrative, e.g. that of Alter, below.

Of the variants in Genesis Gunkel regards the Hagar (Ishmael) stories of chs 16 and 21:8ff as the most important ones, followed by the Wife-sister stories of chs 12:10ff, 20 and 26:7ff and the related legends of the treaty of Beersheba (1901:xlv, ET 99).[61] Of the Wife-sister stories Gunkel dates ch. 12 as the earliest, followed by chs 20 and 26, as ch. 12 conforms most closely to the folkloristic pattern (1910:226).[62] However, Gunkel acknowledges that a variant does not necessarily change equally or evenly in all its detail and thus in some aspects a later version may be more original than an older one. Thus, for instance, according to Gunkel the Pharaoh of Egypt is secondary to the King of Gerar in the Wife-sister stories; as "it was forgotten who the king of Gerar really was (20:26), ...the king of Egypt was put instead (12:10ff)" (1901:xlvi, ET 102). A similar development, Gunkel contends, can be traced in the Hagar stories, where ch. 16 represents the earlier version, but ch. 21 preserves some older features, such as Hagar's tribal identity (190:xlvi, ET 102).

For his interest in tracing the development of the single narrative units to larger oral collections anticipating the composition of J and E, Gunkel has also been credited with pioneering another line of enquiry, that of the history of traditions, *Überlieferungsgeschichte*.[63] Here, again, many of his conclusions are suggested by the study of variants.

Gunkel regards the single oral story as the basic compositional unit in Genesis. Gradually, as several stories were attached to the same person or place, as people were "no longer satisfied to tell a single legend by itself" and "learnt to construct more considerable works of art", small clusters of stories, *Sagencomplexe,* developed, often involving the "splicing" of one legend and

---

61 The list of double narratives Gunkel recognizes is fairly long and ranging from the Creation and Flood narratives to Jacob's device for breeding sheep and the deception by which he gained Isaac's blessing (1901:1vi-1vii, ET 99-103), but does not add anything substantial to those already observed by Wellhausen and others. From outside Genesis Gunkel recognizes Judges 19 as a parallel to the Sodom incident in Gen. 19, as is the meeting of Moses and Zipporah in Exodus to that of Jacob and Rachel in Genesis, while the renunciation of old gods under the oak at Shechem is told of both Jacob and Joshua (1901:xliv-xlv, ET 96-100).

62 The Abraham in Egypt story of ch. 12 can be regarded "as very old" since "it is very brief, has a primitive local coloring, and does not idealise its personages" (1901:liii, 1910:lxxv, ET 117). See Chapter 3 below.

63 See e.g. Whybray 135. Where exactly the line between form criticism and tradition-historical criticism should be drawn is mostly less than clear. For the purposes of the present study I would suggest that the recovery of the folkloristic pattern is clearly in the realm of form criticism, while discussing the impact of any laws of change on narratives already falls under the domain of tradition-historical criticism – as does, of course, the question of how larger collections of narratives developed.

the insertion of another into the gap, as well as inventing connecting material (1901:xxxvii, 1v, ET 80, 123).[64]   Gunkel credits this activity of forming clusters already with the term "collecting", *Sammlung*, and suggests that is first took place in oral form (1901:lv, ET 123).   As the survival of the storytelling tradition then faced a threat and the culture became more disposed to authorship, the second phase of collecting, the process of committing the legends to writing, started (1901:lv, ET 123-4). This, too, took place over a long period of time and involved many "hands" and two main stages: first the formation of J and E, and later a "thorough revision", *durchgreifende Umarbeitung*, which resulted in P (1901:lvi, ET 124).

Contrary to many of his predecessors Gunkel thus regards J and E as collectors, or even more properly, schools of collectors, of primarily oral materials, rather than authors, and the resulting collections as "codifications of oral traditions" (1901:lvi, ET 125).[65] Gunkel does, in fact, state explicitly that there was "no literary connection between J and E", and where verbal agreement does exist it must be "on the basis of a common original source" (1901:lvii, ET 127).[66] This conclusion is, in Gunkel's estimate, suggested by both the disparate character of the materials, often recorded "essentially as they were found" in the two collections, and the examination of the nature of variants in them (1901:lvi, ET 125). This view of J and E as primarily oral collections is particularly significant from the point of view of the methodological issues posed by Gunkel's view of double narratives, to be discussed below.[67]

Gunkel sees the collectors as "servants", *Diener*, rather than "masters", *Herren*, of their subject (1901:lviii, ET 130). Reverence "for the beautiful ancient stories" inspired them to reproduce them as faithfully as possible – even if they at times did not quite understand them (1901:lviii, ET 130). This, Gunkel suggests, explains the existence of many peculiarities in the Genesis narrative, as well as, at least to a large extent, the presence of doublets per se. As the collectors on the other hand "were secretly offended by many things in the tradition" and perceived anomalies in them, they "here

---

64 Gunkel suggests that the more important story was split, the less important one inserted:
    e.g. the Jacob-Esau story was spliced with the insertion of the Jacob-Laban story
    (1901:xxxvii, ET 80).
65 Gunkel also uses the term "schools of narrators" of J and E thus underlining his concept
    of the oral stage as the formative period for the two collections (1901:lviii, ET 130).
66 However, it has to be pointed out that despite these very clear claims Gunkel's actual
    treatment of the extent of orality at the various stages of the development of the tradition
    and the interplay of the oral and the written, is at times at best ambiguous.
67 See Chapter 3.

and there combined different versions" to smooth out contradictions, added detail and the favourite variants of their own, and generally engaged in remodelling that reflected their own religious, aesthetic and ethical values (1901:lviii-ix, ET 131). Though Gunkel refuses to be drawn on the question of what portion of these modifications took place at what stage, he generally speaking credits the oral tradition itself with "certain artistic inner modification" of the material, the collectors with more superficial additions and omissions (1901:lix, ET 131).

The concept of a "law", or a principle, of change being at work in the development of variants at the oral stage is an assumption fundamental to Gunkel's understanding of double narratives and remains an important feature in form and tradition-historical criticism after him, particularly, as will be seen below, in the work of Koch and Van Seters. The fact that Gunkel describes the law of change as "universal", suggests, however, that oral narratives not only change reflecting the society that generates and preserves them, but do so in some decodable, and eventually predictable, way typical of oral narratives as a phenomenon. This concept of oral tradition being bound by intrinsic inner laws or tendencies of composition and transmission does not originate with Gunkel, but is already evident in contemporary literary and folkloristic scholarship. It is explicitly articulated by Axel Olrik in his epic laws, which appeared a few years after the publication of Gunkels' *Genesis,* as well as in various laws of change, suggested by a number of other Fenno-Scandian scholars.[68] Thus, as the idea that oral narrative change according to a predictable pattern has come under scrutiny in various quarters, particularly among folklorists, the validity of Gunkel's observations concerning oral variants will also have to be reevaluated.

1.5. Form and Tradition-historical Criticism After Gunkel

1.5.1. Gressmann

Among Gunkel's successors who developed his lines of methodology the first most notable ones were Gressmann and Alt, followed by von Rad and Noth. It is these scholars who produced much of the formative form-critical

---

68 See below, Chapter 3.

and tradition-historical scholarship,[69] and in whose works we see the continuing preoccupation with double narratives in what now becomes the attempt to unravel both the written traditions of Israel and their assumed oral antecedents. What thus becomes obvious is the magnitude for subsequent scholarship of the methodological implications of Gunkel's notion of doublets as oral variants, as form-critical concepts of biblical narrative as oral tradition are now established and implemented alongside source critical premises intended to deal with narratives as literature. What emerges, perhaps all too slowly, is the tension between these widely different critical models and, in fact, their potential methodological incompatibility, which a scrutiny of the role of double narratives in the creation of these critical methodologies reveals.

Gressmann in his work explores issues relating to double narratives in two areas in particular. In *Mose und seine Zeit*, 1913, he endeavours "to uncover all stages ('Schichten') in the formation of each tradition about Moses"[70] to arrive at the "Ursagen", on which the history of the period could then be based (Gressmann 1913:367). The additions that thus emerge at each level "are conceived to be variants within oral tradition".[71] The same kind of inquiry continues in *Anfänge Israels*, 1922, extending the strata analysis and the search for the "Ursagen" from Exodus to Judges and Ruth. Thus while Gunkel scrutinized Genesis for variants through which the development of Israel's tradition could then be interpreted, Gressmann widens the search to include a much larger body of Israel's narrative literature.

Another dimension of Gressmann's work sheds light both on the development of *Sage*-variants as such, and the wider issue of the origin and relationship of early oral and literary traditions in Israel. In *Die älteste Geschichtsschreibung und Prophetie Israels*, 1921 (ET 1991), Gressmann searches for the roots of history writing, particularly in the context of the Books of Samuel and Kings, and finds them in the *Sage* (ET saga). It is in the *Sage*, then, which for Gressmann, as for Gunkel, is the basic

---

69 How these methodological developments should from now on be termed and differentiated, and what they are understood as entailing particularly in relation to their focus on
either the aspect of tradition (*traditio, traditum*) itself, or its history/transmission (*Überlieferungsgeschichte*), is a matter of debate, with each scholar developing a somewhat
different emphasis. For a comprehensive summary of the various terms used for the
post-Gunkelian, particularly tradition-historical, scholarship and the views held, see
Knight 1975:21-9. Here the terms will be used as "umbrella terms" for the two trends of
scholarship that originated with Gunkel.

70 Knight 1975:85.

71 Knight 1975:85. See Gressmann 1913:360-8 in particular.

compositional unit in Israelite tradition, that we have the roots of two lines of development (1991:12-3). On the one hand, Gressmann, like Gunkel, sees the *Sage*, originally the (oral) work of an individual, as becoming "the common property of many", i.e. of the group its creator belonged to, "the class of the popular narrator" (Gressmann 1991:13). In this group the *Sage* was transmitted by continual repetition, shaped and worked on, possibly with the result of having its beauty marred by "inept additions", until it became part of either the "Yahwist" or the "Elohist"[72] (Gressmann 1991:13). On the other hand, Gressmann argues, from the *Sage* evolved a related, literary, genre: history writing (1991:13-4). The two genres differed in their subject matter,[73] the length of the unit and the literacy of their composer[74] (1991:13-15). Both, however, Gressmann suggests, shared the same technique: "the history writers were", after all, "schooled among the saga-narrators", and the boundaries of the two genres remained at times fluid (1991:13-15).[75]

1.5.2. Alt

With Alt, Knight observes, "we approach the blossoming of 'tradition history' into a field of study in its own right" (Knight 1975:92). For biblical criticism as such Alt's importance as a developer and consolidator of methods initiated by Gunkel and as a teacher of Noth can hardly be overestimated. For the study of double narratives, more specifically, his significance has been perhaps less obvious, stemming not so much from the conclusions he arrived at in his seminal work "Der Gott der Väter", 1929 (ET 1966), but the methodological convergence that took place, and was accepted by scholars at large, in accomplishing it.

In "God of the Fathers" Alt affirmed the form-critical notion of the "independent single saga"[76] as the basic compositional unit of early Israelite tradition and used it to uncover an aspect of the earliest form of Israel's

---

72 Gressmann, as Gunkel before him, regarded the "Yahwist" and the "Elohist" not as "personalities but schools of narrators" (Gressmann 1991:13).

73 The *Sage*, Gressmann argues, "is mostly comprised of events in the distant past", while "historical narrative chooses its subjects from the present or the immediate past" (1991:14).

74 The orally transmittable *Sage* was usually short, while the unit in historical narrative was usually, but not always, longer (1991:15).

75 Thus "history writing" could sometimes be transformed into *Sage*, as "gradually imagination gains the upper hand over the evaporating reality" (Gressmann 1991:15).

76 Alt 4, ET 6.

religion, as well as its development, yet at the same time accepting the source-critical division of the tradition as the starting point for the process. On the basis of the contrasting usage of the names of God in the triplet of the Call of Moses[77] Alt was able to propose the antiquity of the tradition about the God of the Fathers in Israel, and the relative lateness of the usage of the name Yahweh (10-1, ET 11). The E-version of Moses' call, Alt argu-ed, was the link between the Elohist *Sagen* of the patriarchs and those of Moses, and had the function of making "the reader conscious of the complete contrast in the sight of God between the time of the patriarchs and that of Moses", yet on the other hand "smoothing the difference again into a higher unity by presenting the same God as bearer of the old and new divine names"[78] (10-1).

What we have in Alt's work, then, is on the one hand the pivotal impor-tance of a doublet (triplet)-study: it is the contrasting of the E and P versions, in particular, of the Call of Moses, which in Alt's opinion confirms what the comparison of "Elohist presentation with the other narrative works in the Pentateuch" also suggests, namely that the Elohist "was the first to bring the naming of the God of the Fathers into the story" (13, ET 13). But what we also have in Alt's work is a jump from source-critical premises to form- and tradition-historical ones, as Alt, having marked the limits of the sources, moves to consider the nature of the "simple original saga (*einfache[n] ursprüngliche[n] Sage)*" unit behind the sources and to surmise on the tensions it could or could not have contained, and to propose that it must have been the unfixed and ununified state of the tradition, which enabled the divergent E and P accounts to emerge (12, ET 12).

In a way, then, Alt's work contains an anomaly, yet one that has not been recognized as such in Old Testament studies until perhaps very recently, and even then with not much force, namely that the assumptions that led to the source critical division of the call narratives of Moses may be in part inherently incompatible with the principles that are used to trace the oral form and tradition-historical development of the same stories.[79] That is, there may be an inherent contradiction in the position that a narrative could bear

---

77 E: Ex. 3:1, 4b, 6, (a lacuna), 9-14, 18-23*; J: Ex. 3:2-3, 4a, 5, 7-8a; P: Ex. 6:2-8, (Alt 10-1, ET 11-12).

78 Translation mine.

79 Knierim recognizes this problem and explains it (away?) by suggesting that "Gunkel did not intend to introduce a new method *in addition* to the literary criticism prevailing at his time", but to "*replace* literary criticism with a superior holistic method" (149, emphasis mine). In practice, of course, Gunkel was very much tied to some of the source-critical premises as well as the actual document divisions worked out by earlier scholars.

the literary "hallmark of the author" and yet have the "simple original" oral form recognizable in it at the same time.

1.5.3. Von Rad

Von Rad and Noth usually share the accolade of being the "'fathers' of modern tradition-historical research" (Knight 1975:143).   Von Rad's contribution to the study of double narratives is less explicit than Noth's, stemming as it does from the totality of his work, i.e. the wealth and breadth of his analysis of the oral and literary components of Israel's traditions particularly in his seminal effort to tackle the "The Form-Critical Problem of the Hexateuch".[80]   The hermeneutical perspective for this analysis, and consequently von Rad's treatment of doublets, is provided by the central thesis of his work on the Hexateuch: The Hexateuch as a whole is a creed, one hugely ramified and elaborated on, but nevertheless practically identical in content with the older, crystallized forms of creed found in such passages as Deut. 26:5b-9 and Deut. 6:20-24.   The stages of development of this massive statement of belief, von Rad maintains, can still be seen even in the finished work, though only in rough outline, and they betray the "theological penetration and manipulation of the traditional deposit", now amply evident in its variants, that went into achieving the current form of the Hexateuch (1938:3, ET 3). Thus for Von Rad the double narrative phenomenon has a particularly theological emphasis.

This theological penetration becomes most obvious in the different versions of the same account, such as the "Manna"-passages of Ex. 16 and Deut. 8:3 (von Rad 1938:45, ET 49-50). Von Rad points out that in Ex. 16 the Yahwist account is "still quite intelligible as a story, although full of historical difficulties", while the priestly version, though "ostensibly" presenting the incident as "a wholly factual matter", does it in such a way that "no reader will dwell upon the externals", but "can readily grasp the hidden spiritual import" (1938:45, ET 49). Thus the miracle, once occurring "at a particular time and place", has so been generalized in the priestly account that it has acquired "something of virtually timeless validity" (1938:45, ET 49). This, von Rad suggests, is no longer a storyteller speaking but a theologian "who has clothed his meditations in a highly transparent garment of historical narrative" (1938:45, ET 49).   The deuteronomist account, on the other hand, in Deut. 8:3, von Rad argues, "wholly abandons

---

80   "Das formgeschichtliche Problem des Hexateuch", 1938 (ET 1966).

the original significance of the story" and instead in "prosaic language" recounts "what weighty spiritual significance really underlay the outward events even at the time of the occurrence" (1938:46, ET 50).

Similar examples of theological comparison of doublets could be cited from von Rad's Genesis commentary, *Das erste Buch Mose, Genesis*, 1958, (ET 1972), in which von Rad attempts to understand "the purpose and theological character" of Genesis within the Hexateuch and the role of the Yahwist in particular in forging the traditions of Israel, now detached from their original contexts, into a literary framework (1972:13, 29, 42).

1.5.4. Noth

It is in the work of Martin Noth, however, that we have the clearest and most developed articulation of the tradition-historical method of criticism and its bearing on the interrelationships of double narratives. The task Noth sets for himself in his *Überlieferungsgeschichte des Pentateuch*, 1948 (ET 1981), is to investigate the "whole process" of the development of Israel's traditions "from beginning to end", i.e. from its "many roots" through long periods of circulation and oral transmission to writing down, redaction and consolidation as the Pentateuch (1948:1, ET 1). The focus of Noth's work is, however, on the early, pre-literary part of this process as he feels that the later, literary stages have already been exhaustively, if not conclusively, investigated (1948:1, ET 1).

Noth starts his investigation with the concept of Israel as a covenant league of tribes that confessed its communal faith by retelling the story of its life, and proceeds to trace the history of its formation in terms of five themes which, in Noth's view, expressed this common faith and formed the core of its tradition.[81] Two aspects of Noth's work are of particular interest for our present research: the centrality of double narratives for Noth's methodology, and Noth's concept of how oral tradition developed, evident in guidelines that he suggests for its unravelling.

In Noth's view after decades of historical-critical investigation "fundamentally only one of the usual criteria" remained "really useful" for understanding the disunity of the pentateuchal traditions: doublets (1948:21, ET 21). Noth accepted the fact that scholarship preceding his own had shown the debatable status of such criteria as the "alternation of the two

---

81 For a summary of these themes, see B.W. Anderson xx-xxi.

divine names",[82] but maintained that "the unquestionable fact, attested time and again throughout the tradition, of the *repeated occurrence* of the same narrative materials or narrative elements *in different versions*" could not be meaningfully explained in any other way than by the assumption of parallel narrative strands underlying the pentateuchal traditions (1948:21-2, ET 21-2).[83] But then this one criterion, i.e. doublets, Noth argued, was in itself quite adequate for "thoroughgoing literary analysis" (1948:21, ET 21). In emphasizing the importance of the double narrative criterion Noth goes as far as to argue that it should be "a principle of any sound criticism of the Pentateuch not to assume literary disunity unless the occurrence of variants... *compels* such an assumption" (1948:24, ET 24).[84] The pursuit of the doublet-criterion is then much in evidence in Noth's literary analysis, which, according to Anderson, can be distinguished as "as refined as that of the most orthodox Wellhausen disciple" (B.W. Anderson xv).

For Noth, like the other "post-Gunkelian" scholars reviewed above, source division was only the starting point for the study of the pre-literate stages of Israel's traditions. Noth, like Gunkel, regarded the creative stage of these traditions as oral and suggested certain guidelines that could help in the recovery of the earliest stages of these traditions and their development.[85] One of these guidelines is particularly characteristic of Noth's work and relates to one of the major issues in his work, namely the question of the priority of the patriarchs. According to Noth the "earliest traditions usually lie in the background and stand awkwardly in the received Pentateuchal narrative".[86] Thus, for instance, within the theme of "the promise to the

---

82 Noth 1948:23, ET 23, italics omitted. Noth regarded this criterion as "never one hundred percent reliable", but nevertheless usually indicative of source division (1948:23, ET 23).

83 Thus Noth rejects any theory which explains duplication as either "secondary accretions" upon a unified narrative or new editions of older narratives intended for the replacement of the older versions (1948:21-2, ET 21-2).

84 "Obvious seams and secondary connections" could, however, in Noth's opinion also be indications of disunity (1948:24, ET 24).

85 Noth does not provide any systematized presentation of these principles, but a summary list of six "guidelines" is suggested by B.W. Anderson in his introduction to Noth's work (xxiii-xxv). The four guidelines not illustrated below are, according to Anderson's numbering: 1. "Earliest traditions are formulated in small units and in concise style in contrast to later material which tends to appear in larger units composed in discursive (*ausgeführt*) style." 2. "Earliest traditions are attached to places (e.g. Shechem, Bethel, Beer-Lahai-Roi) and frequently end with an etiology of the place name." 3. "Earliest traditions are usually 'cultic' or 'theophanic' in character." 6. "The cases of bracketing together (*Verklammerungen*) of discrete units of tradition are secondary."

86 B.W. Anderson xxiv, guideline 5.

patriarch" in the final form of the Abraham and Isaac-tradition "Isaac seems to be completely overshadowed by Abraham" (Noth 1948:113, ET 103). This fact that the Isaac narrative now "recedes into the background", Noth argues, immediately speaks for its priority (1948:113, ET 103). At some stage then, according to Noth, Abraham usurped the place of Isaac and left the original Isaac narratives to appear as doublets to Abraham (Noth 1948:123, ET 112).[87]

Similarly, in Noth's view, "earliest traditions tend to be anonymous and to deal with typical figures, while later traditions are more specific and individualized".[88] Thus in the introductory narrative to the plagues-episode, in Ex. 5, Noth regards the overseers and elders as the original Israelite "spokesmen to the Egyptians" (5:6 and 19), preceding the incorporation of the figures of Moses and Aaron into the tradition (5:1-3) (1948:76, ET 71). Thus, according to Noth, it was the leaders and overseers that originally went to the Pharaoh to ask for permission for a feast to be held in the wilderness, before Moses and Aaron provided an alternative introduction and the elders and overseers negotiating with the Pharaoh concerning the Israelites' workload were left as a "fossil" in the narrative (1948:76, 179-80, ET 71, 163).

1.5.5. Post-Gunkelian Scholarship: Appraisal

The study of double narratives in the post-Gunkelian period of consolidation, surveyed above, is characterized by much work on the meaning of individual doublets on the assumption that the religious and cultural notions expressed in them reflect various phases in Israel's development.   But, perhaps with the exception of Noth, very little interest has been shown in critical methodology as such. What is methodologically most significant in this period is the extent to which form-critical and tradition-historical methodology is now implemented alongside source criticism in a way which suggests that these two major approaches are merely continuous with each other. The very same doublet can now be taken as the starting point for

---

87 Noth attempts to trace this process by starting from Jacob as the original patriarch of the promise, to whom a genealogy was first attached (Noth 1948:86, ET 79). Abraham and Isaac were then incorporated into the tradition as they were figures similar to Jacob (Noth 1948:112, ET 102). As their native areas were geographically close they became related to each other and, as the people of Abraham's territory overran that of Isaac, Abraham became the dominant one of the two (Noth 1948:123, ET 112).

88 B.W. Anderson xxiv, guideline 4.

unravelling the history of Israel's oral traditions as well as its literary development, with little or no acknowledgement of the fact that the former method assumes certain characteristics in the text to witness to its anonymous, oral composition and long and undateable periods of oral transmission, while the latter may see in the same characteristics the dateable hallmark of an individual author or redactor.

Some discomfort concerning this methodological marriage has, however, surfaced. First of all it has become obvious that although some scholars, notably Noth, have set out with an all encompassing agenda intending to discuss the whole tradition-historical process from beginning to end, from individual oral units to the final literary form of the Pentateuch or the Hexateuch, no clear presentation has emerged of the stages of this process. Thus some of the most debated questions concerning variants still remain without a satisfactory explanation, namely whether double narratives are an oral or literary phenomenon, whether variants have both oral and literary characteristics and how to determine the difference, and why the variants are included in the final text.

Consequently, in the wake of the "post-Gunkelian" scholarship two lines of investigation have emerged which in various ways have attempted to confront the above mentioned issues. In Scandinavia tradition history and the reliability of oral tradition became the focus of research to the exclusion of any interest in, even acceptance of, source criticism. Elsewhere others, such as Koch and Van Seters, have, in turn, expressed renewed interest in one of the most persistently difficult, yet intriguing, areas in double narrative studies: the oral/written interface and the use of epic laws to determine characteristics of oral composition and transmission.[89]

---

89 One of the most significant recent developments in tradition-historical criticism with major implications for biblical criticism as a whole, is the work of Rolf Rendtorff. In *The Problem of the Process of Transmission in the Pentateuch*, 1990 (German original 1977), Rendtorff intends to propose a new method of pentateuchal study with the aim of achieving "a coherent view of the history" of pentateuchal growth, which he feels Noth promised, but failed to deliver (1990:177). This work has great future potential for double narrative studies as Rendtorff sets out to outline, step by step, how the tradition of Israel, now found in the Pentateuch, developed from the smallest form-critically established unit to its final literary form, with a particular focus on the role of the "larger units" of Israel's tradition, the "hitherto neglected stage of formation of the tradition" between the "smallest units" and the Pentateuch as a whole (1990:177, cf. 31ff). However, Rendtorff does not translate his rather theoretical and abstract presentation to the study of actual variants, so in this respect, his promise awaits realization.

1.6. Scandinavian Scholarship

In Scandinavia the form-critical and tradition-historical research pioneered by Gunkel developed in a somewhat different direction from the predominantly German scholarship reviewed above. The Scandinavian approach, though by no means uniform,[90] or even exclusively Scandinavian, is nevertheless characterized by certain presuppositions and methodological features that make it stand out from the tradition-historical scholarship practised elsewhere. These features include "a high regard for the reliability of tradition", "the stressing of oral transmission as the predominant means used in the formation and transmission of the majority of Old Testament traditions",[91] and an ambivalence toward, or even a rejection of, literary criticism as a means of explaining the composition of the Scriptures (Knight 1975:219).

This preoccupation with oral tradition in Scandinavian scholarship[92] has made an important contribution to the debate about how double narratives developed and came to be in the final text of the Old Testament. Thus, even taking into consideration the fact that the main focus of Scandinavian research has undeniably been on prophetic-oracular, rather than narrative, materials, several scholars, such as Nyberg, Engnell and Nielsen, address the question of variants in the Old Testament, particularly in the Pentateuch, directly and at some length.

---

90 Knight in his extensive assessment of tradition-historical research divides the Scandinavians into three main factions, mainly on the basis of their objection to source criticism and emphasis on orality: the "hardliners" (Nyberg, Engnell, Kapelrud, Nielsen, Carlson), the critics of the "hardline" (Widengren, Bentzen), and the eclectics (Mowinckel, Ringgren) (Knight 1975:217).

91   Italics omitted.

92 Widengren credits Nyberg for being the first Old Testament scholar to focus on the question of the means – whether oral or written – by which the tradition was handed down, while in his estimate "Gunkel and Gressmann and their School" had only been interested in how and where the text had originated (Widengren 5). Though this claim does not seem to be entirely accurate – Gunkel had, after all, already developed a thesis of how oral narratives evolved to *Sagenkränze* (1901:lviii-ix, ET 129-133) and Gressmann had also written extensively on the matter (see e.g. 1913:386ff) – it is true that the question of the nature of transmission assumes a far higher profile in Scandinavian scholarship than amongst the preceding Germans.

1.6.1. Nyberg

It is hardly possible to review Scandinavian biblical scholarship without mentioning the contribution of Mowinckel,[93] one of the early champions of the "spoken word" in Scripture, not only in Scandinavia, but among biblical scholars in general. It would not be unreasonable to assume that it was Mowinckel's notion of prophets as speakers rather than writers, and prophetic books as collections of oracles, somewhat in the way of the Gospels, rather than written compositions,[94] that sparked off the interest in oral tradition among Scandinavian scholars. It was in the work of Samuel Nyberg, however, that the recognition of the prophetic word as spoken word first developed into a thesis of predominantly oral composition and transmission of practically all Old Testament material and, maybe even more significantly, to a view of tradition historical criticism as incompatible with, even antithetical to, literary criticism.[95]

---

93 Nielsen calls Mowinckel, with Sweden's J. Lindblom and Denmark's J. Pedersen "the three grand old men" of Scandinavian scholarship (1983:138, italics omitted).

94 These ideas were already expressed in Mowinckel's *Statholderen Nehemia*, 1916, where he famously suggested that "the prophets did not write; they talked" (116, cited in Knight 1975:221n2). In *Prophecy and Tradition*, 1946, Mowinckel addresses the question of oral tradition and the interrelationship of various critical approaches with the intention of "show[ing] that, and how, the traditio-historical point of view in the investigation of the O. T. has long been a fruitful tendency" and "that the method has neither taken, nor must necessarily take, an exclusive, alternative, attitude to literary criticism" (7). Mowinckel, as we have seen in connection with his work on Genesis 1-11, embraced the literary-critical method and did not seem to find a conflict between it and form-critical or tradition-historical approaches. However, Nielsen points out that "the importation of the theory about the significance of 'oral tradition' into Norway by Harris Birkeland in 1938 led Mowinckel to abandon the notion of an E source in fixed (i.e. written) form running parallel to J" and to suggest instead that "some of J's materials had survived orally for some time after J was written down" (Nielsen 1983:139). On the whole it seems then that later in his career Mowinckel becomes increasingly persuaded by the arguments of the "oral school" and consequently de-emphasises the role of source analysis, embraces "epic-artistic laws" and emphasises orality in variant development (1946:10ff).

95 See Knight 1975:234. Knight traces the roots of Scandinavian antipathy towards literary criticism, now brought to bloom by Nyberg, to Pedersen (Knight 1975:224-5). Pedersen rejected the Graf-Kuenen-Wellhausen theory as the solution to the pentateuchal problem, seeing it largely as too evolutionary a result of Hegelian philosophy that had reached Wellhausen via Vatke, as well as of a failure to appreciate ancient Israelite psychology (Pedersen 1931:166-174; 1940:725). Instead, Pedersen regarded

In a brief introductory section to his *Studien zum Hoseabuche*, 1935, Nyberg discusses critical methodology and rejects the contemporary scholarly view that the Old Testament came into being through literary activity and that for its transmission "wir haben mit einer ununterbrochenen schriftlichen Tradition vom ersten Schriftsteller bis zu M[T] zu rechnen"[96] (1935:5).   Instead, Nyberg proposes a thesis of orally composed and transmitted traditions of Israel that included not only prophetic and poetic material,   but   "die   konkrete   Geschichtsüberlieferung,   die   epischen Erzählungen, die Kultlegenden, zweifelsohne auch im allgemeinen die Gesetze",[97] which were then only fixed in writing by the Jewish community after the exile (1935:8).[98] And even when they were written down they were recorded as "the writers heard them",[99] as Nyberg points out in a later work, while the narrators themselves did not use written sources but only oral tradition, *mundtlig tradition* (1947:247).

As a process, Nyberg argues, oral transmission was a reliable one. In fact, by being passed on orally "die primitiven Stoffe viel besser bewahrt blieben, als wenn sie früh schriftlich fixiert worden wären"[100] (1935:8-9).   For, Nyberg goes on to claim, "auf primitiven Kulturstufen ist die Schrift noch kein geeignetes Mittel, der Nachwelt Erzählungen und Gedichte zu vermitteln: das primitive Gedächtnis ist viel zuverlässiger"[101] (1935:9). But this did not mean that the transmission process had been one of mechanical repetition.   Rather, it had been "a living transformation (*lebendige[r] Umformung*), where the material was shaped by the "circles of traditionists (*Traditionskreisen*)" that preserved it and passed it on (1935:8). The stages of these transformations were, however, Nyberg contends, now lost: it was

---

JE, D and P as labels for parallel collections which in their present form come from the post-exilic time but in terms of their material stem from much older times, even "the old chieftain" and "regal" periods (1931:178; 1940:725). As for repetition, the key criterion of the documentary theory, Pedersen maintained that the importance of this "has been greatly exaggerated" and argued instead, speaking particularly of Genesis, "that the narratives as a rule are naturally coherent" (1940:727).

96 "We have to reckon with an uninterrupted literary transmission from the first author to the MT."

97   "The concrete historical traditions, the epic narratives, the cultic legends, undoubtedly also the laws." Cited in Knight 1975:235.

98 What preceded the Exile, Nyberg reckons, "war sicher nur zum kleineren Teil schriftlich fixiert" (1935:8).

99 "Så som nedskrivarna hörde dem."

100 "The content of the tradition was better preserved than if it had been fixed in writing at an earlier time."

101 "On a primitive cultural level writing is not a suitable way to convey narrative or poetry for posterity: the primitive memory is far more reliable."

doubtful that scholarship could ever recover "the actual words", the *ipsissima verba* of a prophet or a narrator, but should be content with the traditions about these words (1935:9).

For Nyberg, the concept of oral predominance in Old Testament traditions seems to have arisen from his understanding of the literary processes of the ancient Near East and the "mind", i.e. the psychology, of its people. Both of these areas become central to Scandinavian scholarship after him as sources of evidence, even courts of appeal, in the attempt to understand the nature of the biblical traditions. In this way Scandinavian research continues the quest already established in Old Testament scholarship for parallels, or "empirical models", from outside its own immediate sphere to justify, or at least to illustrate, Old Testament methodology.

In Nyberg's understanding then, transmission in the Near East had always been, even up to the very recent past, by and large oral in nature. "Fast jeder Niederschrift eines Werkes", Nyberg argues, "ging im Orient bis in die jüngste Vergangenheit hinein eine längere oder kürzere mündliche Überlieferung voraus"[102] (1935:7). And even after the recording oral transmission remained "die normale Form für die Fortdauer und die Benutzung eines Werkes"[103] (Nyberg 1935:7). This had been the case with the Quran and the recitation of the Yasni by Parsi priests, Nyberg argues, and as the "practices (*die Verhältnisse)*" in these areas were overall quite similar in the Near East, it was mistaken to attribute the Old Testament with a special place in the history of the process of transmission of the Near East, as had been done by literary critics (1935:7). As further evidence of its orality Nyberg gives the fact that the Old Testament impresses one as oral literature – "eine schriftlich fixierte Literatur legt in ganz anderer Weise ihrem Benutzer einen Zwang auf"[104] (1935:128).

Having established Israel's traditions as orally composed and transmitted, in a later essay "Korah's uppror" ("Korah's Rebellion"), 1947, Nyberg addresses the question of double narratives more directly with a detailed discussion of the Korah incident in Num. 16-17. Nyberg rejects the literary critical way of explaining the Num. 16-17 narrative which divides it between two sources, JE and P, each reporting different rebellions that originally had nothing to do with each other and were only combined by a post-exilic editor (1947:242, 245). "As a matter of fact", Nyberg argues, "repetition", such as

---

102 "Almost every recording of a work in writing was preceded in the Orient, up to most
    recent times, by a longer or shorter oral transmission." Cited in Knight 1975:234.
103 "The normal form for continuing and using a work." Cited in Knight 1975:234.
104 "A literature fixed in writing places constraints on its user in quite a different way."
    Cited in Knight 1975:235n4.

is provided by Num. 16:6-7 and 16-17, "forms a conscious stylistic feature"[105] in the narrative, and provides "clarifications (*preciseringar)*" (1947:234-5). Nyberg contends that had the "double line (*dubbla linjen)*" not already belonged to the tradition the narrator of Korah's rebellion was utilizing, he would not have taken such trouble to pursue it (1947:248). For when a story has a "flowing course of events where everything comes together nicely",[106] it as a rule rests on a weak tradition foundation, which does not limit the storyteller's imagination. In contrast, Nyberg argues, a less polished story, such as Korah's rebellion, goes back to a stronger tradition that has been more difficult for the storyteller to handle (1947:239). Thus the double line in the story is "original (*primär)*", and moreover, evidence of great antiquity (1947:248).

Thus when we find a story repetitive or "dragging (*släpande)*", Nyberg contends, it may be because the storyteller "had to handle double-lines in the narrative and bring them forward in parallel",[107] or, in order to bring "dramatic tension"[108] to the narrative, he used a "retarding technique"[109] elaborating on the high points of the story (1947:247). On the other hand, Nyberg argues, what a *reader* of the story may find "slow moving (*långsläpigt)*" often impresses a person *listening* to it in a completely different way (1947:247). It is then just the reiterations in the narrative that belong to the oral technique and are our best evidence that the story was "orally composed and orally performed"[110] (1947:247). Thus the unevenness in the redactor's material is not evidence for "disparate and contradictory written sources", but rather for "diverse streams and complex traditions which intersect with each other"[111] (1947:246).

It is abundantly clear then that for Nyberg any duplication in the story is oral in nature. What is not as clear, however, is how he envisages these features to have arisen: whether they are "original" in the sense of going back to the original, first composition of the narrative, its "folkloristic pattern" – to use Gunkel's terminology,[112] or whether they are original in the sense of having developed in the oral transmission of the story, through "laws of

---

105 "I själva verket ligger i upprepningen ett medvetet stildrag."
106 "Ett jämnt flytande händelseförlopp, där allt går restlös ihop."
107 "Han hade att handskas med dubbla linjer i berättelsen och att föra den parallellt."
108 "En dramatik spänning."
109 "Retardande teknik."
110 "Componerad muntlig och framförd mundligt."
111 "Disparata och motsägande källskrifter", "olikartade traditionsströmmar och -komplex, som korsa varandra." ET cited in Knight 1975:237.
112 This seems to be Knight's reading of the matter.

change". Nyberg's reference to stylistic features seems to support the former view, his concept of a later storyteller grappling with the double line of strong tradition could suggest the latter. It may, in fact, be that Nyberg did not make a conscious distinction between the two types of variation and their development, perhaps being precluded from such analysis by the preoccupation of Scandinavian scholarship with the final form of the tradition. The lack of any such distinction or definition does, however, inevitably undermine Nyberg's otherwise well-argued treatment of the Korah doublet, and open his work to the criticism sometimes levelled against Scandinavian tradition-historical method that it is all about tradition and not at all about history! It will also make it difficult to find a meaningful context, such as folklore studies, for instance, could provide for assessing the methodological claims involved.

1.6.2. Engnell

At the centre of the Scandinavian approach to biblical criticism lies the work of Ivan Engnell.[113] His views of the composition and transmission of biblical material emphasize orality even more than those of his predecessor Samuel Nyberg, whose thesis Engnell "sought to apply thoroughly and consistently to the whole of the Old Testament", and his attitude to literary criticism is perhaps even more emphatically negative than Nyberg's (Knight 1975:260). In Engnell's opinion both literary criticism and form criticism had failed in the task of explaining how Old Testament literature developed. Thus, what in his view was needed was not a mere modification of the old method, but a radically new "no compromize [sic]" approach that would replace the old method, such as he hoped his tradition-historical research would provide (1960:21).[114] This method Engnell outlines in two major

---

113 See Knight 1975:260. Knight regards Engnell among "all his colleagues" as "the one most closely identified with the characteristic direction taken by the Scandinavian tradition historians" (1975:260).

114 See also Engnell 1970:53. Engnell argues that we must "free ourselves" from what he perceives as "the modern, anachronistic book-view" of interpreting biblical tradition (1970:3).

works, *Gamla Testamentet*, I, 1945,[115] and articles in *Svenskt Bibliskt Uppslagsverk*, 1962.[116]

The key concept in Engnell's tradition-historical approach is the notion that practically all the significant development of Israel's traditions took place at the oral stage. "Not only the smaller units", Engnell argues, "but also larger complexes – partly, whole collections or tradition works – had already reached a fixed form in the oral tradition stage" (1970:6). The writing down of the traditions was then not a compositional development at all, but just a setting down in a different mode of something that already existed, that had been "firmly formed and fixed already at the oral stage"[117] so that the written form implied in itself "nothing new or revolutionary" (1945:29; 1970:6). Engnell goes on to suggest that written and oral transmission do not need to be seen as antithetical and mutually exclusive but rather "they should be thought of as running parallel and as complementing each other" (1970:65). However, this does not seem to be a partnership of equals: with compositional developments having taken place at the oral stage the written form becomes only a corollary to the "living oral traditions"[118] that continue their life in oral form even after they have been committed to writing (1945:29, 40).[119]

Thus what is important in Engnell's view for appreciating biblical literature and essential for understanding its development, is recognizing the fact that it "has the character of an oral literature which was written down only at a relatively late period" (1970:6). What is crucial to meaningful biblical criticism is to "appreciate better the function, extensiveness, and significance of the oral tradition stage" (1970:53). This is the task for the tradition-historical method which, in Engnell's view, encompasses all the critical questions that have to do with the tradition (1945:28-30).

---

115 The second volume never appeared.
116 A Swedish biblical encyclopedia. Thirteen of Engnell's major articles from this work have been translated into English and published in Britain as *Critical Essays on the Old Testament*, 1970.
117 "Fast utformade och fixerade redan på det muntliga stadiet."
118 "Levande muntliga traditioner."
119 Thus, with the Pentateuch Engnell rejects the idea that any "parallel, continuous, written sources" such as "literary critics presuppose" ever existed (1970:53). Instead Engnell credits "the vast and multifarious traditional material of the Pentateuch" to two collections (Tetrateuch and Deuteronomistic history) with separate and now largely inaccessible transmission histories (1970:58-9). Engnell concedes that some writing down of traditions did take place at different times in the transmission of the material, but knowing this does not in his opinion contribute anything essential to unravelling the text's tradition history.

The most prominent feature of the oral stage, Engnell argues, and the best evidence for the fact that much of the biblical narrative material[120] was transmitted in oral form – and in fact the only plausible explanation for the phenomenon – is the presence of variants in the text (1970:54). "Variant narratives", Engnell emphasizes, "are the best and clearest evidence for oral transmission of material"[121] (1945:191). For, Engnell maintains, the variants and doublets are the result from the fact that at the oral stage "the material comes together according to... the epic law of iteration"[122] and "is arranged according to the principle of association"[123] (1970:54). Though Engnell nowhere explains fully what he understands by this law of iteration the reference seems to be to the epic laws of Axel Olrik,[124] espoused by Gunkel as well as many other Old Testament critics and well patronized in Scandinavian religious and literary scholarship of Engnell's time.

Engnell takes his concept of the dynamics of oral composition and transmission even further by linking the law of iteration with other literary patterns in the Old Testament, such as "the compositional technique of the so-called alternating pattern – the pattern in which doom and hope alternate (especially for portions of the prophetic literature)" and "the technique of *parallelismus membrorum* in both poetry and prose" (1970:8).[125] By combining the "laws of iteration" with other literary schemata in the Old Testament Engnell goes further than any Old Testament scholar before him in trying to come to grips with the overall literary patterning in Scripture. These observation may be partly credited to Engnell's insight into larger literary constellations in traditional materials, but perhaps also partly to the fact that Engnell sees the boundaries between poetry and prose, as well as different genres of prose, as rather fluid (1945:95-6). Unfortunately, like Nyberg before him, Engnell does not go any further in discussing the dynamics of oral composition and transmission and how exactly he sees the variation to have arisen. This may be because Engnell regards the oral process itself as being either of secondary importance – or impenetrable!

---

120 Engnell is here referring to the Pentateuch in particular, but in *Gamla Testamentet* he extends the discussion to include some other narrative traditions as well (1945:96ff).

121 "Variantberättelser äro emellertid alltid det bästa och klaraste beviset för en muntlig tradening av stoffet."

122 See also Engnell 1945:191 for "upprepningens episka lag".

123 This principle is clarified by the editor of Engnell's work (Ringgren?) as "the way different tradition units are linked together by means of associations of ideas or words" (1970:8n10). See also Engnell 1945:191.

124 See Egnell 1945:191n2; Olrik 1909.

125 See also Engnell 1945:36-8.

1.6.3. Nielsen

Another Scandinavian Old Testament critic who has pursued lines of argument similar to those of Nyberg and Engnell is Eduard Nielsen. In his main work on biblical methodology, *Oral Tradition. A Modern Problem in Old Testament Introduction,* 1954,[126] Nielsen sets out a threefold agenda for his attempt to explore the role of orality in Israel's traditions. This agenda consists of setting forth "some fundamental points of view" concerning the problem of oral tradition and illustrating them "by means of testimonies from the ancient world outside the Old Testament", examining "the role of oral tradition in the different kinds of Old Testament literature", and finally, giving some examples[127] of how Old Testament texts can be treated by the tradition-historical approach (1954:17).

Nielsen's reasons for taking up the defence of oral composition and transmission against the emphasis on writing are similar to those of Nyberg and Engnell and consist mainly of a perception of literary criticism as reflecting a western "book view" anachronistically projected on to ancient Israelite traditions, ignoring the psychology of the ancient Semites, and misunderstanding what Nielsen sees as the almost universal nature of traditions. However, Nielsen goes much further than either Nyberg or Engnell in two areas of the orality debate: in his search for potential ancient Near Eastern – and other! – parallels[128] to the Old Testament tradition process, and in attempting to establish criteria by which orality in the text could be determined.

Our particular interest here is with the latter of the two preoccupations, the criteria Nielsen uses to establish orality, as these are central not only to Nielsen's double narrative methodology, but to the form-critical approach as

---

126 This book is a translation of four articles that first appeared in the *Dansk Teologisk Tidskrift*, 1950 13:129-145, and 1952 15:19-37, 88-106, 129-146.

127 The main narrative example Nielsen employs is the Flood story of Gen. 6-9 (1954:93ff). However, after rehearsing the main points of, and his objections to, the source analysis of the story, the alternative approach Nielsen somewhat hesitantly offers is less than conclusive, consisting mainly of the suggestion that the author of the story obviously used a "definite chronological scheme" and that he was not an editor but must have been "a great artist" (1954:102-3).

128 Nielsen's examples range from ancient Near Eastern diplomatic correspondence and Homeric epics, via Rigveda, Talmud and Koran to Icelandic sagas (1954:18ff).

a whole. Nielsen divides these criteria into two different categories: firstly, indications of orality in a single account,[129] and secondly, in doublets.

The characteristics in the form of a single narrative which, Nielsen argues, make it possible to decide with "a reasonable degree of probability whether it may have been handed down orally", consist of the following:

> a monotonous style, recurrent expressions, a fluent, paratactic style, a certain rhythm and euphony which are specially noticeable when one hears the account, and finally anacolutha which a literary writer would hardly have let pass, but which may have been accompanied by a gesture in oral delivery or even have come into existence by the incorporation of a 'stage direction'[130] in the text (1954:36).

Besides these criteria Nielsen also enumerates some of Olrik's epic laws,[131] particularly the "law of repetition", the "law of number three" and "the scenic law of the number two", as evidence of orality, and also makes reference to "memory words" and "representative themes" as indicators of "an organic connection with oral tradition composition" (1954:36).

As for "double accounts", Nielsen suggests, another set of criteria is needed to detect whether the variation has arisen in oral or in written form, and whether one of the doublets is dependent on the other (1954:36). With variants, whether in prose or song, Nielsen argues, it is not "the greater or lesser similarity" in the accounts that determines whether the development has been written or oral, but "the kind of similarity", whether "graphic or phonetic" (1954:37). "Written variation" may thus be distinguished by the following characteristics: "errors of the copyists, words *read* wrong, or interchanged, sentences omitted through dittography or haplography, words in the text revised" (1954:36-7). If, on the other hand, "a larger or smaller passage has been lost", Nielsen maintains, in the case of a written variation it can either be supplied from memory or "interpolations are made from other sources at the disposal of the copyist" (1954:37). In contrast oral variation is typically indicated by evidence of "errors in hearing, or the confusion of words that *sound* alike", also a whole episodes may be forgotten or wrongly added from memory (1954:37).

Nielsen does not indicate how he arrives at the list of oral characteristics of the single story, except when Olrik is credited. It seems, however, that he is following the work of the Norwegian saga scholar Liestøl, whose

---

129 Nielsen refers here mainly, but not exclusively, to prose narratives.
130 As an example of this Nielsen mentions Mark 2:10b.
131 Nielsen remarks that "most" of Olrik's laws can be added to the criteria he himself uses, but does not specify any that cannot be included (1954:36).

characteristics of the oral "saga style" Nielsen's list resembles.[132] Nielsen's laws for variant transmission also come from Liestøl, but bring a twist into the debate about the transmission of biblical traditions: Nielsen seem to have in mind the transmission of a fixed text – this is the context of Liestøl's criteria[133] – and also his list of characteristics of variation in written transmission echoes some of the main canons of how textual variants develop in scribal transmission.   In that sense Nielsen laws, or his concept of oral transmission as such, are not directly comparable with, for instance, Gunkel's laws of change or what is generally thought of as the fairly flexible process of oral transmission amongst form and tradition-historical critics.

1.7. Koch, Van Seters

The interest in oral and literary laws, or "laws of composition and change", first expressed by Gunkel and since then pursued by several form and tradition-historical critics, has most recently been taken up and most comprehensively developed by Klaus Koch in *Was ist Formgeschichte? Neue Wege der Bibelexegese*, 1964 (ET 1969),[134] and by John Van Seters in *Abraham in History and Tradition*, 1975.   Though neither of these works discusses double narratives as a phenomenon – Van Seters limits himself to the Abraham tradition and Koch to just two sets of doublets – they nevertheless represent the most focused efforts to date to deal with the issue of double narratives.   The contribution these works make to the study of doublets is twofold.   Firstly, they attempt to make an appraisal of the methods by which biblical criticism has handled double narratives in the past. Secondly, by taking the task of defining methodology to the point of articulating "laws" designed to determine the interrelationship of variants and their origin, and illustrating these laws in some detail in relation to actual

---

132 See e.g. Liestøl 1930:29-30. Liestøl is a proponent of the "freeprose", as opposed to "bookprose", approach to Icelandic saga origins, i.e. that the sagas are "oral narratives *written down*", rather than "*compositions* in writing" (Liestøl 1930:26ff). The two schools of thought very roughly resemble source criticism and form criticism, both in methodology and underlying assumptions.

133 See Nielsen 1954:36n2; Liestøl 1930:35-7. List Liestøl's criteria for oral and written transmission are, however, somewhat problematic, in that Liestøl's concept of transmission is a mixture of scribal rigidity and creative, almost compositional editing (see Liestøl 1930:34-8). Nielsen seems to ignore this point which does, however, amount potentially to a considerable difference in the nature of the transmission process.

134 *The Growth of the Biblical Tradition.*

doublets, Koch and Van Seters manage to "concretize" the often rather nebulous discussions about the transformations of narratives during, particularly oral, transmission.

1.7.1. Koch

Koch's work provides perhaps the best attempt at a cohesive summary of the basic principles, as well as the application, of the form-critical method since the time of Gunkel. In *Was ist Formgeschichte?* Koch deals with all the issues central to the form-critical method, from the delineation of literary units, definition of genre types and their *Sitz im Leben*, to their application to both the narrative and the poetic texts of the Old Testament, and as such his work is of major interest for the study of the theory of critical method. Our interest in Koch's work relates, however, mainly to his use of compositional and transmissional laws in his attempt to analyse variants, i.e. the Wife-sister triplet of Gen. 12, 20 and 26, and the stories of David sparing Saul's life in 1 Sam. 24 and 26, in terms of their relative originality and types of change they have undergone. For although much interest among biblical scholars has been expressed in folklore studies in general, and the epic laws in particular, Koch's work is in fact the first practical attempt to confront the applicability of such laws to biblical narrative since Gunkel's pioneering work on the subject. We will focus here on the former of Koch's two case studies, the Wife-sister stories.

Koch starts his discussion of the Wife-sister triplet by an investigation of the self-sufficiency and extent of the literary units in question (127, ET 115). He concludes that though the situation with the last of the narratives, in ch. 26, is "a little more complicated" than with the two others, the Isaac story being "only intelligible as a component literary type in a complex unit",[135] there must have been a time when "all three tales about the ancestress of Israel circulated as... independent oral narratives" (130-131, ET 118). Then, after determining the literary type of the stories, in each case as an "ethnological saga (*ethnologische Sage*)",[136] Koch sets out to search for the "original version of the story" and to trace its transmission history, now evident in its variants (133ff, ET 120ff).

---

135 Koch suggests that the ch. 26 variant "had become part of a series of sagas about Isaac" already in oral tradition (131, ET 118).
136 Koch is indebted to Gunkel for this definition (Koch 133, ET 120).

Koch's analysis of the three narratives reveals that their present sequence in Genesis also reflects, in the main, their historical priority and interdependence (139, ET 125). This conclusion Koch reaches mainly on the basis of certain (though imprecisely articulated) oral laws, for which he seems to be mainly indebted to Gunkel. Thus the fact that Gen. 12:10-20 is the most ancient version is, in Koch's estimate, attested by the fact that it is "brief and fluent", reflects the least moral scruples, pictures God's intervention through a foreign soothsayer[137] and has "no inessentials, only external events" (136, 139, ET 123, 125). In comparison the other two stories manifest "long conversations" (ch. 20) or are "broken up by speeches" (ch. 26), become "more sensitive in sexual matters" and also at times "double back" to previous parts of the story: all signs of later transmissional developments (136-9, ET 123-5). However, Koch also argues, influences in the stories have not moved just one way. Thus although Gen. 12 must on the whole be regarded as the original version, Gen. 26 retains the earliest story in certain aspects. These include the identity of the hero of the story, Isaac, rather than Abraham, as well as the identity of the foreign king and the location of the incident, Abimelech in Gerar rather than the Pharaoh in Egypt (139-40, ET 125-6).[138]

In relation to the question of the level at which these developments took place, i.e. whether they are oral or literary, Koch seems to all but exclude the possibility of the latter. "The divergences in the three narratives", Koch argues, "do not seem to have arisen intentionally, but rather through the course of oral transmission", possibly "in different regions" and "at different times" (136, ET 122). These conclusions enable Koch to articulate four laws, which in his estimate have general application to the development of variants during oral transmission (141, ET 126-7):

a) The narratives become elaborated by speeches, which gradually achieve a status equal to the deeds of the hero. Through them the thoughts and impulses of the people are expressed...
b) Moral sensitivity becomes gradually stronger. Sexual matters become treated with more and more restraint.
c) God's intervention is less tangible in the later versions. Divine action is understood in a more universal way....

---

137 This fits less well with the later attitude in the Old Testament than the way Sarah's identity is discovered in the other stories, and therefore, Koch suggests, speaks for its originality.

138 For this conclusion Koch evokes the "general rule in the transmission of the saga", namely that "the least known figure is the original (140, ET 126); cf. B.W. Anderson xxiv; see also p. 33 above.

d) During the story's development there is a tendency to transfer the action of the story to more familiar people and powers.

The transmission history of the story, Koch points out, does not, however, end with the version in Gen. 26, or its incorporation into the writings of the Yahwist and the Elohist. The study of later developments, such as the deuteronomistic revision reflected in Gen. 26:5, the additions in the Samaritan Pentateuch and the LXX, even the Genesis Apocryphon and the book of Jubilees, would widen the picture of narrative transmission (148, ET 132)! Koch does not, however, elaborate on how these further developments could best be traced and analysed.

Like Nielsen before him, Koch does not declare the source of his laws of transmission, although it is obvious that they have all already appeared in Gunkel's work.[139] This lack of credit does, however, raise an important methodological point for Old Testament scholarship in general and this present research in particular: in biblical criticism there seems to exist a concept of what an oral narrative is "like" and how it changes in the course of oral transmission. But, as we can see in Koch's case, there is tendency to simply recycle these laws from scholar to scholar, often as "givens". But what kind of evidence is there for the reliability of these assumptions – short of making Gunkel, or a saga scholar such as Liestøl, an ultimate authority? This issue will be central to the attempt to evaluate some of the foundations of form and tradition-historical criticism in Chapter 3.

1.7.2. Van Seters

Van Seters, in his *Abraham in History and Tradition*, addresses the issue of methodology needed in establishing the possible oral or literary nature of patriarchal narratives, its doublets in particular, even more extensively than Koch, and with the benefit of the latter's work. Van Seters has "two primary foci" in his work: "the form and development" of the Abraham tradition and "its function or intention" in its socio-historical context (1975:3). It is the first of these foci that leads him to an extensive exploration of the variants in the tradition. Van Seters describes his approach as "a literary study with a scope broad enough to include the consideration of any possible preliterary form of the tradition as well" (1975:3). In terms of methodology Van Seters proposes a new "fresh, unbiased approach", not only a "slight modification" of the old (source- and form-critical, tradition-historical) method evident in

---

139 See Chapter 3 below.

the work of scholars such as Gunkel, Alt, Von Rad, Noth and Westermann (1975:148). Van Seters expresses his disapproval of the way these critical approaches have developed in the first place, and also points out how, in his eyes, they have failed in their task by not being able to make a clear case for "the traditions of Genesis as either ancient or deriving from an oral base", or establishing "the form of the stories, their function, the identity of the bearers of these traditions, or the process by which they might have arrived at their extant shape" (1975:148).

The starting point for Van Seters' "fresh approach" is the recognition of the plurality of sources in the Abraham tradition, i.e. rejecting it as "a unified work, the product of a single author" (1975:154). As evidence for this lack of unity Van Seters cites the presence of doublets of the same story plot in the tradition. This assumption locates his work in the main stream of traditional Old Testament scholarship but sets it apart from more recent literary approaches.

The doublets Van Seters recognizes in the Abraham tradition are the Wife-sister stories of Gen. 12:10-20, 20 and 26:1-11, and the stories of Hagar's flight in Gen. 16 and 21:8-21. He also finds a "double presentation of a kerygmatic theme" in the two covenants God makes with Abraham in Gen. 15 and 17 (1975:154). Contradictions or points of tension between stories are, on the other hand, created by the birth of Isaac in Gen. 21. Thus although the promise of a child in ch. 18 is made to an aged couple, in ch. 20 Abraham passes Sarah off as his sister, presumably because of the danger created by her beauty, even though the context suggests that she is by now both old and pregnant (1975:155). Similar problems are created by Isaac passing Rebekah off as his sister in Gen. 26, as according to ch. 25 they already have two grown sons, and by Hagar carrying off the child Ishmael in Gen. 21:8-21, when, according to 17:25, he must already be about 16 years old (Van Seters 1975:155).

Together these features, doublets and tensions in the chronology of the frame story, suggest, in Van Seters' estimate, that the Abraham tradition was collated from originally independent stories (i.e. sources), which the framework now artificially holds together (1975:155). The boundaries of the sources, Van Seters suggests, would be recoverable by using doublets as the prime indicators of sources and by aligning other, single stories with the duplicates on the basis of similarity and internal connection (1975:155).

Before such source-critical judgements can be passed, however, Van Seters insists that certain form-critical tasks must be accomplished, namely establishing the limits, unity, form and structure of an individual story (1975:157). Besides just an intelligent reading of the text to spot inconsistencies and additions and some structural analysis, Van Seters turns folklore research on narrative genres and Olrik's epic laws to accomplish these form-critical tasks (1975:156ff). These laws, Van Seters contends, are a most valuable tool in attempting to evaluate the extent and role of oral components in a given part of tradition – a fact that in turn is crucial to understanding the interrelationship of variants (1975:165). For this latter task Van Seters utilizes other, less well-defined oral and literary laws.

Equipped with these two basic assumptions, the plurality of sources in the Abraham tradition and the recoverability of their original form through the application of folklore methodology, Van Seters then turns to the question of "how to evaluate the relationship of the sources to each other, and particularly the problem of variants" (1975:161). He attempts to tackle this problem in two stages: by establishing first the nature of the variants in the Abraham tradition and then by suggesting laws that could explain their interrelationship.

Van Seters proposes that in the kind of literary tradition that possibly has an oral background, such as the Abraham tradition is commonly accepted to be, four different kinds of variants are possible: "written and oral transmission variants", and "written and oral composition variants" (1975:164). Each of these variants presumes a certain situation where the variant has arisen and a concept of the kind of literature involved. Thus, transmission variants would presume a concept of a fixed text, or a fixed oral tradition (1975:161). Written transmission variants are thought of as scribal errors and they fall within a well-established spectrum of deviance (Van Seters 1975:161-2). Oral transmission variants, in the context of the Abraham tradition, would, on the other hand, presume that "through the whole course of Israel's history from the United Monarchy to the Post-exilic period the various literary sources of the Pentateuch were all dependent upon a body of fixed oral tradition but quite independent of each other" (1975:164). Van Seters rejects both of these alternatives, thus rejecting a concept of a fixed *Grundlage*, whether oral[140] or written, from which the variants in the Abraham tradition could have arisen (1975:164).

The two remaining options that Van Seters is left with are oral or written composition variants, which have to do with "similar material occurring in different works by different authors" (1975:162).[141] Were the doublets in the Abraham tradition shown conclusively to be written compositional variants,

---

140 Thus contra Nielsen.

141 Composition variants is perhaps somewhat of a misnomer for what Van Seters seems to have in mind, in that what he is describing is a process of "recomposition", i.e transmission, but of a non-fixed tradition, while his transmission variants deal with transmission of a fixed tradition.

this, Van Seters argues, would establish the sources they represent as dependent on one another. Conversely, oral compositional variants would suggest the independence of the now written sources (Van Seters 1975:164).

Besides Olrik's epic laws,[142] already mentioned above, Van Seters proposes two other sets of guidelines to determine the type of the variants in the Abraham tradition. The first set is intended for the comparison between oral and written composition variants and has three criteria (1975:163):

1. Oral variants will usually be in the same genre but differ in the non-typical detail. A theme may go from one genre to another...but a combination of genres is a literary phenomenon.
2. Oral variants do not summarize, and any new material is added in the same genre.
3. Oral tradition does not assume knowledge of various aspects of the story, so the 'blind motif'[143] does not exist. If an important aspect has been lost from lapse of memory the story-teller will have to supply it with something new.

Were the doublets in the Abraham tradition found to be of the written compositional type, the question of interrelationship would then be one of literary dependence.[144] Van Seters suggests a further set of four guidelines for determining the direction of dependence in such cases (1975:162-3):

1. The account with the simplest form and structure will most likely be the earliest one.
2. The second version often shortens or summarizes the material that it borrows from the first one, although by adding new material of its own it may result in a longer story.
3. Occasionally, in a later version there occurs a 'blind motif'; ... [T]his is a clear indication of literary dependence and the direction of borrowing.
4. The strongest evidence for literary dependence is verbal similarity.[145]

A major part of *Abraham in History and Tradition* consists of the application of this "fresh literary approach", outlined above, to the narratives, particularly the doublets, of the Abraham tradition. As the Wife-sister stories come under consideration first and receive the most extensive scrutiny, the

---

142 See Van Seters 1975:160-1.
143 I.e. "some unexplained action or detail that assumes consciously or unconsciously that the earlier account is known" (Van Seters 1975:163).
144 In Van Seters' opinion such cases are demonstrated in a number of other literatures: Assyrian and Babylonian royal inscriptions, Icelandic sagas, the Synoptic Gospels and early Arabic literature (1975:162).
145 Thus, conversely, Van Seters argues that "variation in oral composition means that basically the same theme or plot is used in more than one tale or song by either the same, or a different, singer or story-teller", and the question of sources or dependence is not very significant (1975:163).

summary of their treatment will serve as an example of how Van Seters applies his methodology.

Looking at Gen. 12:10-20 first in terms of its form and structure Van Seters observes that "it corresponds rather closely to a folktale model", such as is outlined in Olrik's laws, in that it portrays (1975:168-170):

a. A crisis: A famine in Canaan compels Abraham and Sarah to travel to Egypt.

b. A plan to deal with a difficult situation, here the danger to Abraham's life: Abraham decides to introduce Sarah as his sister.

c. Execution of the plan and complications: Danger to Abraham is averted but complications arise as Sarah is taken to the royal harem.

d. Unexpected outside intervention: God sends plagues on the Pharaoh for the implied adultery.

e. Fortunate (or unfortunate) consequences follow: The Pharaoh "merely expels" Abraham from the country and Abraham is "greatly enriched by the whole turn of events".

In short, measured by these standards, Van Seters regards Gen. 12:10-20 as having a balanced narrative structure, "well suited to popular storytelling", in a clearly self-contained unit that is not tied to its present context (1975:169-170). The story, Van Seters proposes, is a fine illustration of Olrik's epic laws and shows "very little adaptation to…the Abraham tradition as a whole" (1975:169-170).

As Gen. 20 and 26:1-11 are placed against the same criteria a vastly different picture emerges. Gen. 20 lacks an "effective point of departure" (a) for the story, and reduces the two following elements, plan (b) and complications (c) into half a verse, 20:2a, thus producing a very unbalanced structure (Van Seters 1975:171). Abraham calling Sarah his sister in 20:2 produces a "blind motif", "inexplicable in its present context" and a "feature of literary style" rather than of storytelling (Van Seters 1975:171, 183). Also other features, such as the great length of the narrative, while details on issues essential to the plot are at times minimized, as well as important events occurring without preparation or explanation, lead Van Seters to conclude that Gen. 20 is "a deliberate literary recasting of the story" (1975:172-3). Some other elements, such as the concentration on "God's relationship to the innocent king" (20:3-7), "Abraham's reply to the king's accusations" (20:8-13), and the king's relationship to Abraham after that (20:14-17) indicate, Van Seters suggests, that the story seeks to address "some important theological and moral issues" which had been "inadequately treated in the earlier account" (1975:173). Van Seters therefore concludes that the Gen. 20 narrative is a literary compositional variant of Gen. 12:10-20 (1975:183).

When the criteria are applied to Gen. 26 in turn, it becomes clear, Van Seters observes, that "we are not dealing with an independent folktale" as epic laws are poorly observed and there is "considerable lack of clarity and focal concentration" (1975:176). In Gen. 26 there is "no interest in the storytelling aspect", nor can the variant be regarded as a "theological revision" (Van Seters 1975:183). In conclusion, then, Van Seters argues that in Gen. 26:1-11 we have another compositional variant, which is directly dependent on the previous two versions and is, in fact, a "literary conflation" of both of them and as such creates "an artificial literary tradition about Isaac based directly on the traditions of Abraham" (1975:183).

Van Seters's extensive use of Olrik's – and other oral and literary – laws complete the picture of how principles of oral and literary composition and transmission have been appropriated in Old Testament criticism. What is most useful in his approach is the decisive and unambiguous way he applies these principles to the biblical narrative, thus providing a forum for discussion of the potential value of such a method. What is most problematic in Van Seters approach, as was in Nielsen's and Koch's, is the rather indiscriminate borrowing of such laws from various branches of folklore scholarship, Icelandic saga studies in particular,[146] and their "litmus test" like application to biblical tradition, divorced from the wider context and discussion of how these laws developed.

1.8. "Holistic" Approaches to Double Narratives

The approaches to double narratives can, with some generalization, be divided into two overall categories: those, discussed above, which emphasize the heterogeneous nature of biblical tradition as the origin of the double narrative phenomenon, and those, to be taken under scrutiny next, which, accepting or rejecting the concept of sources to various degrees, see the phenomenon in terms of an authorial, more controlled and intentional act.

Generally speaking the approaches in the second category are less well established and less well known than those offered by the traditional schools of source, form, and tradition-historical criticism. They also tend to be more

---

146 For his list of oral composition variants Van Seters' relies mainly on the work of Einar Sveinsson who, as opposed to Nielsen's source Liestøl, is an advocate of the "bookprose" approach to saga origins (Van Seters 1975:162-3n18-21; Sveinsson 1958; 1971). A major weakness in the way Van Seters arrives at his laws is the fact that some of them are dependent on a single, passing observation in, for instance Sveinsson's work, rather than a systematic study of large numbers of narrative folklore.

recent, but gaining momentum, as the crisis concerning the Documentary Hypothesis deepens and alternatives are explored. These holistic approaches include both detailed critiques of the Documentary Theory and "unrelated alternatives", approaches unconcerned with historical critical scholarship. Some of the approaches are proclaimed by solitary voices only, some, as is the case with the new literary criticism, have in the past two decades emerged as a major force in the study of the Old Testament.

Because of their diversity the holistic approaches are difficult to categorize. Loose groupings could, however, be proposed on the basis of common central features. Thus in the first group Cassuto, Sandmel, Segal and Whybray all reject the source-critical explanation for the double narrative phenomenon, but engage in dialogue with the Documentary Hypothesis as they seek for an alternative to it emphasizing authorial intent. In the second group Alter and Damrosch represent the new literary criticism and the attempt to explain doublets as a literary phenomenon.

1.8.1. Authorial Intention

1.8.1.1. Cassuto

One of the first, and most authoritative, critical reactions to the Documentary Hypothesis and its way of explaining double narratives came from Umberto Cassuto.[147] Cassuto discusses variants already in his *La questione della Genesi*, 1934,[148] but offers a more succinct presentation of the matter in *The Documentary Hypothesis and the Composition of the Pentateuch*, 1961,[149] where duplications and repetitions form one of the "five pillars"[150] of the Documentary Hypothesis, which Cassuto sets out to refute (1961:14, 98). Many of the individual doublets Cassuto then explores further in his commentaries *Genesis*, 1964, and *Exodus*, 1967.

In the *Documentary Hypothesis* Cassuto suggests that "duplications and triplications" in the pentateuchal narrative "are of two kinds". When

---

147 There were, of course, many reactions to Wellhausen's thesis before Cassuto's, but as most of these do not enter the critical debate, but reiterate existing positions, they will not be reviewed here.

148 See esp. 255-318.

149 Hebrew original, 1941.

150 The other four pillars relate to the use of different names of God, variations in language and style, contradictions and divergences of view, and signs of composite structure (Cassuto 1961:14).

"parallel sections appertain – or are considered to do so – entirely to one subject, which is depicted in each of them in a different form and with variation in detail", Cassuto calls them "duplications" (1961:69). When such parallel passages concern events which are "unrelated to each other but yet are so similar in their principal motifs, that one may conjecture that they are simply divergent developments of a single narrative", they may be termed "repetitions" (Cassuto 1961:69). Creation story would then fit the former category, duplication, the Wife-sister stories the latter category, repetition, Cassuto suggests (1961:69).[151] Cassuto also finds a kind of parallelism, for which he does not suggest a specific term, between larger, less obviously interrelated passages of the Pentateuch, such as Abraham's and Sarah's journey to Egypt in Gen. 12:10ff and those of Jacob and his sons in Gen. 43:1ff and 47:1ff, as well as Abraham's first journey to Canaan and Israel's later conquest of the land (1961:78-81).[152]

Cassuto in no way denies the pre-history of pentateuchal narratives, but, like most Old Testament scholars, concedes that before the Torah was written, various traditions existed among the Israelites, for instance, "concerning the creation of the world and the beginning of human life upon earth" or "involving the Matriarchs of the nation" (1961:71; 1964:339). Thus, Cassuto proposes, there were narratives that were "handed down in the circles of the sages and philosophers", as well as "folk-tales that circulated among the broad masses of the people",[153] and it is even possible that variants, such as the Wife-sister stories, may have grown from "one ancient saga" and in the process of being handed down from generation to generation assumed their different detail (1961:71; 1964:339).

In Cassuto's view, however, the existence of such oral traditions does not explain the presence of doublets in the Pentateuch any more than the assumption of written documents does. For Cassuto the real question concerning repetitions and duplications is not their possible prehistory, but why they appear in the Torah as it is (1961:82; 1964:339). The answer to

---

151 Cassuto does not recognize the compositeness of stories such as the Flood narrative, but interprets the perceived duplications in terms of a "literary technique" (1961:84ff).

152 Cf. e.g. the motif of "famine" in Gen. 12:10 and 43:1, that of "danger to life" in Gen. 12:12 and Ex. 1:16, and the itinerary in Canaan first in relation to Abraham in Gen. 12:1-9, then in relation to Israel in Joshua 7:2, 8:9 and 8:30 (Cassuto 1961:78-81).

153 The Creation story in Gen. 1, Cassuto suggests, comes from the first of these circles of tradition, the sages and philosophers, and intends to teach us that the world was created "by the fiat of the One God", instead of various and quarrelsome pagan gods, while the Gen. 2 story aims "to make the early history of Adam and Eve a source of moral instruction" and reflects the "traditions current among the multitude" (1961:72).

this, Cassuto suggests, comes from understanding the purpose of the Torah, namely that of religious and ethical instruction (1961:72). Thus when the Torah was written, Cassuto argues, it did not ignore the many traditions that already circulated not only among the Israelites, but all the peoples of the ancient Near East, concerning, for instance, the origins of the world. Rather, the Torah took up "an attitude towards them" in order to "teach us how to extract their kernel and to throw away the husk", i.e. "how to distil from them what ever is good and true" and "purify them" to "conform to the religious conscience of the Israelites" (1961:71-2). The existing traditions thus served as "raw material" for the Torah, but they were "purified and refined" to suit the Torah's own moral and educational aims (1961:72).

Stories were thus included in the Torah because of their intrinsic value and if two, even three, variants of the same story all "harmonized with and promoted the Torah's aim, there was no reason to exclude them" (Cassuto 1961:82). However, at the same time such "a method of recapitulation" in the Torah is always intentional and reflects the "Semitic practice of using parallelism in order to give emphasis and prominence to an idea" (1961:83). Thus in the Wife-sister stories the "teaching and promise" of the Gen. 12 episode was "corroborated and confirmed" by the events of ch. 20, and finally "strengthened and consolidated" by ch. 26, as "everything that is done twice or thrice is to be regarded as confirmed and established" (Cassuto 1961:82-3). Similarly, in parallel sections events and themes, such as journeying in Canaan, were repeated "to teach us that the acts of the fathers are a sign unto the children" (1961:81).

1.8.1.2. Sandmel

Another approach to double narratives focusing on the question of authorial intent is suggested by Samuel Sandmel. Sandmel's views are best articulated in his article "The Haggada Within Scripture", 1961, and to a lesser extent in other works, such as *The Hebrew Scriptures*, 1978. Looking at some of the biblical double narratives in terms of the characteristics of post-biblical midrashic literature Sandmel argues for the interpretation of the double narrative phenomenon as haggadic embellishments.

The context of Sandmel's discussion, as of Cassuto's, is the questioning of the validity of the Documentary Hypothesis, particularly in its classical form.[154] Sandmel recognizes that the division of the Pentateuch into source-documents arose from a need to meet problems within the Scripture itself, namely contradictions and duplications, but argues that instead of having to postulate diverse hypothetical documents, or oral sources to solve these difficulties, there is "an easier, simpler explanation" (1961:105-9). This explanation arises from Sandmel's attempt to understand the composition of the Pentateuch in the light of later developments in Jewish, particularly midrashic, traditions, and to a lesser degree the Gospels, and New Testament apocrypha (1961:109).

Sandmel argues first of all that the "embellishments" we find in such biblical double narratives as the Wife-sister and Hagar stories do not differ essentially, in either character or purpose, from those found in, for instance, Josephus or Genesis Rabbah (1961:110-1). What we have in both cases is "haggada, in short,... the fanciful retelling of tales", but, Sandmel argues, only when we find them in "Gen Rabbah instead of Gen 20" do we recognize them as such! (1961:110-1). Sandmel also uses examples from the Gospels, such as the baptism of Christ, to demonstrate how a single (historical) event can give rise to diverse literary traditions, each witnessing to the *Tendenz* of the writer in choice of material and presentation (1961:109-10).

To illustrate the workings of the haggadic process in the Scriptures Sandmel peppers his discussion with a liberal spread of biblical examples. The texts quoted include most of the best known double narratives: the Wife-sister and Hagar stories, David's introduction to Saul's court and his sparing of Saul's life in the cave, but also the origin of the divine name, the origin of circumcision and the characterization of Reuben and Judah in the Joseph-cycle (Sandmel 1961:111ff). Though the scope of these examples is substantial, very few of them are discussed in any detail with regard to the haggadic elements in them. The variants that do, however, get a thorough treatment are the Wife-sister stories of Gen. 12 and 20,[155] and these will serve as an illustration of Sandmel's approach.

Sandmel sees Gen. 12:10-20 as the original Wife-sister story of which Gen. 20 is "a haggadic retelling" (1961:110-11, 117). In Gen. 12 the incident is reported with sparse detail: Abraham takes Sarah to Egypt and passes her off as his sister; she is taken to Pharaoh's harem; God brings plagues on the Pharaoh who then sends Abraham away (Sandmel 1961:110). In Gen. 20,

---

154 The focus of Sandmel's discussion is J and E – with P he has "no great quarrel" (1961:116).

155 The "triplicate" in Gen. 26 is dismissed as a story that was "simply retold" (Sandmel 1961:112).

where Abraham and Sarah are in Abimelech's court, five significant embellishments have developed (Sandmel 1961:111):

1. The random plague of Pharaoh becomes the plague of sterility.
2. The deity intervenes.
3. Sarah's virtue is unimpaired.
4. Not only has Abraham not committed a prevarication, but also he is a prophet.
5. Abraham was not lying: Sarah is his half-sister.

The main motive behind such embellishments, Sandmel suggests, is the need to recast a leading figure, in this case the patriarch Abraham, in a more favourable light by removing unflattering and questionable traits (1961:112, 116). Such a need could have arisen, Sandmel contends, at the time when "folk heroes were turned into ancestors and thereby symbols of the collective people" and would have been part of the "nationalizing" of the tradition (1978:345; 1961:116). Thus, for instance, Jacob, originally "a folk character of low moral attributes...needed to be transformed from a mere ancestor into a respected ancestor, and from a respected individual to a national symbol" (Sandmel 1961:116).

The literary method used by the haggadist Sandmel describes as "disinclination to expunge", counterbalanced by a "process of neutralizing by addition" (1961:120). What this means is that instead of removing from the biblical text something that had come to be regarded as unacceptable, such as Abraham lying about Sarah, the story is retold in such a fashion that the patriarch's behaviour appears acceptable. Once such an embellishment is added, the original story has the same meaning to the haggadist as the emendation (Sandmel 1961:120). In other words, "the Abraham of Gen 20 determines the character of the Abraham of Gen 12:10-20" (Sandmel 1961:120).

According to Sandmel's haggadic approach Scripture grew by accretion as smaller and larger items, verses, incidents, new versions, were added to the text, the margin, and even the end of the scroll, yet without removing the text that had "bothered" the haggadist (Sandmel 1961:120-2). What is central to Sandmel's thesis is that no one involved in the process was a mere recorder all – the parties were "involved", shaping the text out of conviction (1961:121). Sandmel does not deny the existence of Israel's traditions in different shapes at various stages – oral, written, canonical, midrashic – but insists that the process of transformation is a continuous and always an intentional one, never involving "disinterested writing" or "automatic copying", such as the Documentary Hypothesis, in his estimate, represents (1961:121-2).

1.8.1.3. Segal

An even more strictly authorial view of double narratives than those suggested by Cassuto and Sandmel, yet sharing important features with them, is proposed by Moses H Segal. In his *The Pentateuch*, 1967, Segal rejects the "complicated, artificial and anomalous" Documentary Hypothesis which, he feels, is "based on unproved assumptions", "uses unreliable criteria" and with all its analysis has "reduced the Pentateuch to a mass of incoherent fragments" (22). Instead Segal suggests a "method of synthesis" as an alternative approach to the composition of the Pentateuch and its doublets (22).

The basis of Segal's approach is "the traditional claim of the Mosaic authorship" (25). Segal sees the individual books of the Pentateuch, as well as the composition as a whole, as "the work of a single inspired author and literary artist who composed it with a definite and preconceived plan and with fixed purpose" (1967:30).[156] This purpose was for the Torah to serve as "a book of instruction and edification and legislation" for the nation of Israel, and the composition of the work can be best understood in relation to its "real theme", which runs through the entire composition climaxing in the end, namely "the selection of Israel from the nations and its consecration to the service of God and his laws in a divinely-appointed land"[157] (23-4).

The double narratives within this scheme Segal dismisses as either just "apparent" doublets or as results of "incorrect exegesis" (32). Consequently Segal offers no overall method for the interpretation of the variants in most of the Pentateuch, choosing instead to look at certain cases on an individual basis. The Hagar stories of Gen. 16 and 21, Segal argues, for instance, "are not duplicates", but rather "they record two events which are entirely different in character" (33). The same holds true for the stories of Abraham's and Isaac's covenants with Abimelech in Gen. 21 and 26 (33). The story of Abraham's covenant with God in Gen. 17 Segal, on the other hand, interprets as "a reaffirmation of the covenant concluded many years before in 15", while some other "alleged cases of duplication", such as have been detected in the Flood story, have resulted from "breaking up integral narratives...into incomplete parallel accounts" (33).

---

156 Segal is here commenting on Genesis in particular, but this statement holds true for the entire work (cf. Segal 24).
157 Capitalizations and italics omitted.

Segal does, however, make a distinction between these seeming duplications and "parallel narratives", stories such as the "appointment of chiefs and judges in order to relieve Moses of the burden of ordinary administration", which are first found in Exodus-Numbers and then retold in Deuteronomy (90). These can generally be explained on the basis that the use of the narratives for different purposes resulted in differences of style. While the narrative in Exodus-Numbers is historically inclined, the purpose of the book of Deuteronomy requires a more rhetorical style (90). This "possibility of choosing varying details in the narration of the same events", Segal argues, "springs from the peculiar character of ancient Hebrew story-telling" (90).

What is significant in Segal's approach is that although firmly claiming Mosaic authorship as the unifying factor in the composition of the Pentateuch, Segal does not exclude the author's use of different traditions, at least some of which must have been oral, or the possibility of some later additions (24). The presence of the two Creation stories in Genesis, for instance, can be explained on the basis that the author may have used different traditions and written the stories at different times (32). On the other hand, and akin to Sandmel, Segal admits that "many passages and also longer sections" have been added to the Pentateuch in later times and that these usually "serve to explain or to develop or to supplement the older text" (25). However, Segal insists that these additions are not "inventions by later writers" in their content but orally transmitted traditions of Mosaic origin that have expanded in post-Mosaic times, i.e. part of the Oral Torah (25).

1.8.1.4. Whybray

The latest and most thorough "holistic" rethinking of the pentateuchal question, and the problem of double narratives in relation to it, has been presented by Whybray in *The Making of the Pentateuch*, 1987. The added merit of this work, besides its comprehensive discussion of doublets, is the fact that Whybray also comments on some of the other challenges to the Documentary Hypothesis, including those posed by Cassuto and Sandmel, and the new literary approach of Alter, to be discussed below. The starting point for Whybray, too, is his dissatisfaction with the Documentary Hypothesis, as well as the other critical approaches he sees as stemming from it (namely form and tradition-historical criticism), which in Whybray's estimate have failed to address the question of authorial intention in the composition of the Pentateuch, including its phenomenon of variants, and have tolerated considerable inconsistency in the use of source-indicating criteria, such as duplication.[158]

Whybray sees the Pentateuch as the product of a sixth century historian (242). Though not denying the use of sources, written or oral,[159] he nevertheless regards double narratives "as a deliberate literary device", "integral to the literary effect intended by the author", rather than necessarily a reflection on any variance in the received materials (76-7). Thus, for instance, in the case of the Hagar stories, the author may have intended "by placing the story of the miraculous birth of the true heir between the two stories about Hagar and Ishmael...to draw attention to the way in which God faithfully and effectively overcame, on two separate occasions, the threat to the true succession to Abraham" (76). A very similar explanation of God's faithfulness to his promises could be given of the Wife-sister stories which, Whybray observes, occur "at crucial points in the total narrative" and also provide, as in the case of Gen. 20, "a dramatic suspense" (77).

Although interpreting doublets as a literary device, Whybray makes a distinction between his concept and some other literary approaches to the phenomenon, such as Alter's type-scenes.[160] Alter's model, which treats doublets as resulting from the use of a literary convention, dismisses, Whybray argues, "the striking similarities between the stories", i.e. the fact that "they are not simply similar stories perhaps made more similar in the telling, but *the same story* told twice with variation at different points of the total...narrative" (75). Whybray does highlight the main oversight in Alter's use of the type-scene convention – and is the only commentator on Alter's work to do so.

Sandmel's idea of doublets as "rabbinic improvers" Whybray, on the other hand, sees as amounting to a kind of supplementary hypothesis which ignores the question why, after the new version was composed, the older version was still retained (75-6). Thus, Whybray points out that when some doublets, such as the Wife-sister stories, occur "at crucial moments" in the larger cycle,

---

158 See Whybray 47-53, 74ff.

159 Whybray's emphasis is however on written sources, as in his estimate attempts to establish the orality of pentateuchal narratives in the now written text have proved unconvincing (235-6). For the author-historian's use of the written sources Whybray allows a far more generous scope than most "holistic" scholars, as, he suggests, "already existing works" may have been incorporated "in their entirety without alteration" or they may have been "excerpted, adapted, expanded, summarized, or simply used as source-material" in the composition of the Pentateuch (236).

160 Whybray, however, firmly seconds some of the other views on repetition as "consummate literary skill" expressed by Alter (see Whybray 81).

the literary skill of the author is in the use of "the *repetition* of what is basically the same story" to show how "God intervened *not once but three times*" to safeguard his promises of progeny (77-8).

The main contribution to the double narrative discussion that Whybray makes is, however, his attempt to define the phenomenon, at least within the Pentateuch. Thus he looks at a range of narrative pairs that have been significant to the formation of the Documentary Hypothesis, such as the Hagar and Wife-sister stories, Joseph's dreams, the Plagues of Egypt, Manna in the wilderness and the Creation stories. The criterion for "doublets in the strict sense of that term", Whybray suggests, is that they are "based on a common narrative source" (79). According to Whybray, the Hagar stories, for instance, would then qualify as a genuine doublet, that is, a story told twice with variation, while the Creation stories would not (75). Succession of doublets "with no other material intervening", such as Joseph's dreams in Gen. 37:5-11, Whybray recognizes as another side of the literary technique of repetition, of which the doublets occurring in different points of the total narrative are also a manifestation (78-81). Finally, and uniquely among the commentators on double narrative, Whybray draws attention to the fact that double narratives have been studied very selectively by source critics in particular: some doublets have consistently been neglected, while their "neighbours" have received large amounts of attention. Whybray also hints at the possibility – argued by this present research – that not all doublets may have arisen in the same way (78-82).

1.8.2. New Literary Criticism

1.8.2.1. Alter

Within the last few decades looking at the Bible "as literature" has become increasingly popular among both literary and biblical scholars.[161]

---

161 As a method the literary study of the Bible is usually traced back to Erich Auerbach's comparative treatment of Gen. 22, the sacrifice of Isaac, in his *Mimesis*, 1946 (ET 1953). Placing the terse, high-lighted and economically worded story of Isaac's sacrifice alongside a detailed, excursive and expansive scene from the *Odyssey*, the recognition of Odysseus by his old housekeeper because of a scar on his thigh, Auerbach contrasts the vastly different, yet equally praiseworthy, literary styles by which the two works in question achieve their effect (1953: 3-23). For this treatment of Gen. 22 Auerbach was soon hailed as a trailblazer "in showing the way toward a reunion of the secular with the religious critical tradition" (Alter and Kermode 1987:4). It was

The ensuing, diverse trend of scholarship has been variously termed "literary criticism",[162] "new" literary criticism, or "the Bible as literature" approach. One of the first to give serious attention to double narratives amongst the prolific group of scholars that have pursued this approach was Robert Alter.

In his *The Art of Biblical Narrative*, 1981, Alter attempts to explain repetition of basically the same narrative episodes in the Scripture as a literary convention. Borrowing the notion and the terminology from Homeric studies Alter designates this convention "type-scene" (1981:50).[163] Alter suggests, again on the basis of Homeric scholarship, that type-scenes arose from "the special needs of oral composition": there were "certain fixed situations" which the poet was "expected to include in his narrative" and which he had to "perform according to a set order of motifs" (1981:50). In biblical literature examples of such situations, or type-scenes, Alter argues, include such "recurrent narrative episodes" as the annunciation of the birth of a hero to his barren mother, the encounter with the future betrothed at a well, the initiatory trial, and the testament of a dying hero (1981:51). These situations then usually occur at certain stages of the careers of biblical heroes and are narrated with the help of a "fixed constellation of predetermined motifs" (1981:50-1).

Alter uses the betrothal scenes of Gen. 24:10-61, 29:1-20 and Ex. 2:15b-21 to illustrate his notion – but includes the Wife-sister and Hagar stories in the same category (1981:49, 52ff). In the betrothal scenes the dominant pattern[164] pictures the hero journeying to the "world outside" to find a bride; a meeting takes place at a well; water is drawn; and eventually a marriage is arranged (Alter 1981:52). The reason for the repetition of these scenes in the Bible is the use of the convention, but the art of the convention, Alter explains, is not the pattern, the schema itself, which remains fairly consistent, but the individual application of it, the innovations and refashionings of it "for the imaginative purposes at hand" (1981:52).

The benefits of recognizing this convention, Alter suggests, have first of all to do with enabling the reader of the Scriptures to discern the artistry

---

hoped that "all manner of new possibilities" would emerge as biblical texts "that paradoxically had been neglected even as they were venerated and studied" could now be reread with literary-critical awareness (Alter and Kermode 1987:4).

162 Creating confusion with source criticism, also so called by many – hence the designation "new literary criticism" used in this current reseach.

163 Alter recognizes his indebtedness to Walter Arend's *Die typischen Szenen bei Homer*, 1933 (Alter 1981:50).

164 There are other betrothal scenes that differ from this pattern, e.g. in 1 Sam. 9:11-2, Ruth, and Judges 14, and the "suppression" of one in the David narrative (Alter 1981:58ff).

imbedded in the text. It is "through our awareness of convention", Alter argues, that "we can recognize significant or simply pleasing patterns of repetition, symmetry, contrast; we can discern between the verisimilar and the fabulous, pick up directional clues in a narrative work, see what is innovative and what is deliberately traditional at each nexus of the artistic creation" (1981:47). Secondly, and this, Alter testifies, was what led him to his "heureka" experience concerning doublets, understanding such conventions enables us to attribute repetition to something else than "duplication of sources", i.e. "a kind of recurrent stammer in the process of transmission, whether written or oral" (1981:50).

Besides type-scenes Alter also discusses another kind of repetition in the biblical narrative which, he suggests, uses "composite materials", sources of various kinds, but through literary artistry achieves "a comprehensiveness of vision that is distinctly biblical" (1981:133). In this category of composite narrative Alter includes the rebellion of Korah, Num. 16, where he finds two accounts of rebellion "superimposed upon one another" leaving several contradictions in the narrative, and the Joseph-story, where, Alter suggests, minor duplication and seeming contradiction are tolerated for the sake of the two axes of the story: the "moral-psychological" one and the "theological-historical" one (1981:134, 140). A somewhat different case of "two axes", on the other hand, Alter argues, is seen in the two stories of David's introduction to Saul's court. The narrative of 1 Sam. 16:14-23 represents the "more concise, more symmetrically stylized, 'vertical' view" of David, followed by the "human-centred, richly detailed 'horizontal' view", and corresponds to an extent with the private David and the public David: the David Saul loves and the one he hates (Alter 1981:152).

Fundamental to Alter's approach to double narratives – and to the whole of the biblical text, for that matter – is the concept of the "intricately interconnected unity" of the text (1981:11)[165]. This view, shared also by some other literary scholars,[166] has been most explicitly articulated by Alter, who insists on not only a final editorial unification of the text, but on its whole development as if according to a grand scheme. To quote Alter, the text is "a real narrative continuum...a coherent unfolding story in which the meaning of earlier data is progressively, even systematically, revealed or enriched by the addition of subsequent data" (1981:11). Alter sees this

---

165 Text-critically this view is of course very problematic – what Alter seems to have in mind is only the Masoretic Texts.

166 Cf. Josipovici's explorations concerning whether the Old Testament is a narrative, or contains narratives (1988).

approach to the text as an innovation and goes on to suggest that in biblical narrative, "perhaps for the first time in narrative literature", meaning "was conceived as a *process*, requiring continual revision – both in the ordinary sense and in the etymological sense of seeing-again – continual suspension of judgement, weighing of multiple possibilities, brooding over gaps in the information provided" (1981:12). This approach, Alter argues, makes it possible to see connections between texts that are traditionally regarded as interpolations in their contexts, such as is the case with the Tamar story, Gen. 38, in its Joseph-cycle framework, which also serves as a good illustration of Alter's method.

Crucial to Alter's treatment of the Tamar story is the parallelism of certain key words and concepts. At the end of Gen. 37 (vs. 32) Joseph's brothers, having sold Joseph into slavery, show his tunic which they have stained with blood to Jacob and say: "'This (*zot*) have we found. Please recognize (*haker-na*), is it your son's tunic or not?'" And Jacob "recognized it (*vayakirah*), and he said: 'My son's tunic!'" (Alter 1981:4). The story is one of deception, and Judah, Alter points out, is "the leader of the brothers in the deception" (1981:10).

The next chapter, Gen. 38, the story of Tamar and Judah, then balances the scales by recalling how the deceiver becomes deceived (Alter 1981:5ff): Tamar, Judah's daughter-in-law, dressed as a prostitute, tricks Judah into sleeping with her, seeing that her rights for marriage have been neglected after her husband's death. Tamar becomes pregnant and, having received a death sentence from Judah, reveals the valuables she has received from Judah as pawn for payment at the time of their sexual encounter. Then "as she was being taken out, she sent word to her father-in-law, 'By the man to whom these belong, by him am I with child.' And she added, 'Please recognize (*haker-na*), to whom these belong'". And Judah recognized (*vayaker*) them" (Gen. 38:25-6) (Alter 1981:9-10).

The Judah-Tamar story, Alter argues, is thus an intentional analogue to the Joseph story of Gen. 37 and the occurrence of "the formula of recognition, *haker-na* and *vayaker*", used of both Jacob and of Judah, "is manifestly the result not of some automatic mechanism of interpolating traditional materials but of careful splicing of sources by a brilliant literary artist" (Alter 1981:10). By the careful use of the formula of words, Alter points out, the deceiver of the first story becomes unmasked by the deception of the second (Alter 1981:10).

1.8.2.2. Damrosch

Another scholar widely utilizing literary analysis, but within the context of historical criticism,[167] is David Damrosch. In *The Narrative Covenant*, 1987, Damrosch takes up and develops some of Alter's concepts, such as the type-scene, but also deals with a number of other issues integral to the study of double narratives. Though perhaps most readily bracketed under new literary criticism, Damrosch's work defies categorization in that it is an attempt to bring together all relevant critical approaches to bear on the text, illustrated in his study of doublets.

The purpose of Damrosch's study is "to explore the origins and growth of biblical narrative" (1). His concern reaches from the early compositional stages of the traditions to the finished canonical form of the text, with much of the emphasis on the literary developments and adaptations that must have taken place in between (2-3). Thus, Damrosch explains, his study is really one of genre, which he defines as "the narrative covenant between author and reader, the framework of norms and expectations shaping both the composition and the reception of the text" (2). His approach to the study of genre is one of combining the forces of three fields of inquiry, "the comparative study of Near Eastern literature, the historical study of the sources within the biblical texts, and literary analysis of the text as it develops into its canonical form" (2-3).

With such a wide brief Damrosch's work has a bearing on many aspects of the study of double narratives. Without too much generalization, however, his main points concerning double narratives can be presented as pertaining to the two areas of the nature and the meaning of narrative doublings. The first category has to do with the types of duplication found in the Old Testament, the second with their meaning and function in the development of the text.

Firstly, reflecting on the nature of duplications, particularly in the context of the David story of 1-2 Samuel, Damrosch observes that doublings occur "both on the level of content and on the level of form" (233). Doublings of content appear mainly as "thematic linkages" of "character and event" (Damrosch 234). Thus, Damrosch argues, Saul, for instance, becomes "a

---

167 Damrosch argues that "source study does not deserve its continuing neglect by literary students of the Bible but, on the contrary, is essential to understanding the dynamics of literary transformation that produced the canonical form of the text" (2).

new Isaac, a new Eli, a new Goliath" as various episodes in Saul's life echo or are modelled on other Yahwistic or deuteronomistic incidents, resulting in "a series of repetitive transformations of earlier events" (234).[168] Alongside these thematic linkages come "doublings of form", or "narrative doublings", that concur more with the conventional definition of double narratives, as "Goliath is joined by a second Goliath; Saul is rejected twice by God, meets David twice, is spared by him twice" (234).

For Damrosch the thematic linkages in the biblical narrative are myriad: his treatment of 1-2 Samuel bristles with "intertextuality". Even a quick perusal of his treatment of the Books of Samuel points the reader to more than a score of possible narrative connections one is unlikely to have encountered elsewhere in Old Testament scholarship. Thus, for instance, David refusing Saul's robe in the Goliath-story links with him dancing naked in front of the Ark on its return to Jerusalem; the five stones David had when confronting the Goliath are echoed by the five tumours the Philistines sent back with the Ark after God had "duelled" with Dagon, just as David had with Goliath; Dagon lying headless in front of the Ark recalls David cutting off Goliath's head; Eli's grief after his sons were killed anticipates David's grief over Absalom (182ff).

A thorough illustration of this methodology of linkages is Damrosch's treatment of the Ark Narrative, 1 Sam. 2:12-17, 22-25 and 4:1b-7:1, in which he sees "the Yahwistic Exodus story" used as the "most basic unifying element" (182-8). At least six points of contact stand out (188-192):
1. The wickedness of Hophni and Phinehas, 1 Sam. 2:12-7, 22-25, is described in a "language associated with the departure from Egypt". Thus, for instance, the brothers "did not know the Lord", which is a "hallmark" theme also in the Exodus story, cf. Ex. 5:2 (188-9).
2. Similarly, the sons, when warned by Eli, "'would not listen to the voice of their father'", 1 Sam. 2:25, just as the Pharaoh refused "to listen to the voice of the Lord", Ex. 5:2 (189).
3. Learning that "the Ark has been brought into the battle" the Philistines recall the Exodus story, 1 Sam. 4:7-9 (189).
4. The Philistines "view the appearance of the Ark as a unique event ('nothing like this has happened before')", 1 Sam. 4:7, thus echoing

---

168 According to Damrosch, Gen. 27, with its language of "sonship and fatherhood" and Isaac's non-recognition of his son and blessing of the younger instead of the elder, stands behind the shaping of the 1 Sam. 24 and 26 encounters of David and Saul (see e.g. 1 Sam. 26:17 and 25) (211-2). For the links between Eli and Saul and Goliath and Saul, see pp. 215ff and 230ff.

Moses' words to the Pharaoh concerning the plagues that will be such "'as neither your fathers nor your grandfathers have seen'", Ex. 10:6 (190).

5. As the Philistine priests "recommend returning the Ark", they again make reference to the Exodus: "'Why should you harden your hearts as the Egyptians and Pharaoh hardened their hearts?'", 1 Sam. 6:6 (190).

6. Just as the Israelites took golden jewelry from the Egyptians, the Philistines return the Ark with golden tumours and mice, Ex. 3:22 and 1 Sam. 6:8. Damrosch points out that in both cases the same term, *keley zahav*, is used (191).

Alongside these doublings of content Damrosch differentiates an another type of duplication, that of form, the "narrative doubling". These duplications match more closely the conventional concept of double narratives. As an example of narrative doubling Damrosch discusses in some detail the various Goliath stories, finding two variants conflated into one in 1 Sam. 17 and four further, more historically original references to the killings of various Philistine warriors in 2 Sam. 21:15-17 (193ff).

As a third type of duplication, besides content and form, Damrosch also employs the concept of the type-scene. The type-scene under Damrosch's scrutiny is the "announcement of battle news" of which he cites three examples in the Books of Samuel: the bringing of the news of the captured Ark to Eli, the announcement of the death of Saul and Jonathan to David, and of the death of Absalom, again to David (250ff). Interestingly enough, however, Damrosch maintains that none of these represent the pure form of the type-scene (256).

Secondly, when discussing duplication in the Bible, Damrosch's main interest is not in the relative authenticity or interdependence of the variants, but in their meaning, that is, in how they function in their larger narrative framework. The Goliath story Damrosch regards as the key element in the (re)shaping of the history of David's Rise (195). Dislocated from its original place at the end of the History, Damrosch points out, the story causes disruption both in terms of narrative flow and genre (195). But this disruption is tolerated for a purpose: the Goliath story provides a frame in which the History of David's Rise both begins and ends with confrontation with the Philistines, with David and Goliath in the beginning, and the "decisive vanquishing of the enemy" in the end in 2 Sam. 5 (197-8). Moreover, Goliath becomes a theme that runs through the whole History, as David, Saul, and Nabal all in turn take up the role of Goliath, in some aspect, or reversal of an aspect.

Looking at the meaning of narrative doublings, particularly in the books of Samuel, Damrosch argues that they are essentially a compositional tool

(238). Along with many other scholars he sees the origin of the variant phenomenon in oral tradition and the practices of storytelling. He suggests that the first two stages of the phenomenon becoming literary, "simple collection, and literary revision of oral material", are evident in such doublets as the Wife-sister stories, which could well be "independent variants" that were "brought together and then edited into a progressive relation" (236).[169] But, he argues, a further third stage can be often seen "in the far-reaching doublings in 1-2 Samuel: purely literary composition on *analogy* to oral composition" (236-7). Thus in 1-2 Samuel he sees the whole structure of the book is having been built out of variants of individual stories (238).

Damrosch sees two main factors contributing to this development. First of all the cultural context was familiar with storytelling and the forms of oral narration, from which the biblical narrative grew (237). Biblical writers thus "found in oral variants a powerful compositional tool" (238). Secondly, Damrosch suggests that during the period of growth of biblical texts a "complex interplay" must have taken place between "theme and form" – as, for instance, "a metaphoric view of character and history inspired the seeking out of such analogies" – enhancing the development of such patterns (234).

Varied as they are the "holistic" approaches to double narratives, reviewed above, nevertheless have certain important common characteristics. The most prominent of these is the emphasis on authorial intention as the prime cause for duplication. Whether for the purpose of theology, ethics or literary artistry, duplication is nevertheless seen as a part of the design of the narrative, rather than an evolutionary accident only at best "managed" in the final literary product. How this view of "narrativeness" can be understood is an issue that will come under discussion in Chapter 2.

1.9. Summary

As we have traced the role of double narratives in the development of Old Testament criticism from its tentative beginnings till the present, we have seen the extraordinary extent to which the double narrative phenomenon has been influential in the formation of biblical critical methodology. The three main historical critical schools of source, form, and tradition-historical criticism are all to a large degree indebted in their concepts of biblical

---

169 Damrosch regards his view as a "middle" position between the concept of the stories as
    oral variants and the view that the second and the third are literary products, the second
    building on the first, the third on the second.

composition to their perception of double narratives. Similarly in the "holistic" approaches, of which new literary criticism has become a major force in biblical studies in recent years, ideas about literary artistry or theological intention evident in the composition have been largely defined by reference to double narratives.

As we have also seen, within these approaches a large number of explanations have been suggested for the presence of doublets in the biblical tradition. Methodologically, however, these hypotheses offer only three main alternative juxtapositions. Firstly, there are the concepts of heterogeneous versus homogenous origins of doublets, and biblical tradition in general, polarized in the historical-critical approaches on the one hand, and the holistic approaches on the other. Yet even though this is perhaps the most obvious juxtaposition in biblical scholarship, it should be pointed out that since the time of Astruc no truly homogenous critical model of biblical composition has been mooted – even the most integrated ones, such as the approaches by Cassuto and Segal, accept an amount of use of sources. Conversely, it should also be noted that the "clarity of vision" that the Four Document hypothesis offered of the heterogeneous origins of biblical narrative at its formulation, was a transient experience in Old Testament scholarship, soon to be followed by the – still raging – controversy over the role of sources in the Bible.

Secondly, there is the issue of the nature of doublets as literary verses oral phenomenon. The juxtaposition here is in the realm of what various narrative characteristics are indicative of in terms of their authorship and mode of composition, and whether there are any criteria, or "laws", by which the issue of oral verses written composition can be unravelled.

Thirdly, there is the question of what constitutes a double narrative or a variant in biblical composition. This question has come to the fore with new literary criticism discovering previously unnoticed repetitions, yet without significantly contributing to the definition of what constitutes a doublet – i.e. whether all repetitions are equal?

There are still other realms of biblical criticism where double narratives have been discussed, such as structuralism and some of the postmodern approaches, such as psychoanalytic and feminist criticism, which have not been reviewed in this research.[170] The reason for this is that in these approaches double narratives are not used for the development of methodology, but simply in application of already existing approaches. Also being fully "text immanent" these approaches do not enter the debate about

---

170 See e.g. Brenner 1997; Culley 1974, 1976; Exum 1993; Rashkow 1993.

origin and development of biblical literature so prominent in the methods
surveyed in this chapter.

Chapter 2: Double Narratives as Indicators of Documents or Literary Artistry

2.1 The Nature of Biblical Criticism: The Role of Models in Methodology

In Chapter 1 we looked at the role of double narratives in the birth and development of Old Testament scholarship, from its conception to its most recent ramifications. What this exercise has demonstrated is the seminal importance of the double narrative phenomenon to the very fabric of the biblical critical discipline. Thus we saw how all the major critical approaches, and many of the minor ones, from the earliest source-critical reflections to the latest literary ones, have used the phenomenon to develop their methodological premises and/or to demonstrate them. What is remarkable here is that this has resulted in double narratives being used to form and demonstrate not only a variety of more or less complementary notions of the Old Testament text, but completely contrary ones!: Double narratives have been used to argue for the heterogeneous, composite origins of the Pentateuch and other narrative parts of the Old Testament, as in the main critical approaches, as well as for the homogeneity of the authorship, as in the more recent literary methods; they have been used as proof for the literary (written) nature of biblical composition, as well as to demonstrate its oral origins.

Naturally this situation is not completely satisfactory. We may able to rationalize that some seemingly contradictory notions are complementary rather than contradictory by, for instance, claiming differences between diachronic and synchronic approaches. But it is not possible to use the same aspects of doublets as evidence for opposing arguments: It is not possible to reconcile the notion of double narratives existing in the biblical text because works of many authors, which included some of the same material, have been compiled together, and that these very same variants signify the literary artistry of a single author. For the former concept suggests that double narratives just "happened", as if by accident, the latter that they are an integral part of a master design. Nor is it easy to see how we could argue for doublets to be a literary phenomenon (Wellhausen) and at the same time accept them as evidence for the oral origin of the Old Testament tradition (Gunkel). We must then question the compatibility of the various Old Testament methods as far as they are based on the observation of doublets and also ask to what extent such methods are in fact suggested by the presence of double narratives in the biblical text. Furthermore, we must ask whether the various critical approaches have in the development of their respective notions taken into account double narratives as a wider phenomenon, i.e. whether an understanding of the number and variety of double narratives in the biblical text as a whole would suggest the same methodological conclusions as have been arrived at by the observation of the particular variants that have been so central to the development of each successive approach.

Given such centrality of the double narrative phenomenon to the development of biblical studies, a scrutiny of the various Old Testament schools of criticism with respect to their methodological integrity and the role of doublets in them is not, therefore, misplaced – nor premature! And even if, as is realistic to expect, no "one" meaning or explanation for the phenomenon could be found as a result of such an exercise, a clarification of the issues on which such methodological disparity, even contradiction, hinges, would forward our understanding of the composition of biblical narrative and the methods appropriate for its study a great deal.

The object of the following three chapters is then to assess critically the methodological notions attached to double narratives by various forms of scholarship that have sought to explain their presence in the Old Testament text, and to suggest more meaningful and comprehensive ways of dealing with the doublet phenomenon in the Old Testament. What should come under scrutiny here are the types of evidence that have been used to explain the double narrative phenomenon and thence to justify the relevant critical methodologies based on the observation of the phenomenon.

First of all literary assumptions have been attached to doublets – such as aesthetic or other culturally governed notions of what narrative literature "should be like" in terms of repetition – i.e. whether such duplication as is found in the Old Testament narrative literature suggests compilation of documents, as claimed by source critics, literary artistry, as proposed by new literary critics, or implies orality, as argued for by form critics. These assumptions have mainly been used as *a priori* statements, from which other reasons for the existence of doublets in the text have followed. The circularity of the process has sometimes been pointed out,[1] but usually tolerated because of the strength of the conviction of the rightness of the assumptions. We need to look at how these assumptions have arisen and find the intellectual context in which they can be evaluated. The main vehicle for this assessment will be the isolation of the conceptual models operative in the biblical critical approaches in question. This will be our task in the present chapter.

Secondly, in form and tradition-historical criticism the concept of double narratives is often discussed with recourse to folklore studies, "oral laws" in particular. We need to look at the status of the tenet "duplication indicates oral variation" in the context of folkloristics and establish whether oral laws do have bearing on the doublets in the Old Testament. This will be investigated in Chapter 3.

Finally, I would like to add another, previously neglected dimension to the assessment of the methodological significance of doublets: the question of what methodological implications might be found by looking at the pattern of duplication in the Old Testament, i.e. the double narrative phenomenon as a whole, and to what extent this dimension has been taken into consideration in the formulation of various critical approaches. This will be our domain in Chapter 4.

2.1.1. Nature of Critical Tenets: Method, Theory and Model

One of the fundamental tenets of source criticism is the proposition that duplication, whether of complete narrative variants or repetition of detail, indicates that combination of material from more than one original source has taken place: the present text is a result of independent and separate narratives having been "woven together in double or threefold cord" (Wellhausen 1883:310, ET 295). This has been a basic methodological guideline for source criticism since Astruc first used it, together with the names of God, to separate two documents within Genesis, and has an overwhelmingly central role in Wellhausen's Four Document thesis. Achieving almost dogmatic status in biblical criticism soon after its conception this notion that duplication indicates sources has been the single most influential concept for

---

1   The process by which the criteria for source division was arrived at has been particularly vulnerable for such circularity, as highlighted by Whybray (1987). However, a number of "practising" source critics have always admitted to as much, thus underlining the hypothetical nature of the process. Similar observations are beginning to emerge concerning other approaches, see e.g. Greenstein 1989:54 for the interpretational process in general, Barton 1984a:5 for biblical critical methodology as a whole.

the shaping of Old Testament methodology[2] in its approach to the biblical text, which then has been understood as a heterogeneous entity, originating from a protracted literary process of composition, editing and collating by a number of authors and editors.

More recently scholars, such as Alter, have made what amounts to an opposite claim, namely that duplication in biblical narrative is a literary, artistic device, indicative of single, or at least homogeneous, authorship. This approach has been steadily gaining popularity, being most attractive perhaps because it seems to provide an explanation for the text as it is, in its canonical form, without cumbersome investigations into its pre-history.

That the notion "duplication indicates sources" and its opposite "duplication indicates literary artistry" thus lie in the heart of biblical methodology, with vast ramifications for the questions of date, composition and authorship of the Scriptures, is easy to see. What is far harder is to assess is the validity of these notions. For, as pointed out before, both concepts have often been used as *a priori* statements and evaluated in terms of their success in explaining the problems and inconsistencies of the biblical text – an exercise which can, of course, be highly subjective and circular. It is therefore of paramount interest for the present research to explore the nature of these notions and establish some parameters within which they can be debated and evaluated more objectively. A way to do this, it seems to me, is to open biblical criticism up for critique from other related disciplines, with which it naturally overlaps and shares (consciously or unconsciously) methodology, such as history, philosophy, folkloristics and poetics.

What then is the nature of biblical critical tenets, such as "duplication indicates sources", or its opposite, "duplication is an artistic device"? The answer to this question depends largely on how we perceive the Bible as a document, i.e. what we perceive to be its mode of expression and the type of knowledge it is attempting to communicate, and thence, what we understand the nature of biblical criticism to be as an enterprise. For instance, the Bible is now a literary, i.e. a written, document, but is it then also literature, to be evaluated according to literary canons, such as there may be, just as any "other" literature? Or should the Bible be seen more as a historical document, or as an example of folklore, attempting to convey facts about the events of the ancient world, its demography, geography, etc., or its meanings and beliefs, according to the conventions of the time and the genre? Or, because of its nature as a religious work, should all knowledge on biblical issues be the matter of divine illumination, sometimes defying all other kind

---

2   See e.g. Greenstein's comment on how source criticism has been "virtually equated...with Biblical criticism" (1990:31).

of logic, with either the individual or the church as an interpretative body, much as the Church has thought over the centuries?

Over the past two centuries of biblical criticism a variety of perceptions concerning both the nature of the Bible and that of biblical criticism have been held, but perhaps the only clear demarcation line that has merged is to see the task of biblical criticism as separate from the religious search for spiritual meaning as such, or the Church's task for doctrinal clarification or application. Biblical criticism in this respect is a "secular" enterprise, akin to other humanistic and scientific disciplines that emerged from the Enlightenment, or were redefined by it.

Establishing a self-identity for biblical criticism has not been an easy exercise. When biblical criticism first started to take firm shape in the eighteenth and nineteenth centuries, there were some who, in fact, wished to present it as a branch of exact science. In this respect biblical scholars reflected the general mood of the time pervading the intellectual world, humanists and natural scientists alike, which did not see different realms of knowledge as fully separate[3] and was excessively optimistic about the results new disciplines, often drawn on the models of natural sciences, could yield.[4] It was not unusual to see biblical criticism labelled as a "science",[5] and eventually to feel that the Documentary Theory, no longer remembered as the Documentary *Hypothesis*, had received the status of a proven law.[6]

---

3 The gradual, though still incomplete (Berlin argues), emergence of sciences and humanities as separate spheres of knowledge has been discussed at some length by Isaiah Berlin in "The Divorce between the Sciences and the Humanities" (1981 [1974]). Berlin points out how in the first half of the seventeenth century "theoretical knowledge was still conceived as one undivided realm; the frontiers between philosophy, science, criticism, theology, were not sharply drawn" (cf. Leibniz) as "all the spheres of human activity" were thought of as sharing "eternal, timeless truths" recognizable in one way only: "by means of reason" (cf. Voltaire) (I. Berlin 84, 88). Berlin sees the divorce between science and humanities beginning to emerge at the turn of the eighteenth century in Vico's (1668-1744) distinction between positive knowledge (single corpus of knowledge governed by single universal criteria) and understanding, but only becoming more generally known in the late eighteenth-century reaction, championed by Herder, to the above-mentioned "classification of all human experience in terms of absolute and timeless values" (I. Berlin 92, 104-5). However, Berlin points out that some scholars still believe that "methods and goals are, or should be, ultimately identical" throughout "the entire sphere of human knowledge": a reflection on the fact that the respective roles of sciences and humanities have still not been fully thought out – as attested also by the need for our present discussion (I. Berlin 80).

4 See Weiss 1-2.

5 E.g. Robert Lowth describes biblical criticism as "a particular department of science" (Lowth cited in Norton II:61).

Since then the expectations concerning the yields of biblical criticism have been adjusted at least to an extent, due perhaps in the first instance to the emergence of competing critical approaches, such as form criticism and tradition-historical criticism, which destroyed the illusion of one all-sufficient theory, and more recently the application of the new literary approaches to biblical studies. In the context of such plurality many scholars today tend to be much less ambitious – or more vague? – than their nineteenth century colleagues concerning the sufficiency and comprehensiveness of any particular approach. However, the emulation of scientific language has also persisted in some quarters and if anything, has been on the increase, as first structuralism in the 1970's, and more recently, poetics, have made their bid to be the newly (re) discovered "science of literature".[7]

All this is symptomatic of the fact that although biblical criticism is now well established as a discipline and is firmly recognized by most scholars as belonging to the humanities,[8] there has been remarkably little reflection in biblical scholarship on the nature of the discipline itself as a scholarly pursuit, and thence, the nature of its underlying tenets.[9] Thus what the apparent modesty in the claims made for various critical approaches may, in fact, betray, is not so much a hard-earned perception of the realistic limits of the scholarship as some confusion about its nature and capabilities. Consequently, although there has been something of an explosion of new ideas and approaches in the scholarship, as among other things "secular" literary criticism has been adopted to Old Testament studies, these methods have seldom been able to build on, or even relate to, each other's results, and have instead appeared as isolated and mutually exclusive claims for truth.[10]

---

6   The search for "laws" is one of the most central characteristics of the post-Enlightenment endeavours to understand the world we live in and to classify our knowledge about it. E. H. Carr points out that "throughout the eighteenth and nineteenth centuries, scientists assumed that laws of nature...had been discovered and definitely established, and that the business of the scientist was to discover and establish more such laws by process of induction from observed facts" (51-2). Carr argues that "students of society, consciously or unconsciously desiring to assert the scientific status of their studies, adopted the same language and believed themselves to be following the same procedure", hence, for instance, Adam Smith's "laws of the market" and Marx's "economic law of motion of modern society" etc. (52). This tendency is much in evidence in early biblical criticism as well, as seen e.g. in the source critical-insistence on the definiteness of the source-dividing criteria and, even more conspicuously, in the form-critical search for oral and literary laws.

7   See e.g. A. Berlin 15; Longman 29-30; cf. Culley 1985:174-5.

8   See Barton 1984a:6.

9   Cf. Tsevat, who draws attention to this fact (219).

In the last few decades a few scholars have, however, attempted to break these isolationist tendencies by bringing the nature of biblical criticism into focus. The works most relevant to our present discussion are Barton's seminal exposition of Old Testament methodology, *Reading the Old Testament*, 1984a, Alonso-Schökel's article "Of Methods and Models", 1985, and Greenstein's "Biblical Studies in a State", 1990, and "Theory and Argument in Biblical Criticism", 1989.[11] I will use these works as a catalyst for the discussion on how biblical critical tenets can be evaluated.

2.1.2. Barton, Alonso-Schökel, Greenstein

The object of Barton's work is to explore "the place and proper understanding of *method* in a discipline like Old Testament studies",[12] and the issues most relevant to our present study in the work are Barton's discussion of the relationship of method and theory, and the "metacritical" question of the nature of theory as such.

Barton points out how the prevalent concept of method in contemporary Old Testament studies is that of "a set of procedures which, when applied to the text, elicit its 'true' meaning" (1984a:205).[13] This concept, Barton argues, has equated biblical criticism with "procedures of technology",[14] which "process the text" rather than read it, and have subjected the scholarship to unrealistic expectations of scientific correctness and comprehensiveness (1984a:5). Disagreeing with this model for biblical criticism Barton argues that "biblical 'methods' are *theories* rather than methods: theories which result from the formalizing of intelligent intuitions about the meaning of biblical texts" (1984a:205). According to Barton, then, the reader approaches the text with a perception of its meaning, with "certain vague expectations about genre, coherence and consistency", which in the reading are then "either confirmed and clarified, or disappointed and frustrated" (1984a:205). When the reading resumes, it does so "with a sharper focus", and "at the end

---

10 Barton aptly describes this inability to relate as "the tendency of each newly-discovered method to excommunicate its predecessors" (1984a:5), and Alonso-Schökel, speaking particularly of the relationship between historical-critical and literary approaches, as "mutual condemnation" (1985:7, italics omitted).

11 See also Tsevat, 1975; Alonso-Schökel, 1975; and in somewhat different vein, Weiss 1984, chs 1-2.

12 Barton 1984a:4.

13 Cf. "I believe that all are well agreed as to what a *method* is: a defined and controllable way of proceeding" (Alonso-Schökel 1985:4).

14 Or even a "*technique*" (Barton 1984a:205).

of the process there emerges a distinct impression of what the text means, together with an explanatory theory as how it comes to mean" (Barton 1984a:205).

What is primary, then, for Barton is that there is "some prior understanding of the text", a notion of what the text is to be "read as", before any method can be applied or theory formulated: the theory is always "logically subsequent to the intuition about meaning" (1984a:5, 199, 205). These prior ideas, or "intuitions", about the meaning of the text, are then not methods themselves, but "models for understanding what methods are for" (1984a:199, 205).[15]

For Barton, then, biblical criticism is a descriptive, non-scientific pursuit, one of analysis, but not of prescription, and a task he sets for himself is to relieve critical approaches from any misplaced obligations to scientific precision and "watertightness". Biblical criticism, he argues, "needs to be evaluated with the tools proper to the humanities not the sciences" (1984a:6). Though Barton does not elaborate on what these tools might be, he sees "literary criticism in general, in the world of English literature and the study of modern languages and literature", as the only background against which biblical critical methods can "make coherent sense" (1984a:3).

In a similar fashion, though with a different emphasis, Alonso-Schökel attempts in "Of Methods and Models", 1985, to clarify the theoretical framework of biblical studies, this time with the focus on the relationship of methods to models. Alonso-Schökel sees the model as the single most important factor in the shaping of a critical approach: the "model", he argues, "is not dependent on method but rather directs it" (1985:4).

Alonso-Schökel defines a model as "a system of elements constructed to give a unified explanation to a set of observed data", or as "a system already known and tested in one field which is transferred to a new field of investigation" (1985:5).[16] What seems to be the essence of these rather cumbersome definitions is that according to Alonso-Schökel a model is a kind of constellation that provides an operational framework for yet unclassified material and "guides subsequent observation and explanation of

---

15 Tsevat identifies the preconceptions which guide theory formulations as "first principles", which scholars have "implicit recourse to", but seldom state explicitly (218).

16 Alonso-Schökel more or less equates the term model with "paradigm", as used e.g. by T. S. Kuhn, and also with "hypothesis" and "theory", although each term has its individual emphasis. In the main Alonso-Schökel seems to concur with Barbour's perhaps better known definition of a model as "an imagined mechanism or process, postulated by *analogy* with familiar mechanisms or processes and used to construct a *theory* to correlate a set of *observations*" (Barbour 30; cf. Alonso-Schökel 1985:4ff).

data" (1985:5). In this sense the model always has "a surplus meaning" that can be used in service of research in another area than where the model originated (1985:5). In this respect, Alonso-Schökel argues, "the model, once adopted, becomes an *a priori* form of the research and its method" (1985:5).

The way the model operates as an organizing principle has been further developed by Greenstein. Greenstein attacks the idea, expressed, for instance, by Alter, that one can "simply 'infer'…the conventions of the literature 'by a careful inspection of the texts'",[17] and argues instead that "data do not by themselves congeal into theories. Scholars shape the data into configurations of their own imagination".[18] Greenstein points out that we "do not simply see the connections; we first draw them", i.e. our observations are classified and organized on the basis of "models with which we are familiar" without us actually having any choice in the matter, and argues that "each theory's methods select and interpret evidence in order to support or lend substance to the arguments that hold up the theory" (1989:56, 61; 1990:34). Thus, Greenstein contends, "the debate over the composition of the Pentateuch often represents itself as an argument about logic, methodology, and data", when often the contest is, in fact, "between theories or models of composition" (1989:61).

What the works reviewed above have done is to attempt to conceptualize biblical criticism as a discipline and also, to an extent, to clarify its position within the larger framework of human knowledge – both issues that other humanists, historians and literary critics in particular, have in their respective realms been struggling with.[19] With respect to the present research two issues in particular stand out from the reviews above. First of all biblical criticism is affirmed as a humanistic, theoretical enterprise and as such as an essentially circular, or perhaps more aptly, spiral, one, as contrasted with the more linear, cause-and-effect processes of the sciences or the procedures of technology. This suggests certain tentativeness, perhaps even inconclusiveness, about biblical criticism, which is not present in the same sense in the sciences. Secondly, and perhaps even more importantly, the model, i.e. the preconception of the meaning of the text, which guides the processes of observation that are then consolidated in a subsequent theory, emerges as the key conceptual and organizing element in biblical criticism.

---

17 Greenstein 1989:56, citing Alter 1983:118.
18 Greenstein 1990:30. See Greenstein 1989:56-7 for a further discussion on the role of perception in theory making.
19 See e. g. Carr in relation to history.

Much has been written in Old Testament scholarship about the relative sequence, or even necessity, of historical (source-critical, diachronic) and literary (genre-oriented, new literary, synchronic) investigations in the critical process.[20]   The argument has frequently been put forward, particularly by the proponents of the latter – literary – priority in the above dilemma, that if we allowed "the text to speak for itself", approached it "neutrally" and objectively" the problem would be solved as the necessary conventions would "arise" from the text more or less on their own accord.[21] The concept of the process of the critical study of Old Testament, reviewed above and most succinctly summarized by Barton's description of the process of reading, from its beginning with "vague expectations" to its resumption with "a sharper focus",[22] could be easily taken as a vote for the genre-priority position in the sequence debate. It is however an indictment of posing such a dilemma in those terms in the first place and can be taken as a priority statement only with a twist: in the wider sense the choice of the historical approach qualifies as a "genre decision" as much as the literary approach does, for neither is apparent in the text itself, but is preceded by the model for the text, i.e. the decision to read the text as one or the other.[23] There is no neutral observation of "naked facts" on the basis of which a theory could then be construed. The priority of the model in the critical process means that a preconception colours not only the type of theory that can be constructed, but the very choice of facts to support or criticise it, and the observation processes with which this is to be accomplished.[24]

---

20 See e.g. Polzin, who calls this "the very first question" confronting today's biblical scholars (1). This is an issue that is very much alive also in literary criticism in general, cf. Pomorska 276, and Sötér 85-6.

21 Cf. Alter 1983:118.

22 Barton 1984a:205.

23 Thus in my view the claim made by, for instance, Polzin that "scholarly understanding of biblical material results from a *circular* movement that begins with a literary analysis, then turns to historical problems", finally returning to inform "one's literary critical conclusions", indicates a choice of a model, rather than a neutral starting point (Polzin 6). The process is indeed a circular one, but for that very reason cannot begin in any one set place. Rather, there is more than one model-dependent option for the start, end and length of the process. Cf. statements similar to Polzin's made by literary critics Pomorska (276), and Sötér (94).

24 In presenting such a model of the biblical critical process the scholars reviewed above resonate the wider academic community of the late 1950's onwards that reacted strongly to the prevailing empiricism, which had by then permeated both humanities and sciences (Barbour 3). The empiricist view saw the scientific process as a purely objective one, starting from "publicly observable data which can be described in a pure observation-language independent of any theoretical assumptions", and included the notions that "theories can be verified or falsified by comparison with this fixed experimental data"

But where does all this leave us in trying to address some of the most fundamental questions in biblical criticism, i.e. the nature of its basic tenets, on which the definitive theories of biblical criticism have been construed? What has emerged from the discussion above is the crucial role of a conceptual framework, a model, which enables a theory, in our case of the composition of parts of the Old Testament, to take shape by providing a meaningful language necessary for the task and by guiding the observation processes involved. The two critical tenets under scrutiny here, "duplication indicates sources" and "duplication indicates literary artistry", are not models themselves but, rather, they reflect models in which such explanation for duplication is perceived to be true. Thus in the case of our present research not only are the notions "duplication indicates sources" and "duplication indicates literary artistry" preceded in a scholar's mind by either a document-related model or a literary model but furthermore, the very observation of duplication must be recognized in the first place as presuming some model of the kind: the recognition of doublets in the Old Testament text is in itself "theory-dependent" – a fact testified to by the relatively late "discovery" of the phenomenon.

What is essential then for the present research, is to identify the models in question and to find some way of evaluating their appropriateness for the material they have been used for in the Old Testament. With reference to the latter of these tasks, the evaluation of theories and their tenets, some qualification may be appropriate. Even though appeals for "testing" of critical notions in biblical studies are periodically made with "empirical models" as the suggested vehicle,[25] I do not consider it to be possible to

---

and that "the choice between theories is rational, objective and in accordance with specifiable criteria" (Barbour 3). To this scholars, such as Kuhn, retorted that "all data are theory-laden; there is no neutral observation-language", that "theories are not verified or falsified; when data conflict with an accepted theory, they are usually set to one side as anomalies, or else auxiliary assumptions are modified", and that "there are no criteria for choice between rival theories of great generality, for the criteria are themselves theory-dependent" (Barbour 93, italics omitted).

25 Information deduced from the observation of traditions, deemed in some aspects to be comparable to the Scriptures, has been used to argue for various compositional and scribal practices in the making of the Old Testament, which are assumed to have contributed to the double narrative phenomenon. Such analogues, usually drawn from the wider cultural context of the Old Testament, i.e. types of ancient Near Eastern literature, but also from more recent epic or saga traditions, are usually called "empirical models". These models have had a significant role in the debate concerning double narratives and their function in the Bible right from the early days of biblical criticism, and have had a particular appeal to source and form critics. However, to discuss the importance and function of these models in any meaningful way falls outside the scope

prove or disprove biblical critical theories by such – or any other – means, as invaluable as they are in their place, only to clarify the evidence and thus affect the balance of probabilities. Evaluation here will therefore first of all mean identifying the intellectual and historical context of the models in question.

2.1.3. Identifying Models for Duplication: "Nature", "Archivist-Historian", "Historian", "Literary Artist"

What then are the models the two tenets in question reflect? It is one of the ironies of the debate on the nature and significance of doublets in the Old Testament narratives that the two, quite diametrically opposed, schools of thought on the issue both have characterized their pursuit as "literary criticism" and regard duplication as a literary phenomenon. It seems that with regard to the source-critical notion "duplication indicates sources", as well as its more recent counterpart "duplication indicates literary artistry", the issue is that both notions have been perceived, if in somewhat different ways by their respective advocates, as literary concepts, arising from a concept of what literature is or "should be" like. What is meant by literature or why certain expectations are placed on it is, however, not made very clear, although in the more recent literary scholarship there has been at least an attempt to define "literature", and thus one of the central issues in our task here is to clarify this question.

In the history of Old Testament scholarship several models have been identified for the composition of, in particular, the Pentateuch. Alonso-Schökel recognizes three models, two of which are of particular interest for our present study. The model employed in source criticism, Alonso-Schökel contends, is that of a historian, for "historians, critical or otherwise, make use of *sources* in writing their works: oral and written sources, monuments, documents" (1985:5). (New) literary criticism, on the other hand, Alonso-Schökel argues, is modelled on the "literary work and its author" (1985:9). While the expectation of coherence for the former model is "a certain homogeneity within each narrative, heterogeneity with respect to the other accounts", in the latter the coherence one expects is "specifically poetical or literary, not necessarily logical" (Alonso-Schökel 1985:5, 9). Similarly,

---

of the current research. See Tsevat 219ff, for the extent to which the search for empirical models is sometimes taken, Tigay 1985, for the use of empirical models in source criticism.

while the former model presupposes "pre-existing narratives which are continuous, datable and relatively complete", in the latter model "what the author consciously intended to communicate is indeed a main factor in the meaning of the work" (Alonso-Schökel 1985:5, 9).[26]

Greenstein, in turn, contrasts two compositional models in pentateuchal studies, one operational in "the classical Documentary hypothesis", the other in the more recent challenge to the traditional hypothesis, which he terms the "Winnett-Van Seters theory" (1990:31). Greenstein argues that the model represented by the Documentary theory "regards the redactor of the Torah as an ancient Jewish predecessor of the author of a synoptic Gospel, redacting together two or more sources into a new version", while in Van Seters' approach the author of the Torah is seen as "a contemporary of Herodotus, composing history using similar methods" (1990:31).[27]

In a somewhat different vein, focusing in their search for models on biblical scholarship rather than biblical traditions themselves – although the two are interlinked – scholars such as Weiss and Polzin see source criticism, or even biblical criticism as a whole, including modern literary approaches, as reflecting a model based on natural sciences. Thus Weiss describes "a science of literature analogous to the natural sciences" being created in the nineteenth century and this forming the context also for biblical (source?) criticism (1-2). Polzin entertains the same natural science model, but finds for it an even wider application than Weiss – and negative consequences: "if there is a crisis in biblical scholarship today", as is often suggested, this crisis, Polzin argues, "does not consist in the present, almost healthy tension between historical and literary criticism but rather in the destructive self-image both may mistakenly have concerning their status as scholarly disciplines modeled after the natural sciences" (2).[28]

---

26 Alonso-Schökel contrasts the "historian" model of source criticism with the "story-teller" model of form criticism, but also brackets the two together under the "sedimentation" model of redaction analysis, thus contrasted with the "literary work and its author" model of new literary criticism (1985:5-9). The storyteller model will not be discussed here as it does not directly relate to either of the duplication-tenets under scrutiny in this chapter, but assumes a third tenet, "duplication indicates oral composition and transmission", to be discussed in Chapter 3.

27 Greenstein recognizes these as "opposing models" with "profound" implications for the reconstruction of Israelite history (1990:32). The first of these models compares closely with Alonso-Schökel's "historian", the second comes closer to the "literary artist", though assuming a distinct historical context.

28 In some contrast to the above models, identified by scholars as formative to various already existing critical approaches, new models, such as the "biological" model and the "house building" model, are also mooted as a basis for future, potentially revolutionary, theories of biblical criticism, see Weiss 22ff.

All the models outlined above have their merits and, perhaps most importantly, illustrate the way source- and literary-critical approaches are perceived in recent scholarship. However, it is obvious that the models have been suggested, as it were, in passing, as there is no accompanying discussion on the reasons for the suggestions, or reference to scholars in question or the context of their time to substantiate the claims.

Our task here then is twofold. Firstly, we need to relate the discussion on models more specifically to the issue of duplication and the two opposing tenets, "duplication indicates sources" and "duplication indicates literary artistry". Secondly, we need to deepen and concretize the discussion by moving it to the context of actual scholarship, rather than discussing models in the abstract or in relation to biblical criticism in general. And lastly, we need to relate this to the larger framework of the intellectual history of the time of the scholars in question. What is particularly important here is to see whether there is anything in the early critical scholarship itself that suggests – or precludes – such, or other, models as suggested above. In what follows the three main models of "nature", "historian" and "literary artist", and an intermediate model, "archivist-historian", will be used as a basis for discussion.

2.2. The "Nature" Model: Spinoza

The "discovery" of the double narrative phenomenon occurred, as outlined above, in the seventeenth century, with the first work dealing extensively with the issue appearing in the mid-eighteenth century. Three scholars, Spinoza, Simon and Astruc, usually share the accolade of the "father" or "founder" of biblical criticism[29] and it is in the works of these men that the double narrative phenomenon is first observed and an explanation for it is attempted. The context for the early work on doublets, and any conceptual model it may be based on, is thus the late Renaissance and early Enlightenment of northern continental Europe, France and the Netherlands in particular.

Although the influence of the early critics on the subsequent development of Old Testament criticism has been well documented and commented on, not much work has so far been done, within biblical scholarship at least, on the forces that produced and shaped this new thinking, i.e. the intellectual history of the ideas that form the foundation of biblical criticism even

---

29   See e.g. O'Doherty 300; Popkin 1996:404; Savan 97; Strauss 1965:35; Yovel 19.

today.[30] Even though a full investigation of this topic would naturally have to be a work in its own right, it is nevertheless vital for our task that we understand something of the intellectual context in which the first critical observations concerning doublets, and the Bible in general, arose.

Of the scholars who first observed the double narrative phenomenon, Spinoza is one of the earliest, the most original and the most important for our present interest, as he not only provides us with observations on doublets but also outlines the larger hermeneutical framework of which they are a part.[31] His significance for subsequent scholarship is also unrivalled, as his work on the Bible in the *Tractatus Theologico-Politicus* is often hailed as the first modern, scientific hermeneutic, not only of the Bible but of historical texts in general.[32]

Perhaps the first point to keep in mind in connection with Spinoza's observations on duplications in the Bible is that they were not the focus of his study – nor of Simon's after him: not until Astruc's *Conjectures* is the phenomenon looked at in any detail and in its own right. Spinoza's remarks on doublets in *Tractatus Theologico-Politicus* are part of his attack on the

---

30 Thus, e.g. the handful of articles on Astruc that have appeared in biblical journals in the last century (Alphandéry; de Vaux; Lods 1924a, 1924b; O'Doherty) have tended to concentrate on his biography, the influence of *Conjectures* on biblical criticism, even the state of Old Testament studies before Astruc. There has been very little analysis, however, of Astruc's indebtedness – or otherwise – to his predecessors, his conceptual framework or place in the scholarship of the time. More has been written on Spinoza and Simon, but mainly in French scholarship (see esp. Armogathe (ed.); Auvray; Zac; but also Craigie; Sandys-Wunsch).

31 Goshen-Gottstein points out that Spinoza may not have been the first person to comment critically on the Bible, "mais on peut dire que c'est par son intermédiaire que ce fait a pénétré la conscience européenne moderne" (36). Various scholars and ideas have been identified as influences on Spinoza's biblical critical thinking. The authorship of the Pentateuch had been questioned by several scholars, such as Hobbes, the reliability of the transmission of the biblical text by e.g. Samuel Fisher, while the Socinian movement as a whole fostered a rationalistic approach to the Scriptures (Strauss 1965:52; Popkin 1987:86, 1996:388-99; but cf. Curley 71, 95-6, 96n46). The role of the main influence on Spinoza in matters of biblical criticism is, however, often given to Isaac La Peyrère, whose hermeneutic has been characterized as "naturalistic and rationalistic" and as "an attempt to reconcile the history of salvation with the new natural science" (Popkin 1987:1; Strauss 1965:64-5, 71; but cf. Curley 72ff). Interestingly, in his main work, *Men Before Adam*, 1656, La Peyrère, too, wrestles with the presence of doublets in the Bible. Eventually he ends up using the two Creation stories as evidence for two separate creations of mankind and attempting to explain inconsistencies in the Pentateuch on the basis that "*Moses* made a Diarie of all those wonderfull things which God did for the people of *Israel*": This "diarie" was then copied into the Bible with increasing confusion as the process went on (La Peyrère, Book IV:205-6).

32 See Savan 97.

authority of the Bible in general, which he saw as the main obstacle to free investigation, and the Mosaic authorship of the Pentateuch in particular.[33] In their context his observations are meant to emphasize the human, thence inconsistent and at times irrational, character of biblical composition, or at least of its transmission.[34]

In Spinoza's opinion the Bible was "a literary document like any other", and should be studied as such (Strauss 1965:35). Yovel points out that the "humanists had turned the Bible from mere story into a 'text', while Spinoza's second revolution turned it into a 'document'", and crucially, "a *secular* document" (Yovel 19).[35] The criteria, by which this "document" should then be studied, Spinoza's hermeneutic or method, are outlined in the *Tractatus Theologico-Politicus*. They are inseparable from Spinoza's overall philosophical orientation, which was above all rationalistic,[36] and can be encapsulated in two words: reason and nature. It was Spinoza's "first principle", as Strauss has pointed out, to place "full trust in the findings of his own intelligence" (1965:113). For Spinoza the universe was "inherently continuous and rational": what was knowable at all was so through "reason and experience" (Wild xxii; Yovel 17).

This approach had two main consequences. On the one hand it meant the rejection of revelation, as well as any "preestablished schemes" of interpretation, such as allegorization, as a source of knowledge – a fact that got Spinoza into trouble with the authorities on not a few occasions (Yovel 17). On the other hand the rationalistic approach meant the treatment of the Bible "as a purely scientific object" and the emergence of the notion of the "Bible science" (Yovel 17; Strauss 1965:258).[37]

The analogue or model, which Spinoza used for developing this new science of hermeneutics, was that of nature and natural sciences.[38] It was his intention in the *Tractatus Theologico-Politicus* (ch. 7) to show that "the proper method of interpreting Scripture does not differ from the proper

33 Cf. Popkin 1996:385; Strauss 1965:35, 258; Yovel 3.

34 For Spinoza the question of the inspiration of Scripture was in the final analysis only academic, as the fact that we have no autographs of the texts meant that they had inevitably been "corrupted" in transmission, as is shown by repetitions, discrepancies in chronology, etc. (Strauss 1965:262-8).

35 See also Popkin 1996:403-4; Zac 165-6.

36 Scruton 46ff; Yovel 4; Lagrée qualifies Spinoza's position as "reason directed by multifarious knowledge (historical, linguistic, etc.)" (31), and Sandys-Wunsch as an opposite of, or alternative to, superstition (332).

37 Strauss has pointed out that though Spinoza had his doubts about religion, as a disciple of Maimonides he "never doubted the legitimacy of science"! (1965:251).

38 See Klever 37; Sandys-Wunsch 336; Strauss 1965:258ff; Yovel 16ff.

method of interpreting nature" (Spinoza 84, ET 1862:143-4).   What this
meant was that "as the interpretation of nature consists in the examination of
the history of nature, *historia naturae*,"[39] and drawing conclusions therefrom,
"so Scriptural interpretation proceeds by the examination of Scripture",[40] or
as Spinoza continues: "the interpretation of...almost everything contained in
Scripture, is to be sought from Scripture alone, even as the interpretation of
nature is to be derived from nature" (Spinoza 85, ET 1862:144).

Spinoza's method was then to a large degree an empirical one, just as
much as it was rational, emphasizing above all, as Savan has put it, "the
importance of the careful collection of empirical data" and insisting that
"variations and changes in the data must be noted, compared, and cross
checked" (Savan 99). For the interpretation of a subject, whether Scripture
or nature, "no other principles nor data" could be "assumed" than what can
be gathered from the study of the subject itself and its history (Spinoza 84,
ET 1862:144).

This emphasis on careful observation is very much in evidence in the
comments Spinoza makes in the *Tractatus Theologico-Politicus* on doublets
in the Bible, and echoes the principles enumerated above of noting
"variations and changes" and comparing and cross-checking data, as e.g. "in
the Five Books of Moses", Spinoza observes, "one and the same story is
often met with again and again, and occasionally with very important
differences in the incidents" (117, ET 1862:189). On the other hand Spinoza
sees the inconsistencies in the two introductions of David to Saul's court
implying that the narratives must have been taken from different records, as
the "cause assigned for David's frequenting the palace of Saul is very
different" (117, ET 1862:190).

Two aspects of Spinoza's work and context highlighted by commentators
on the period may help us put Spinoza's "nature" model for biblical criticism
into a wider perspective.   Underpinning Spinoza's "general theory of
method", as Savan[41] terms it, is a concept of "universal laws and rules of

---

39 Curley interprets Spinoza's use of "history" with regard to nature "in a Baconian sense"
    as "a descriptive catalogue of the principal phenomena a scientific theory would seek to
    explain", and with regard to Scripture as "a full description of the life, character, and
    concerns of the author of each book", time and reasons for writing it, its language and
    transmission history (Curley 79; cf. Reedy 25).
40 "Sic etiam ad Scripturam interpretandem necesse est ejus sinceram historiam adornare"
    (Spinoza 84).   ET 1862 is here somewhat less succinct: "Inasmuch as the way of
    interpreting nature consists especially in bringing together, in arranging and contrasting,
    the facts of natural science...so also in interpreting Scripture it is necessary to co-
    ordinate its simple statements and histories" (144).
41 Savan 100.

nature".[42] Thus, according to Spinoza, there ought to be "one and the same method (*ratio*) of understanding the nature of all things whatsoever" as "the laws and rules, according to which all things are changed from form to form, are everywhere and always the same".[43] In other words, in the area of human sciences[44] Spinoza pursues "the same method" he uses in "considering lines, planes, or bodies".[45]

On the other hand, as Strauss has pointed out, Spinoza's biblical method follows hot on the heels of advances in such "strictly empirical sciences as geography and ethnology" that resulted in "the dissemination and extension of empirical knowledge"[46] and changed people's conception of the "world of the Bible", this in turn instigating much of the critique of religion in post-Renaissance Europe (Strauss 1965:70).[47]   The emergence of a "new conception of knowledge" that expressed itself in the "new mathematical physics" – an area of expertise for Spinoza – is also much in evidence in Spinoza's demands for reason and deduction, irrespective of the field of study (Strauss 1965:70).[48]

Despite the emphasis on natural sciences Spinoza's approach to Scripture has also sometimes been seen as historical,[49] but it would be mistaken to attribute to him the proper model of "historian" for his understanding how doublets came to be in the biblical text: Yovel, for instance, maintains that for Spinoza "the study of history is but a branch of the study of nature" and "provides a paradigm case for the kind of natural science of history which alone is possible in Spinoza" (Yovel 23).[50]   Spinoza's concepts of the "secular text" and the "Bible science" do, however, prepare the ground for a future historical discipline.[51] Thus Strauss argues that Spinoza's purpose for "Bible science" was for it to be "a means of unprejudiced understanding of Scripture", and that unprejudiced understanding in turn was equivalent to "historical understanding" (1965:262).   Similarly Popkin sees Spinoza's

---

42 Spinoza *Ethics* III, Preface, cited in Savan 101.
43 Spinoza *Ethics* III, Preface, cited in Savan 101.
44 Here the context is the study of the human mind, emotions in particular.
45 Spinoza *Ethics* III, Preface, cited in Savan 101.
46 Italics omitted.
47 Cf. Maull 9ff; Sandys-Wunsch 328.
48 Savan goes as far as to suggest that "Spinoza saw no incompatibility between the geometrical method" and the study of, for instance, the emotions (101).
49 See Strauss 1965:35.
50 Cf. Frei, who calls Spinoza's approach "a natural history of the development of the Pentateuch" (156).
51 Cf. Zac, who credits Spinoza with "a historical consciousness in embryo" (Zac 1965, referred to in Yovel 23).

"naturalist stance" as the basis for the "rational secularism" that led Spinoza to see the Bible as a "totally secularized" historical document (Popkin 1996:403-4).

The assessment of validity of Spinoza's model will ultimately have to be done in relation to his philosophical framework. What is most significant for our present purpose, however, is to see the interdependence of his biblical interpretation and the larger philosophical context of his thinking and time. It would not be unreasonable to suggest that Spinoza observed repetition and duplication in the biblical narrative very much as a scientist records variation in the natural world and sees it as an indication of growth, evolution and diversity – the "naturalness", i.e. humanness, of the Bible. More than his successors Spinoza's interest in duplication relates to it just "being there", as evidence for diversity, and hence as ammunition against supernatural design, rather than to the literary process that may have produced it.

2.3. The "Archivist-Historian": Simon and Astruc

The critical models used for double narratives by Spinoza's two most important successors, Simon and Astruc, have a less easily definable profile than Spinoza's "nature" model, as the works of the two later scholars lack the extensive philosophical discussion on methodology provided by Spinoza. Neither is there any consensus among intellectual historians of the Enlightenment on the extent of methodological agreement between Spinoza and his successors, Simon in particular: while Popkin suggests that Simon agrees with Spinoza's method but not his conclusions, Moreau argues that Simon's criticism of Spinoza relates particularly to the question of method (Popkin 1996:403-4; Moreau 410).[52] However, Simon and Astruc comment on the double narrative phenomenon more extensively than any other early critics and do leave some clues for their potential conceptual framework in their own work.

What is clear is that Simon's *Histoire critique* and Astruc's *Conjectures* have a widely different context for their exploration of doublets from Spinoza's *Tractatus*, in that both Simon's and Astruc's works are, at least on the surface, apologies for the authority of Scripture, which Spinoza had

---

52 Reedy points out that when Locke read Simon's *A Critical History of the Old Testament* he thought that "Simon was a scientist who amassed raw empirical data and sought a simple way to explain their existence" (Reedy 114).

attacked.[53] It is also obvious that the focus and intention in Simon's and Astruc's work on double narratives are different from Spinoza's, in that Simon and Astruc look to find some kind of unity in the duplication-repetition phenomenon, while Spinoza is more content to point out the fact that the phenomenon exists and emphasize this as evidence for the humanness of the biblical record.

Simon's way of establishing unity despite the duplications is through his theory of "publick Writers (*Scribes publics*)",[54] inspired editors of the Israelite archives, who among other documents used Moses' own work for the creation of the Pentateuch, while Astruc's hypothesis of Moses using *mémoires*, or documents, for his writing of Genesis[55] utilizes much the same model. The framework for Simon's suggestion is his "inordinate historical researches to try to get to the ur-text" of the Old Testament,[56] an area of biblical scholarship in which Simon's erudition far surpasses that of Spinoza and which provides in his *Histoire critique* the first serious attempt at tracing the history of the biblical text, both in the lower and the higher critical senses of the term. In somewhat similar fashion Astruc's *Conjectures* provides the first scholarly attempt to identify the types and limits of documents employed in any biblical book, in this case Genesis.

These two aspects of Simon's and Astruc's work – a more sophisticated and detailed picture of the Old Testament text as one composed of records or documents, and the quest for a unifying factor, whether "publick Writers" or Moses himself, that would explain duplication without compromising authority – suggest at least a tentative model Simon's and Astruc's concept of biblical composition and one different from Spinoza's "nature" model: an "archivist-historian". The assumptions that are endemic to Simon's and Astruc's argumentation, and therefore central to their conceptual model, relate to the expectancy of consistency within a document,[57] allowance of inconsistency and duplication in a "historical" work, i.e. one which has been composed of sources of some kind, and the figure of the "writer", the early

---

53 See Simon Preface * 3, ET Preface a 2; Astruc 439, 453; see also p. 6ff above.

54 Simon Preface * 2ff, ET Preface a 1ff. Woodbridge calls this theory one of Simon's "daring innovations" (1989:202; cf 1988:74), and Reedy Simon's "seminal contribution to scriptural interpretation" (105).

55 See the full title of Astruc's work. Spinoza, too, provided a unifying factor in the person of Ezra, but far more casually than Simon or Astruc.

56 Popkin 1996:404. Simon himself explains his "rules of criticism and translation", which employed a "philological and historical perspective", in the Preface to his *Historie critique* (see also pp. 352-510) (Woodbridge 1988:83)

57 Now based on a kind of "documentary logic", or as Sykes has described it, one of "grammar and philology" (Sykes 195), in contrast to Spinoza's mathematical logic.

historian. The need of this last feature, the unifying "publick Writer" - historian, can be seen as a tacit acceptance from the part of both Simon and Astruc of Spinoza's notion of the "secular text": the expectations of consistency and absence of repetition or duplication Simon and Astruc place on the document the "historian" used, do not in essence differ from Spinoza's characterization of the secular text.

Yovel has argued that Simon's method is less radical than Spinoza's and this is certainly true in terms of the repercussions on the authority of Scripture – although Simon himself by no means escaped from persecution either (Yovel 19). However, Simon's method is different from Spinoza's and is innovative, maybe even radical, in a different way. Strauss has pointed out that, in fact, Spinoza's influence on historical studies was limited as a consequence of his view that "the method of biblical studies is fundamentally the same as that of natural sciences" (Strauss 1965:35). In this respect Simon, and Astruc after him, perhaps have an edge over Spinoza in that it was their model of biblical composition – i.e. the composer – and consequently of the scholar unravelling the composition, the "archivist-historian", one that insisted that it was "impossible to understand Scripture without knowing the different states of the text at different times and places",[58] that became formative for Old Testament criticism for the next two centuries.

If in Spinoza's "nature" model the concept of a historical document that could not tolerate duplication was embryonic, in Simon's and Astruc's "archivist-historian" model it emerges in definite outline, with an accompanying rationale for the presence of duplications in the Bible and an approach for studying them. In fact, the basic expectation concerning what a document may or may not entail, now established, would remain largely unchallenged until the mid-twentieth century and the rise of new literary approaches in biblical criticism.

2.4. "The Historian": Wellhausen

It was, however, nineteenth-century German scholarship, Wellhausen in particular, which in the Documentary Hypothesis worked out the first coherent explanation and rationale for the presence of doublets in the Old Testament and in so doing reflected a vastly different intellectual context and set of premises than what has just been discussed above. In one of the few

---

58 Reedy 104-5.

major studies dealing specifically with the intellectual history of Old Testament criticism, *Bible without Theology*, 1987a,[59] Oden identifies the German nineteenth-century historiography as the conceptual context of the Documentary Hypothesis (1987a:5; 1987b:2).[60] It is against this background that we will look at the model for double narratives employed in documentary criticism in its heyday.

Oden recognizes the time of Wellhausen as a distinct, discernible period in the study of the Old Testament (1987b:1).[61] Reflecting Kuhn's concept of paradigm shifts Oden observes that such periods in scholarship arise and define themselves "in response to the perception of a new setting", i.e. a change in the intellectual context of a discipline which necessitates the reorientation of the discipline and its conceptual basis (1987b:1). Oden argues that in the case of Old Testament criticism it was German historiography which in the third quarter of the nineteenth century "had achieved a confident maturity" and "made such great claims for itself" – claims that had been favourably received – that scholars eminent in their field, such as Wellhausen, "perceived it a necessity to re-establish the foundations of their own disciplines" (1987b:2). As double narratives have such a central role in Wellhausen's work, and source criticism in general, it is to be expected that any reconsideration of foundations be also reflected in how doublets are perceived.

The shift of paradigms which took place in the nineteenth-century thinking, and which Oden is referring to,[62] is a well-recognized fact among the intellectual historians of the period.[63] If in the time of Enlightenment

---

59   See also Oden's article "Intellectual History and the Study of the Bible", 1987b, and a special Wellhausen-issue of *Semeia* (vol. 25) 1982, particularly the articles by Smend and Knight. Most comparable works on nineteenth-century biblical scholarship have concentrated on the question of Wellhausen's alleged indebtedness to Hegel (see Kraus; Perlitt).

60   Cf. Smend: "Wellhausen had lived in complete awareness of his period, which was one of the great intellectual heydays" (8). Oden sees de Wette as the key figure for the transition to historical though in biblical studies, arguing that it was in his work that "the study of the religion of Israel and of the Hebrew Bible had become a part of the broad historiographic tradition", under discussion here. (Oden 1987a:19).

61   Oden recognizes two other such periods within the past century of Old Testament scholarship, the history-of-religions school represented by, among others, Gunkel, and the more sociological approach to Israel's origins and institutions pursued, for instance, by Robertson Smith (Oden 1987b:6ff, 11ff)

62   Oden 1987a:5.

63   Iggers regards German historiography, in which he recognizes a continuous line of thought from von Humboldt and Ranke to Meinecke and Ritter, "as a unique event in the history of ideas" (Iggers 1968:13). The roots of this tradition Iggers finds in certain

"nature and reason" dominated, in contrast, as Mandelbaum, one of the foremost exponents of nineteenth-century scholarship, argues, "one of the most distinctive features of nineteenth-century thought" can be said to have been "the widespread interest evinced in history" (41). The interest, amounting to a revolution in thinking rather than a mere shift in focus, manifested itself, according to Mandelbaum, not only in "the growth and diversification of professional historical scholarship, but in the tendency to view all of reality, and all of man's achievements, in terms of the category of development" (Mendelbaum 41).

As a consequence a historical orientation, or as Iggers has pointed out, "the philosophy and methodology of historicism" came to permeate "all...humanistic and cultural sciences", theology, as well as its sister disciplines, such as philology, linguistics and philosophy (1968:4). This revolution in thinking took place most noticeably, or at least in the most radical way, in Germany, our particular interest here, but was by no way means confined to it.[64] The new mode of thought, or "intellectual paradigm", which crystallizes this historical orientation is "historicism", particularly as manifested in German nineteenth-century historiography (Oden 1987a:5; 1987b:2)

The characteristic central to the historicist position[65] has been defined by Iggers, whose work in the area is widely regarded as seminal, as "the assumption that there is a fundamental difference between the phenomena of nature and those of history, which requires an approach in the social and cultural sciences fundamentally different from those of the natural sciences" (1968:4-5). The difference in the two spheres is that "nature, it is held, is the scene of the eternally recurring, of phenomena themselves devoid of conscious purpose", while "history comprises unique and unduplicable human acts, filled with volition and intent" (Iggers 1968:5).[66]

In the historicist perspective, Iggers argues, the human world came to be seen as one "in a state of incessant flux", but nevertheless encompassing "centers of stability", such as "personalities, institutions, nations, epochs" (1968:5). Each of these centres, in turn, was thought of as possessing "an

---

"broad currents" of seventeenth- and eighteenth-century European thought, particularly reactions against French Reason and Enlightenment, and more immediately, in the philosophy of German Idealism (Iggers 1968:3, 5-6, 29ff).

64 Cf. Iggers 1968:4, 6.

65 For a definition of historicism see also Mandelbaum 42; for the breadth of thought historicism encompasses, see Mandelbaum 41ff; Iggers 1973; and for historicism in relation to nineteenth-century theology more generally, see Scholtz.

66 Cf. Iggers: "Historicism...rejects the idea of static 'Being' as the essence of reality and views 'Being' itself as resting upon action" (1973:456-7).

inner structure, a character", and is seen to be in constant metamorphosis in accord with its own internal principles of development" (Iggers 1968:5). Thus not only human being but institutions, such as nations, came to be regarded as individuals, and as human nature was not constant, but rather "the character of each man" (or institution) was seen to reveal itself "only in his development", history became "the only guide to an understanding of things human" (Iggers 1968:5).

In terms of methodology what this changed perception of human world meant was that while "abstract, classificatory methods" were appropriate for the study of natural sciences, the were to be regarded as "inadequate models for the study of human world" (Iggers 1968:5). Instead, as Iggers observes, "history requires methods which take into account that the historian is confronted by concrete persons and groups who once were alive and possessed unique personalities that called for intuitive understanding by the historian" (1968:5). In other words while in natural sciences one could generalize and deduce from a principle, all matters human[67] had to be studied in terms of particulars, actual occurrences and their (never totally predictable) development.

Oden identifies three tenets in German historiography, outlined above, which he feels are also evident in Wellhausen's treatment of the Old Testament. Reflecting the notion that human and natural sciences are separate and employ different and distinct methodologies, Oden asserts first of all that "the first law of the historiographic tradition" is "to heed concrete data as the human sciences should, not abstract laws" and that his law "the *Prolegomena* obeys" (1987b:5). Thus while "natural sciences can safely and profitably utilize abstractions; history cannot", but must instead be based on "empirical demonstration" and "concrete date [sic] of life", as abstractness and theorization would "risk emptying history of its vital reality" (Oden 1987a:15, 1987b:3, 5).[68]

On one level this dictum, Oden argues, is born out by Wellhausen's work in the *Prolegomena*, which provides copious illustrative material – concrete data – for what Oden describes as otherwise "a fairly simple thesis" (Oden 1987b:5).[69] On another level this preoccupation with actual life-detail not

---

67   Thence the broad designation "humanistic and cultural sciences" (Iggers 1968:4).

68   In German historiography this animosity towards the abstract and the theoretical has come to be known by the term "anti-*Begrifflichkeit*, the rejection of conceptualized thinking" (Iggers 1968:10).

69   Knight also recognizes Wellhausen's efforts "to found his views on the concrete data provided by the text" and observes how this manifests itself in his attention to differences in the style and vocabulary, even "syntactical peculiarities" of the biblical writers,

only results in Wellhausen's interest in, or attention to, the way Israelite life is described, but more importantly for our present purpose, in a value judgement on Wellhausen's part, also typical of the historiographical school, namely that he tends to praise and regard as early, materials that are "based in life" and disapprove, and regard as late, that which is "divorced from everyday activity" (Oden 1987b:5).[70] As an example of this tendency to see "what is fully human" as early and more original, Oden mentions Wellhausen's perception of Israelite religion,[71] but the assertion is equally true of Wellhausen's treatment of individual narratives as well as whole documents and can be easily seen by contrasting variants of the same story.

The comparison of the two Creation stories may serve as a case in point. The aim of the Priestly narrative in Gen. 1:1-2:4a, according to Wellhausen, is a theoretical, rather than purely, or even mainly, religious one: the writer "seeks to deduce things as they are from each other", that is "to give a cosmogonic theory" (Wellhausen 1883:313, ET 298). The world the author of P is contemplating is "not a mythical world but the present and ordinary one", and the question he asks is how the things he sees in it now "are likely to have issued at first from the primal matter" (Wellhausen 1883:313-4, ET 298). By contrast in Gen. 2:4b-3, Wellhausen points out, "the Jehovist narrative does shine by the absence of all efforts after rationalistic explanation, by its contempt for every kind of cosmological speculation" 1883:319, ET 303). Instead of standing "before the first beginnings of sober reflection about nature", as in P, in the Jehovist story "we are on the ground of marvel and myth": "we are in the enchanted garden of the ideas of genuine antiquity; the fresh early smell of earth meets us on the breeze" (1883:320, ET 304).

Such differences in the characterization of the "earthly" JE and the "speculative" P variants is fairly consistent throughout the *Prolegomena*, although Wellhausen by no means ascribes total uniformity to either of the sources. Thus on the whole, as Oden points out, Wellhausen regards the JE-source as one of "'genuine antiquity,' 'sacred mystery' and 'living poetic detail'", while P "represents 'theological abstractions,' 'mere fact,' and the 'pedantry' of theory" (Oden 1987a:23).

---

at a time when "the study of the history of the Hebrew language was very much in its infancy" (Knight 1982:31).

70 Similarly, Barr observes that Wellhausen was "particularly moved by the contrast between the free and natural life of the early Israelites and the fixed, hardened and defined lines of life in the priestly hierarchy with which the Old Testament ended up" (Barr 1981:147).

71 Oden 1987b:5.

Secondly, Oden points out the conviction in German historiography that "nations and epochs are best viewed as individuals" (Oden 1987a:15).[72] This results in the tendency, also apparent in Wellhausen's work, to treat "both entire societies and separate eras" as if they were "living organisms" with their distinct "lives", "deaths" and life stages, and to characterize them by "organic analogies" (Oden 1987a:15; 1987b:3).[73] The clearest manifestation of this tendency is the concept of the *Zeitgeist*, "the spirit of the age",[74] a notion that loomed large in the nineteenth-century German historiography in general and is also much in evidence in Wellhausen's treatment of the stages of Israel's history.[75]

Most importantly for our present research in the historicist perspective the *Zeitgeist* was seen to be reflected in the literature of its era.[76] It is in this connection that Wellhausen so famously explains: "Under the influence of the spirit of each successive age (*des Zeitgeistes*), traditions originally derived from one source were variously apprehended and shaped; one way in the ninth and eighth centuries, another way in the seventh and the sixth, and yet another in the fifth and fourth" (Wellhausen 1883:177, ET 171). It is this determining literary importance of the author and his time that is the basis of Wellhausen's central source-critical tenet and of his understanding of double narratives, clearly distinct from either form criticism or the more recent new literary criticism: as every narrative bears the hallmark of its author and his time the essential features of narratives are literary features; differences in variants are literary differences, variants are literary variants.

The difference in the *Zeitgeist* permeating Israel's literature can again best be seen by comparing variants, even whole sources. The examples that Wellhausen himself regards as the clearest comes from the portrayals of David's life in the two histories of Samuel-Kings and Chronicles. Thus in the rewriting of the accounts of David's foreign wars,[77] Wellhausen argues,

---

72 Cf. Scholtz 149.

73 Oden observes how in dealing with various sources Wellhausen uses adjectives to characterize the materials as "fresh, clear, spontaneous, vivid, heroic, generous, authentic, or confident", if he regards them as early, and "static, abstract, narrow, perverse, anxious", if he thinks of them as late (Oden 1987b:5)

74 See Mandelbaum 51ff.

75 Oden traces this historiographical tenet to Herder, but of the nineteenth-century founders German historiography the concept that "every human epoch bears its own, uniquely individual character", is mostly closely connected with von Humboldt (Oden 1987a:9-11, Oden citing Wach).

76 According to Knight, this happens through "a principle of projection" (Knight 1982:29), cf. Wellhausen 1883:336, ET 319.

Chronicles always "keeps in view its purpose, which is directed towards David as founder of the Jerusalem worship" (1883:184, ET 177-8). The stories of the wars serve this purpose as "those wars brought him [David] the wealth that was required for the building of the temple" (Wellhausen 1883:184, ET 178). In comparison "everything so fully and beautifully told in the Book of Samuel about the home occurrences of that period is omitted, for after all it does not contribute much to the glorification of the king" (Wellhausen 1883:184, ET 178). As a result "statements about foreign wars are torn from the connection with domestic events in which they stand in older narrative" and this happens in a "rude and mechanical manner" (Wellhausen 1883:184, ET 178).

The difference in the spirit of the two periods, according to Wellhausen, is that the David stories of Chronicles are "clericalised in the taste of the post-exilian time, which had no feeling longer for anything but cultus and torah": this is how "the founder of the kingdom" became "the founder of the temple and the public worship", and "the king and hero at the head of his companions in arms" became "the singer and master of ceremonies at the head of a swarm of priests and Levites" (1883:189, ET 182).

The same kind of differences, if in somewhat less striking form, Wellhausen accredits to doublets representing JE and P. Thus the Jehovist miracle of the manna (Ex. 16) "is taken advantage of in the Priestly Code as a very suitable occasion for urging on the people a strict sanctification of the Sabbath" (Wellhausen 1883:374, ET 352-3). According to Wellhausen "this pursuit of a legal object destroys the story and obscures its original meaning" (Wellhausen 1883:374, ET 353). The change in the *Zeitgeist* is best seen in how the eating of the manna is portrayed: it is not "any sign of originality, rather of senility", Wellhausen remarks, "that in the Priestly Code the manna is not eaten raw, but boiled and baked" (Wellhausen 1883, ET 353).

Thirdly, Oden observes that the German historiographical tradition "demanded the emphasis upon *Entstehung* and *Entwicklung*": the historicist thesis stipulated that "to understand any human phenomenon historically…is to investigate above all the phenomenon's origin and development" (Oden 1987b:4).[78] This tenet, Oden points out, follows logically from the previous one, the concept of nations and institutions as living organisms with respective life stages. According to Oden it is also clearly evident in the object Wellhausen sets for himself in the *Prolegomena*, to test the comparative dating of the three sources, JE, D and P, "by reference to an

---

77 2 Sam. 8; 10; 11:1; 23:30-31; 21:18-22; versus 2 Chron. 18-20 (Wellhausen 1883:184, ET 177).
78 Cf. Scholtz 149.

independent standard, namely the inner development of the history of Israel"
(Oden 1987b:6; Wellhausen 1883:13, ET 12).[79] The parallel sources thus not
only reflect the *Zeitgeist* of the different times, but also indicate a
development in Israel's history, and according to the historicist
understanding and the subsequent value judgement from the part of
Wellhausen, this development was above all ethical, moral and indivi-
dualistic (Oden 1987a:21-2).

Again this concept of history stands out most clearly in Wellhausen's
treatment of variants of the same story. The higher moral standard of P over
JE is continuously emphasized. Thus "in the Priestly Code", Wellhausen
points out, "all those stories are absent in which there is anything morally
objectionable", such as the ones in which "the cowardice of the patriarchs
endangers the honour of their wives", or which deal with "Sarah's cruel
jealousy of Hagar" (1883:353, ET 333-4). Where the variants of these stories
do occur in JE, Wellhausen judges that, for instance, the "short and profane
version" of Gen. 26:6-12 is "more lively and pointed" and therefore earlier
than "the long and edifying version" of Gen. 20:2-16 (1883:338, ET 320).

2.4.1. Model Shift

What is important for our current research is the recognition of the shift in
conceptual models employed in the study of double narratives, which has
taken place. Thus while for Spinoza, as we have seen, "the proper method of
interpreting Scripture" did not "differ from the proper method of interpreting
nature"[80] and he dealt with doublets accordingly, by the nineteenth century
humanities had emerged as a separate sphere of scholarship with its distinct
methodology, one dominated by a historical preoccupation, and this in turn is
reflected in contemporary biblical criticism.

The difference between Wellhausen's work and the earlier models of
biblical criticism is not, however, the concept of the document and what can
be tolerated in terms of duplication – this remains fairly constant from
Spinoza to Wellhausen – but the way doublets are approached and the
importance that is attached to them. For Wellhausen variants themselves
have value in their richness, detail and the insight into the *Zeitgeist* they
offer: they are not simply indicative of a process of composition that is of

---

79 That "'the inner development'" should form an "'independent standard'", Oden points
   out, "was self-evident *only* to those who stood squarely" in the historicist tradition of
   historical understanding (Oden 1987a:22).
80 Spinoza 84, ET 1862:143-2.

interest as a phenomenon. This difference in approach is perhaps best summarized by Ranke's observation concerning the role of the historian, who "works as does the artist and the poet, not in the coldly rational fashion of a natural scientist".[81] The historian is thus the nations "biographer", whose work does not demand only exactness and impartiality, but also "empathy" and "intuition"; not only "philology and grammar", but also imagination.[82] In Wellhausen's model this role of the historian is a central one: Wellhausen himself works with the record of Israel's history and the doublets in them on the analogy of the "historian" model he has for the composer of the Pentateuch, not so much in terms of the technicalities of their compilation, but as an interpreter of the development of Israel's cultural and religious life which these doublets reflect.

On the other hand, what our discussion so far on the role of conceptual models in the interpretation of double narratives has also done, is to highlight the fact that although all the commentators reviewed above obviously have definite expectations concerning how biblical literature – the documents, *mémoires* and histories that they postulate – should behave in terms of repetition and duplication, practically no attention is given to the question why this should be so, or even what kind of literary products these expectations apply to. And this is still the case even when the Documentary Thesis is already fully formulated and scholars, such as Wellhausen, describe their approach to criticism as a "literary and historical investigation".[83]

So far many of the expectations scholars have had concerning duplication or consistency in biblical narrative and how they might have understood the Bible as a literary product, have had to be conjectured from the wider intellectual context of their time, and particularly their use of conceptual models which, I have argued, guided the observations and interpretations of early biblical critics on double narratives. And yet it is hardly unreasonable to suggest that to a large extent the whole question of double narratives and their meaning in, and implications for, the Bible as a composition, centres upon the question of what kind of literary product Old Testament narratives represent and whether there are any "rules" for duplication and consistency in such compositions. This, in turn, makes the question of what kind of literature the biblical narrative is perceived to be a crucial one for Old Testament scholarship.

Whybray has suggested that biblical criticism from its beginning until the turn of the twentieth century was "literary" criticism in the sense that the

---

81 See Oden 1987a:12.
82 See Iggers 1973:459; Oden 1987a:12; Sykes 195.
83 "Literargeschichtliche Untersuchung" (Wellhausen 1883:13, ET 12).

question of pentateuchal and later, more widely biblical, unity and authorship was seen as "a purely literary one", i.e. that it was "a problem concerning the compilation of *written sources*", as opposed to having something to do with the oral, pre-literary stages of Israel's traditions, the existence of which was acknowledged, but which were regarded as inaccessible (Whybray 17). It was then thought that these written documents could be identified and separated through the use of literary criteria, such as the analysis of the stylistic features of the text (Whybray 17).

Perhaps in this connection it is helpful to remember that Biblical criticism developed in parallel with the critical study and renewed debate about the authorship and composition of some of the great works of world literature, corresponding particularly closely to developments in Homeric studies. This link with the great classics, coupled with the discipline being termed "literary criticism", led in both cases to some uncertainty as to what was meant by literature in this connection: in what sense was criticism "literary"?

The renaissance of Homeric studies in fact also started with questions being asked about unity, composition and dating of the Homeric epic, the so called "Homeric question",[84] rather than, for instance, with any major advances in the aesthetic appreciation of the work. Thus observations were made concerning differences in "tone" in various poems and the presence of "anomalies" as well as "a large number of variants" in them.[85] It was in the sense of trying to understand such features that the early Homeric scholars engaged in "literary" criticism.

The basic assumption that was shared by all these "analyst scholars", as A. Parry has argued, was that "Homeric poetry was essentially poetry like ours" (xviii). It might not be inappropriate then to suggest that biblical scholars, who in their critical endeavour parallel their Homeric counterparts at practically every point, made a similar assumption and expected biblical documents to resemble writings of their own time. Certainly this suggestion seems to fit the biblical critics reviewed above. For instance Spinoza, whose approach to the Scriptures was based on a naturalistic model, established the Bible as a secular document and seems to have expected from it the kind of logic and consistency that would have been in line with a scientific treatise of his time. In the case of Simon, in turn, it has been pointed out that his

---

84 The formulation of the *Homeric* question is usually traced to August Wolf's *Prolegomena ad Homerum*, 1795, although earlier on Vico had raised the possibility of the epic stemming from a "Homeric school" that had "two preeminent poets", Homer thus being "a collective term for many men's work" (Myres 57; A. Parry xff; R. Pfeiffer 175; Wilamowitz 108).

85 Myres 22; A. Parry xv, xviii.

approach to the biblical narrative was one of "grammar and philology",[86] and that he observed consistencies or redundancies in the biblical text largely in those terms. Wellhausen, on the other hand, who also had a strong philological background but was working in the context of the "historical century", seems to have effected little essential change in the concept of the document, but rather took the exploration concerning the meaning of the differences in the documents into a new direction by seeing them as historical or "biographical" compositions.

2.5. "Literary Artist": Alter

Remarkably then the concept of biblical narrative as "documentary literature", based on the model of treatise or a historical document, has remained basically uniform, if ill-defined, in historical-critical scholarship.[87] The situation only changed, but then did so very dramatically, when a new approach to double narratives, and biblical criticism in general, arose in the mid-twentieth century in the form of the "Bible as literature" approach, or the "new" literary criticism.[88] This approach, hailed by Longman as a "paradigm shift"[89] and regarded by Barton as "the first really fresh departure" from "all the traditional forms of literary criticism",[90] was already intimated in Auerbach's *Mimesis*, 1946, but became clearly articulated in Alter's *The Art of Biblical Narrative*, 1981.[91] Since then the new literary criticism has become a major, if diverse, force in biblical scholarship, but Alter's work has remained a definitive one within the movement.[92]

---

86 Sykes 195.
87 In my view form and tradition-historical criticism do not constitute a paradigm shift in this respect. The reasons they offer for duplication and repetition, which are accredited to oral composition and transmission, constitute a fundamental discrepancy with the source-critical notion of literature bearing the hallmark of its author and his time, but the basic notion of narrative consistency with regard to duplication does not change in essence.
88 A number of terms have been suggested for the approach to avoid the confusion with "traditional" literary criticism, such as "aesthetic criticism" or widening the meaning of rhetorical criticism", but these have not gathered a following (Longman 7).
89 Longman 4-5.
90 Barton 1984b:25.
91 See p. 63ff above.

Central to the new literary criticism is the tendency to view duplication in the biblical narrative as in indicator of the literary nature of the text. The critical tenet intrinsic to this new literary approach is that in the biblical narrative "duplication indicates literary artistry": that is, doublets, long seen as the main evidence for heterogeneous, documentary, origin of the Pentateuch as well as the main historical books of the Old Testament, witness to the "literariness" of the biblical narrative composition, now seen to have been produced by a "literary author" in much more homogeneous a manner than previously suggested by source critics. The "artistry" of the text, evident in doublets, is seen to have resulted from the use of literary "conventions" or "techniques", such as Alter's "type-scene",[93] in the composition of the text.

The basic assumption underlying this view of double narratives is that the Bible is "literature" and that this is how "literature behaves" in terms of duplication and repetition. What is vital for our understanding and evaluation of this approach to double narratives is to explore the sense in which the notion "literature" has been employed in this type of approach to biblical criticism and thus what constitutes the model for the concept of duplication as a literary phenomenon. Secondly, we must attempt to establish how such a view of doublets as literary artistry compares with the understanding of repetition fostered by modern poetics, regarded as the "scientific" side of modern literary criticism.

2.5.1. The Bible as Literature

The issue of the Bible as literature is a complex one, the crux of the problem being the difficulty of defining "literature" – not only in terms of

---

92 Some scholars see the concept of a literary understanding of the Scripture going as far back as the New Testament (Gottcent xxviii) or at least the Church Fathers (see Longman 13ff), with an impressive suggested pedigree of writers and scholars from Milton to Wordsworth embracing the idea (see Norton I:306-7, II:150-2). The literary-aesthetic qualities have indeed long been applauded by scholars, who in no way would then practice literary criticism in its modern sense. As early as 1849, J. Hamilton published a work titled *The Literary Attractions of the Bible*, in which he extolled the literary beauty of the Bible as the way "God had made the Bible, not only an instructive book, but an attractive one – not only true, but enticing" (5), and in 1899 the first *The Bible as Literature* appeared, by R. G. Moulton. In these works "literature" is, however, treated in a very limited, mainly aesthetic sense and, at any rate, the issue of double narratives as a potential literary feature is not addressed.

93 Alter 1981:50. See also A. Berlin 14-20; Wenham 347.

what shared features qualify compositions as literature, but what particular shared features scholars have had in mind when they have applied the designation to biblical narrative. In an extensive survey that traces the history of literary attitudes to the Bible from the antiquity to present time, *A History of the Bible as Literature*, 1993, Norton points out that "there is an unbreakable connection between the history of ideas of literature and the history of literary ideas of the Bible" (Norton I:4). Norton argues that "ideas of what literature is and, particularly, of what might be critically admirable and how that might be discussed have changed radically through time" (I:3-4). The ideas concerning the literariness of the Bible have then also changed, and to determine what a given scholar has in mind when describing a feature of the Bible as "literary" requires more than a recourse to a dictionary definition of "literature",[94] namely understanding the wider conceptual context of the author .

In what sense, then, is the Bible "literature" for the new literary critics? Even in the limited period since *Mimesis,* and the even shorter period since *The Art of Biblical Narrative,* the term literature has been employed in a variety of ways and used as a reference to a heterogeneous collection of works.[95] When Gabel, Wheeler and York pose the question "what does it mean to read the Bible 'as literature'?", they answer with considerable generality "that for the time being one looks at the Bible in the same way that one would look at any other book: as a product of the human mind"(3). "In some fundamental respects", they argue, the Bible ranks with products as diverse as those by Shakespeare, Emily Dickinson, Henry Fielding and Ernest Hemingway (4). However, their actual definition is still much more inclusive, as for Gabel et al. literature "in its broadest sense" seems to mean "writings produced by real people who lived in actual historical times" (Gabel, Wheeler and York 3-4). In a more restricted fashion Barr, on the other hand, observes that "much of literature, to put it bluntly, is fiction" and wonders "what if we were to think of the Bible as a supremely profound work of fiction?" (1990:55). Frye, in turn, famously remarks that "the Bible...is as literary as it can well be without actually being literature" (62).

Alter himself offers a complex definition of the Bible as literature. Writing with Kermode, Alter seems to equate the Bible as "literature" with

---

94 See Norton I:65ff, for such definitions.

95 As the new literary criticism is not a "school" of scholarship even in the sense applicable to source or form criticism, but rather an umbrella term for scholars with certain common goals and sympathies, such plurality can of course be expected. It nevertheless makes any generalization difficult as terms need to be defined practically on individual basis.

secular literature, but with emphasis not so much on the literariness of the actual text as the method of reading it. Thus Alter and Kermode ascribe the use of the term "Bible as literature" to the movement of scholarship that often traces its roots to Auerbach's *Mimesis*, but has gathered momentum only since the mid 1970's, in which the Bible is studied by methods developed by secular literary criticism, and in which "the Bible, once thought of as a source of secular literature...now bids fair to become part of the literary canon" (3).[96]

On the other hand Alter's aim for *The Art of Biblical Narrative* seems to imply a more specific sense of the Bible as literature in that Alter seeks "to illuminate the distinctive principles of the Bible's narrative art" and feels the need to help the reader over, among other things, "one of the most imposing barriers that stands between the modern reader and the imaginative subtlety of biblical narrative art" – namely "the extraordinary prominence of verbatim repetition in the Bible" (1981:ix, 88). Alter also acknowledges that there are features that are "distinctively biblical", in fact, "one discovers that the characteristic procedures of biblical narrative differ noticeably from those of later Western fiction" (1981:131, 133).

Practitioners of the new literary criticism also differ as to whether their approach involves the claim that the Bible is literature or whether it is merely *looked upon* as such, the distinction very often, but not always, stemming from whether they involve the role of authorial intention in their recognition of literary artistry in the text. Thus some scholars, such as Cooper, argue that "advocacy of literary-critical method does not...entail the ontological claim that the Bible *is* literature, only the assertion that it is interesting and enjoyable to read it that way" (65). Others however, and Alter among them, include the authorial dimension in their equation and see the recognition of the Bible as literature as the rationale for their literary approach in the first place.[97] Thus, for instance, Alter describes biblical literary art as "finely modulated from moment to moment, determining in most cases the minute choice of words and reported details", even "a whole network of ramified interconnections in the text" and sees in the Tamar story the workings of "a brilliant literary artist" (1981:3, 10).

---

96 This seems to concur with e.g. Barton who, looking back on the post-Mimesis movement, describes reading the "Bible 'as literature'" as "not in the sense of reading it for aesthetic pleasure....but in the sense of reading it in the same way as literary critics read secular literature" (1984b:25).

97 Thus they continue the trend we have already seen of the correlation between a scholar's approach to the Bible and the model he/she envisages for its composition. With so many literary critics now seeing the Bible as literature, one could perhaps go as far as to suspect that scholars create the composers of biblical narrative in their own image...

What then does characterize the model of literary artistry for the new literary critics of the Bible? In their introduction to one of the main compendia of new literary criticism, *The Literary Guide to the Bible*, 1987, Alter and Kermode make the claim that "literature is a complex language, not necessarily unique, not without significant overlaps with other kinds of language, but distinctive nevertheless" (5). What the practitioners of new literary criticism and their definitions of literature seem to have in common, regardless of their attention to the question of actual authorship, is the assumption that there is something universal, historically indeterminate, about the "literariness" of literature. It is almost as if literature were a language, as described by Alter and Kermode, and one language, if a highly complex one,[98] which once learnt would enable the speaker to communicate with every kind of composition. In Alter's case this universality seems to stretch to oral composition as well, as he treats the "type-scene", which, he observes, arose from "the special needs of oral composition", as literary artistry (1981:50).

The ontological question whether the Bible actually is literature is not the issue for our present research,[99] only establishing the conceptual model that leads to the interpretation of a narrative feature, such as duplication, as a literary one. However, from the point of view of the wider context of biblical criticism, the issue is not without significance. While for many modern literary critics the emphasis on reading "texts as wholes" amounts not to the negation of authorial intention but to relegating the issue to irrelevance, involving the dimension of authorial intent in the discussion, as for instance Alter does, takes the new literary criticism as an approach to biblical methodology from "disengaged synchronism" to the realm of historical critical, diachronic, scholarship. "Duplication indicates literary artistry"

---

98 Alter and Kermode describe the complexity of the "operations of this language" as: "its syntax, grammar, and vocabulary involve a highly heterogeneous concord of codes, devices and linguistic properties", which include "genre, convention, technique, contexts of allusions, style, structure, thematic organization, point of view for the narratives, voice for the poetry, imagery and diction for both, and much else" (5).

99 This question has been debated at length, and without consensus, elsewhere: see e.g. a series of articles in *Prooftexts*, 1981-3, where Kugel seems to present the main dissenting voice (Kugel 1981; 1982). Norton, more recently, has approached the question from a historical angle and argues that the modern sense of "literature" and "literary" only emerged in the time of Samuel Johnson; the phrase "the Bible as literature"', Norton claims, "would have been opaque to anyone living before the latter half of the eighteenth century" (I:66). Norton, in fact, traces the first usage of the term "the Bible as literature" to Matthew Arnold in the mid-nineteenth century, but points out that Byron already had used the practically equivalent phrase "the Scripture as a composition" (Byron cited by Norton II:262).

under those auspices cannot then be simply seen as a synchronic alternative to the diachronic, source-critical claim that duplication indicates documents, but as a rival to it, and it seems, a contradictory one.   The work of Damrosch[100] is important in this respect as it aims to study literary artistry in the biblical narrative, but with full understanding and acknowledgement of historical critical premises.

2.5.2. Poetics, Fiction, and Repetition

The question of how to approach literature, not in terms of its interpretation (*what* it means), but in terms of some general rules concerning its conventions, structure and language (*how* it means it), is almost as old as literature itself, going at least as far back as Aristotle's *Poetics*. Although no universal, immutable laws for literature have ever been established, there is general agreement that no composition can be completely without rules either, if it is to be anything other than "wholly unique", and consequently "completely incomprehensible",[101] at least to anyone else except perhaps its creator. In the second half of last century interest in "how texts mean" has experienced a resurgence and poetics, the "theory of literary discourse",[102] has made a renewed bid to become the "science of literature" and formulator of literary "laws".[103]   More recently poetics has been followed by narratology, the study of discourse with the narrower focus of narratives alone. It is in these realms that the issues of repetition and duplication in literature in general and in narrative in particular, have been most recently and most profitably addressed.

Tzvetan Todorov, one of the most articulate theorists of the "new poetics" and a main contributor to the resurgence of the discipline,[104] has in his seminal *Introduction to Poetics* defined poetics as the discipline that "aims at a knowledge of the general laws that preside over the birth of each [literary] work" (1981:6). Todorov distinguishes "two attitudes" to the text in the general study of literature and sees poetics in contradistinction to both (1981:3-6). The first of the attitudes, "interpretation", Todorov maintains,

100 See pp. 67ff above.

101 Wellek and Warren 18.

102 Preminger and Brogan 930.

103 Similar questions concerning how the text "is made" were already asked by the Russian formalists in the beginning of this century. Some came to the conclusion that "there exists an important distinction between artistic and non-artistic prose" (Pomorska 275-6).

104 See Brooks vii-viii.

regards a literary work as "the ultimate and unique object" and aims "to name
the meaning of the text examined", ideally from within, by making "the text
itself speak" (Todorov 1981:3-5).[105] The second attitude Todorov calls
"science", as it is manifested by disciplines, such as psychology, sociology
and ethnology, which use literature as the object of their study and have as
their aim "no longer the description of the particular work, the designation of
its meaning, but the establishment of general laws of which the particular text
is the product" (Todorov 1981:5-6). "Poetics", on the other hand, Todorov
argues, "breaks down the symmetry thus established between interpretation
and science in the field of literary studies" by, in contrast to interpretation,
seeking to establish general laws concerning literature, instead of meaning,
and in contrast to science, by seeking "these laws within literature itself"
rather than in other disciplines (1981:6). The object of poetics is thus not any
individual literary work, either in terms of its meaning or as a manifestation
of the society it is a product of, but the properties that make a discourse a
literary discourse, i.e. its "literariness" (Todorov 1981:6-7).

For the study of repetition and duplication in their various forms Todorov
divides the field of poetics according to the three principal aspects of the text,
namely the "semantic" aspect, the "verbal" aspect and the "syntactic"
aspect.[106] Cases of repetition or duplication, of which Todorov recognizes
four different kinds, fall within the first two categories.

The semantic aspect of the text, Todorov argues, explores the kind of
operations that allow signification and symbolization to take place in a
discourse (1981:13). As there are potentially "countless interrelationships"
that can be observed in a text, there are potentially countless ways of
addressing this aspect of semantic meaning. Todorov chooses one, which in
his estimate is "the least arbitrary" and divides all the countless
interrelationships into two major groups: "relations between copresent
elements, *in praesentia*", and "relations between elements present and absent,
in absentia" (1981:13). While the relations *in praesentia* link phenomena to
each other by causality, thus forming "relations of configuration, of
construction" between semantic forms and units, the relations *in absentia*
work by a certain phenomenon *evoking* another, thus forming "relations of
meaning and of symbolization" (13-4).

Todorov recognizes two types of semantic duplication in the text,
"repetition" and "polyvalence", both normally representing the second of the
relational categories, relations *in absentia*, therefore achieving their meaning

---

105 Most emphatic italics in Todorov's work are omitted here.
106 Cf. Brooks xiv.

by evocation.[107] "Repetition", Todorov maintains, occurs in a discourse when "the relations of two words[108] are of identity" (Todorov 1981:21). The relationship has, of course, also to be *observed* to be such,[109] Todorov emphasizes, and will be "guaranteed" either by "recourse to schemas readily available to our mind" or "by a particular insistence in the presentation of certain verbal relations" (1981:22).[110]

Another type of duplication in a discourse is represented by "polyvalence". Language, Todorov argues, can also be evaluated in terms of "presence or absence of reference to an anterior discourse" (1981:23). A discourse is *"monovalent"* when it "invokes no anterior 'way of speaking'" and, in turn, *"polyvalent"* when it "invokes an anterior discourse more or less explicitly" (1981:23). Todorov points out that, although well known in the history of literature, polyvalence has been undervalued and treated with much suspicion, particularly in classical literature, where only two forms of polyvalence have been recognized, namely parody and plagiarism (1981:23).[111]

In Russian formalism work has, however, been done more recently on the meaning of this feature of language, now recognized by many as a significant one and termed "intertextual polyvalence".[112] This work has focused on the question of how a "work of art is perceived in relation with other artistic works and by means of the associations the reader makes with them"[113] and it centres on the perception that when a word, or a discourse, is "taken possession of" by a "member of a collective of speakers" he finds it "already inhabited" (Bakhtin 167). Thus there is "no neutral word of language, free from the aspirations and valuations of others, uninhabited by foreign voices" (Bakhtin 167).

Even more recently another "version" of polyvalence has been recognized where "the present text evokes not another individual text but an anonymous

---

107 The line between "presence" and "absence" is not, however, always clear.
108 Or of several words, or units (22).
109 Thus repetition may "objectively" exist in a discourse but "really" only becomes so when perceived as such – a point which may appear self-evident but, nevertheless, reveals a crucial psychological dimension of language and literature.
110 The presence of such a relation as repetition creates a "figure" in the text, the "systematic presence" of any given figure (or other linguistic property), in turn, a "register". This concept of register, Todorov observes, approaches certain usages of the term "style" (Todorov 1981:20-2, 27).
111 In parody an anterior discourse is mocked or disparaged, in plagiarism this critical aspect is missing (Todorov 1981:23).
112 The term is credited to Bakhtin, as is the first formulation of a "true theory" of the phenomenon (Bakhtin 1973; Todorov 1981:23).
113 V. Shklovski, cited in Todorov 1981:23.

ensemble of discursive properties" (Todorov 1981:24). The "discovery" of this new version of polyvalence is the result of the application to non-oral literature[114] of Milman Parry's oral-formulaic theory, originally formulated for the Homeric epics (Todorov 1981:24). In this new form of polyvalence the text is seen as the product of the evocation of "specific ensembles", such as "a certain style, a particular of tradition, a type of usage" (Todorov 1981:25).

In the area of the verbal aspect of the text, which addresses the issues of "mode, time, perspective and voice" in a discourse, Todorov also recognizes two types of repetition. Both of these relate to the dimension of time, i.e. the property in a discourse that manifests the "relation between discourse-time and fiction-time", and its property of frequency in particular (1981:31). In Todorov's estimate there are three possible types of frequency in a discourse, two of which represent a form of repetition. In a *repetitive* narrative "several discourses evoke one and the same event", while in an *iterative* narrative "a single discourse evokes a plurality of (similar) events" (1981:31).[115] The repetitive narrative can result from various processes in a discourse, such as "an obsessive reprise of the same story by the same character", the telling of "complementary narratives by several persons about the same phenomenon" – thus resulting in a "'stereoscopic' illusion" – or the telling of "contradictory narratives" of the same event or phenomenon by "one or several characters" (1981:31).

The potential applicability of these (or any other) categories of repetition to biblical narrative ultimately has to do with the question of the universality of the notion of literature, i.e. whether literature is a universal "language" as seems to be suggested by Alter and some of the new literary critics. Todorov has phrased this question in terms of whether literature is a "historical phenomenon" or an "eternal one" (1990:1). The juxtaposition here, according to Todorov, is between function and structure. That there is something we designate "literature" that has a certain definable function in a given society or culture is, Todorov argues, an undeniable fact (1990:2). But whether by this designation we have also "demonstrated that all the particular products that take on the function of 'literature' possess common characteristics, which we can identify with legitimacy" is, according to Todorov, quite another question to which the answer, so far at least, has been negative (1990:2).

---

114 Most notably by Michael Riffaterre.
115 In a *singulative* narrative a "unique discourse evokes a unique event" (Todorov 1981:31).

The issue that, according to Todorov, should be determined to answer these questions, is "what distinguishes literature from what is not literature"[116] – a dilemma that, as we have seen, biblical criticism, both "new" and traditional, has had to struggle with in its own context. Todorov's tentative conclusions suggest a questioning of "the legitimacy of a structural notion of 'literature'", i.e. the idea of literature as "eternal" or "universal" (1990:11). If this be so for the kind of compositions that fall in the centre, so to speak, of the spectrum of the definition of literature, as Todorov's do, we may want to ask what the implications are for literary products that are on the periphery of the definition to begin with, such as is the case with the Bible? However, Todorov also suggests that with the demise of the controlling idea of an "eternal" literature, we might in fact be gaining "numerous types of discourse", with the emphasis already shifting to establishing characteristics narratives have in terms of their "narration", rather than literariness[117] – a direction that might be profitably pursued by biblical scholarship.

As the model of literary artistry which, I have argued, the new literary critics employ in their approach to duplication in biblical narrative, has as its conceptual context the wider "literary canon" consisting in the main of relatively recent, secular, Western literature, it would perhaps be appropriate to look briefly at how repetition occurring in one of the main genres of that canon, the English novel, has been dealt with.

Hillis Miller in his *Fiction and Repetition*, 1982, one of the few works so far to focus solely on the phenomenon of repetition in fiction, recognizes the importance of repetition for "a long work like a novel", which, he argues "is interpreted...in part through the identification of recurrences and of meanings generated through recurrences" (1). "In a novel", Miller aptly points out, "what is said two or three times may not be true, but the reader is fairly safe in assuming that it is significant" (2)! As Miller then sees a novel as "a complex tissue of repetitions and of repetitions within repetitions, or of repetitions linked in chain fashion to other repetitions", understanding the phenomenon becomes a central issue in a close reading of a text (2-3).

Miller identifies a number of types of repetition in the seven novels under his scrutiny in this particular work and classifies them into two main categories. "On a small scale", Miller proposes, "there is repetition of verbal elements", such as "words, figures of speech, shapes or gestures, or, more subtly, covert repetitions that act like metaphors" (1-2). "On a larger scale", on the other hand, Miller recognizes duplication of "events and scenes",

---

116 Todorov 1990:9.
117 Todorov 1990:11ff.

"motifs" and "characters", which are repeated either in one novel or different novels by the same author (2).[118]

Many of the examples Miller then gives of these various kinds of repetition have obvious parallels in how duplication in the Old Testament narrative has been perceived. For instance, the "cluster of motifs; somnolence, the color red, some act of violence done or received"[119] Miller finds Tess of Thomas Hardy's *Tess of the d'Urbervilles* re-enacting in her life, is not unlike the way motifs, such as deception – even the colour red! – have been found recurring in the life of Jacob. The recasting of Rome as Portland Bill, the home place of the hero in Hardy's *The Well-Beloved*, Miller uses as an example of how people in Hardy's novels tend to "trace likes in unlikes". This echoes the way Old Testament scholars have traditionally found significant places and persons, whether mountains of momentous encounters, or great leaders, reframed in subsequent incidents (Miller 12ff). Miller also comments on the close similarity in the relations of the three main characters in *The Well-Beloved* and *Jude the Obscure* – again a situation for which a counterpart could be suggested in, for instance, Abraham-Sarah-Hagar and Jacob-Rachel-Leah constellation (150ff).

The similarity between the types of repetition Miller finds in his Victorian novels and those that have been alluded to in Old Testament narrative, is considerable. An attempt to approach biblical repetition in similar kinds of terms has been made by, for instance, Damrosch in his thematic linkages (doublings of content). What is, however, most significant for this research is the fact that the wide spectrum of Miller's examples does not include anything that would parallel the most obvious Old Testament form of repetition, and the one that has been undeniably most significant for biblical criticism, namely double narratives or variants, in the sense they were first observed as repetitions of the same, verbally dependent story-base, or unique event.

---

118 The conceptual framework of Miller's work is quite different from the approaches to repetition discussed so far in this chapter in that it is based on the juxtaposition of a "Platonic" theory of repetition as "resemblance" and a Nietschean theory of repetition, which posits "a world based on difference" (5ff). We will not review this model here as it does not affect Miller's perception of the structures of repetition, only their meaning. To my knowledge this model has not as yet been applied to duplication in Old Testament narratives.

119 Miller 1-2.

2.5.3. Appraisal

Looking at how both poetics and literary scholars, such as Miller, have dealt with repetition has revealed many points of contact between the literary study of the Old Testament and the wider world of literary scholarship. A certain preoccupation with repetition as such is one of them, as is the feeling that not all that the phenomenon holds has as yet been uncovered. Undoubtedly even more avenues await exploration as models developed in poetics, narratology and literary criticism are implemented in the study of duplication in biblical narratives. Of the concepts of repetition we have looked at perhaps Todorov's repetitive and iterative narratives suggest the most immediate analogue to biblical doublets – might, for instance, the Wife-sister stories be an example of a "stereoscopic illusion"? However, as these ideas have so far been but sketched, they await more consideration, as does the applicability of the notion of polyvalence. On the other hand the comparison of actual examples of repetition in fiction, such as Miller's study represents, with doublets in Scripture, might make the sometimes abstract discussion about the literariness of the Bible more tangible.

With much potential promise our study of the "literary artist" model has, however, also brought to fore some weaknesses in the concept, or in its application to double narratives. Perhaps the most obvious of these is the rather inclusive and generalized definition of repetition, which seems to offer very little differentiation when applied to actual cases of biblical doublets. This is incongruous in a sense in that the new literary approach has brought to the fore a wide spectrum of examples of repetition and duplication in the Bible. This richness in quantity has not, however, been matched by discrimination in quality.

Some of the difficulties of labelling biblical duplication with terminology employed in poetics, or any other field related to biblical studies, will become more obvious as we will explore the complexity of the double narrative phenomenon below in Chapter 4. However, what the examples of the treatment of repetition in poetics have already demonstrated is that while there is an obvious overlap in the biblical phenomenon of repetition and that perceived in literature in general, and in that respect the adoption of literary models, such as polyvalence, will undoubtedly open new perspectives in double narrative research, nevertheless it seems that the biblical phenomenon of duplication cannot be limited to the terms suggested by poetics, but is wider than what they imply. To put it another way, while all doublets may by definition be polyvalent, not all polyvalence produces double narratives in their, if not unique, at least unusual, manifestation in the Old Testament.

Chapter 3: Double Narratives as Oral Variants

The main theoretical notion contributed by Gunkel to the study of Old Testament narrative was the proposal of oral origin and early oral transmission as the formative stages of certain types of narratives, and therefore the stage at which variants of these narratives developed. Another notion closely related to that was the concept that these narratives had changed according to a "universal pattern" operative in all oral material of the same genre. Consequently, Gunkel argued, the development of these Old Testament narratives could now be unravelled with the help of methodology derived from the field of folklore studies, which had developed ways of determining the patterns of composition in oral narratives, such as epic laws, and also suggested laws of change, according to which these narratives are purported to change in the course of their transmission.

The primary object of such unravelling was, in Gunkel's case, first of all to recover the original form of the Genesis narratives, and then to establish the developmental stages these stories had passed through to achieve their present form. The original form of the stories would then give us insight into the thought of the earliest Israelites and the stages of their psychological, cultural and religious development, witnessed to most clearly by narrative variants, which reflected the changes in society that had prompted them. Thus, Gunkel maintained, it was possible with the help of form and tradition-historical criticism to reconstruct the stages not only of Israel's narrative heritage, but of its religion and society as well.

Both of these notions, the formative role of the oral stage for types of Old Testament narrative and the accessibility of that stage for analysis and reconstruction, became central to much of the form-critical and tradition-historical research after Gunkel, as seen from our survey above in Chapter 1. In Scandinavia this developed between the 1930's and the 1960's into an almost exclusive emphasis on the importance of oral transmission for the biblical narrative and consequent appeals for methodological support to models from other cultures believed to (have) preserve(d) their religious or cultural inheritance in oral form. Elsewhere, and later on, particularly with scholars such as Koch and Van Seters, but also many others, the interest in deciphering any intrinsic differences between oral and written narratives and their transmission has persisted, with periodic surges of interest in devising new oral laws, or utilizing existing ones, to "test" or "measure" the orality of various parts of the Old Testament.

It is thus safe to say that Gunkel's proposal of an oral formative stage for Genesis and eventually other Old Testament materials as well, and their subjection to universal laws of change resulting, and evident, in variants, is the most revolutionary and influential proposition relevant to double narratives since the early source-critical notion that "duplicates indicate sources" and only rivalled by it in terms of its impact on later scholarship. This is particularly so now that more research is being carried out into both the nature of narrative as a medium for the message of the biblical writers, and the role and interpretational implications of orality in the formation of the Scriptures in general.

To assess the importance of Gunkel's work to the interpretation of double narratives as a phenomenon, as well as to Old Testament methodology as such, we need to look at the key concepts underlying his thesis. These consist of three main notions: firstly, the idea that certain types of narratives were oral in nature; secondly, that this orality is detectable, i.e. the story as it now stands is perceptibly different from a story that developed in a written form; and thirdly, that oral composition and transmission is governed by a "universal law of change". To assess the validity and applicability of these notions to biblical scholarship today we need to understand as far as possible the contemporary context in which Gunkel's form-critical ideas concerning orality developed, and then scrutinize these ideas in the light of modern oral narrative research.

The search for the contemporary context and meaning of Gunkel's ideas of double narratives as oral variants reveals three main trends of research: the work of the Grimm brothers on types, or genres, of folk tradition; the ensuing debate on the origins of these genres, the myth in particular, and the way tradition develops; and finally the particularly Fenno-Scandinavian preoccupation with the nature of variant development and its articulation in epic, and other oral, laws. For the assessment of these ideas, on the other hand, particularly in terms of their theoretical and methodological validity, we need to turn to modern folklore studies. Here the modern concepts of genre analysis and the debate about the status of oral laws in folklore research are most pertinent to our understanding of the validity of Gunkel's concepts of orality in biblical narrative.

3.1. Oral Genres and the Old Testament Narrative

3.1.1. Gunkel: Genesis as *Sage*

As a discipline folkloristics only began to emerge in the early nineteenth century as a widely interdisciplinary "sphere of interest" contributed to by philologists, historians, anthropologists and even some theologians.[1] Much of the seminal scholarship in the area was published contemporaneously with the work of Wellhausen and Gunkel[2] and the two emerging disciplines, folklore studies and Old Testament criticism, developed under much the same intellectual and cultural environment and drew from the same contemporary notions concerning the evolution of human culture, literature in particular. As folkloristics has in the past century become very much a discipline in its own right with a well-scrutinized theoretical framework and accompanying methodology, bringing these assets to bear on the study of biblical criticism can produce some very valuable results, and enhance the self-understanding of both disciplines.[3]

The idea of orality underscoring biblical narrative was not a new one or one original to Gunkel. Many scholars before him – Astruc, de Wette, Ewald, Klostermann, Reuss, even Wellhausen – acknowledged the fact that at least some of the Old Testament narrative material had existed in oral form before being set into writing.[4] But they also thought that this stage was now inaccessible and thus concentrated on trying to unravel the development of

---

1   The term "folk-lore" was coined by William Thomas in 1846 as "a good Saxon compound" to replace "Popular Antiquities or Popular Literature" and it soon became the term used to translate the German *Völkerkunde* (Thoms 863). Since then "folklore" has at times been used very widely to encompass practically every aspect of a non-literary culture (or the non-literary aspects of literary cultures), i.e. literature and other arts; beliefs, customs, and rites; crafts; and language or folk speech (Utley 1965:9). Here we will use the term in a narrower sense focusing on what is now often regarded as the most prominent aspect of folklore, i.e. literary traditions that are predominantly (or presumably) orally composed and/or transmitted, i.e. "oral literature". (For the complexities of defining folklore and related terms, see Utley 1965; Kirkpatrick 15-17; and Finnegan 1992:1-24).

2   See e.g. Grundtvig (ed.) 1853-76; J. Krohn 1885, 1888; K. Krohn 1888, 1903-10; Olrik 1892-4, 1903, 1909; Aarne 1913.

3   For surveys of the use of folklore ideas in Old Testament studies, see Rogerson 1974; Culley 1986; Kirkpatrick; Niditch 1993.

4   For Gunkel's recognition of this fact, see Gunkel 1895:143 and 144n2.

Israel's traditions on the assumption that it was the author-writer who left a detectable and dateable hallmark in the text, even when using already existing oral material. What was different in Gunkel's approach was that he saw the oral stage as the formative one and considered the determining factor in the development of a narrative to be its genre, rather than any literary author, even an individual storyteller. In this respect Gunkel's thinking was continuous with much of the folklore research of his day and reflected its major debates concerning the nature of oral composition, the origin of narrative genres, and the historical reliability of oral tradition.[5]

Fundamental to Gunkel's thesis that certain Old Testament narratives are oral in form is his perception of these stories as types of folk narrative, such as myth, *Sage* or *Märchen* in terms of their literary genre. Thus Gunkel's work on the orality of biblical narratives always goes hand in hand with his interest in literary types (genres), and the attempt to understand the dynamics – origin, development, function – of these genres. In this respect Gunkel's interests and goals mirror those of a number of scholars of various types of expertise who, motivated either by the search for national roots and identities that swept over much of Northern Europe in the nineteenth century or by the quest for man's intellectual and cultural origins in general, threw themselves into collecting, classifying and analysing various folk traditions, and interpreting them not only in terms of their immediate cultural context, but in relation to the heritage of classical and biblical literature as well.[6]

Gunkel's understanding of the genres of Genesis, and certain other biblical narratives, is first systematically articulated in his 1901 Genesis

---

5   It is very unlikely that Wellhausen, too, was aware of these debates. Kirkpatrick interprets his "dismissal of the possibility of gaining any historical insight from oral tradition" not as a sign of ignorance, but as "acceptance of a degeneration theory" (Kirkpatrick 119n10).

6   Thus, besides the many collections of folktales that appeared in the wake of the Grimm's *Kinder- und Hausmärchen*, 1812-15, a number of collections of folk traditions previously only known in oral form, such as the Finnish *Kalevala*, 1835, the Estonian *Kalevipoeg*, 1853, were set into writing. On the other hand interest in already existing traditions, such as Icelandic sagas and Scandinavian ballads surged. As approaches to the study of these traditions were developed, the application of folklore methodology was widened to include some of the world's ancient religious and classical traditions, the Indian *Rig-Veda*, the Homeric epics and the Bible. Gunkel was the first biblical scholar to attempt a systematic application of folkloristic principles of the Scriptures. For parallel developments in Homeric studies, see M. Parry 1971, and Foley 1988; for *Rig-Veda* and other Indo-European traditions such as the King Arthur legend, see Cox, 1881. For surveys of the folkloristics as a discipline, see Thompson 1946:367-405; Dorson 1968; Hautala 1969; and Strömbäck *et al* (eds) 1971.

commentary,[7] developed and in part considerably revised in the two subsequent editions of the work, 1902 and 1910,[8] and finally elaborated on and expanded to include a wider range of Old Testament stories in *Das Märchen im Alten Testament*, 1917 (ET *The Folktale in the Old Testament*, 1987). In these works Gunkel proposes that the stories of Genesis are legends, *Sagen*, and the genre is defined first of all by juxtaposing it with history, *Geschichte* (1901:i, ET 1). Historical writing, too, is found in the Old Testament, the story of Absalom's rebellion in 2 Samuel being a salient example, but the amount of history is negligible in relation to *Sage* (1901:v, ET 9-10). Remnants of myth also survive, for instance in the reference to the union of humans and angels (Gen. 6:1-4) and to the Tower of Babel (Gen. 11), while the list of folktale, *Märchen,* is an extensive one but drawn mainly from outside Genesis (Gunkel 1901:vii, ET 14-5; 1917, ET 1987).[9]

In terms of the origin of the various genres, in 1901 when *Genesis* was first published, Gunkel regarded myth as the parent genre from which others derived. "Myths,…stories of the gods (*Göttergeschichten*)", Gunkel contends, "are in all nations the oldest narratives", while "the legend as a literary variety has its origin in myths" (1901:vii, ET 14). Amongst the Israelites the change from myth to legend was prompted by the hostility of the Jahvistic religion to the pagan connotations of myths, which, Gunkel argues, explains both the relative paucity of myths in the Old Testament and the "unspoken aversion to mythology" that dominates early Israelite legends (1901:vii, ET 15-6). As for the relationship of legend and history, Gunkel regards history as a relatively late, "learned literary genre", achieved only by people with certain amount of sophistication, while *Sage* with its simple style and structure and a (quasi)poetic form originated earlier in oral form from the mouths of "unlettered", primitive people (1901:i-ii, ET 1-3; 1917:1, ET 21). Besides such matters of style and origin, the two genres can be recognized on the basis of their subject matter, history being interested in public matters,

---

7   Already in *Schöpfung und Chaos in Urzeit and Endzeit*, 1895, Gunkel expressed a clear conviction that "die Sagen haben schon vor der literarischen Fixierung eine Geschichte in der mündlichen Tradition gehabt" and that "diese, schliesslich allein wichtige, Vorgeschichte ist durch keine Literarkritik zu erreichen" (143).

8   The fact that Gunkel never completed and systemized his revisions of *Genesis* has left many internal contradictions and loose ends in his work on genre and orality. See Rogerson 1974:60-4, and Klatt 129-38, for a discussion of some of the problems thus created.

9   Jacob at Penuel, Gen. 32:23-32, and the Hagar stories of Gen. 16 and 21 are, Gunkel contends, examples of folktales in Genesis (1917:67ff, 75ff, ET 83ff, 90ff). In his classification of the folktale in the Old Testament into twelve categories, these two stories come under "Tales of Spirits, Demons and Spectres" (1917:67, ET 83).

legends in human affairs and domestic issues (1901:iii, ET 4-5). In terms of historical reliability, though contrasted with history, *Sagen* in Gunkel's view were not pure invention but depended for their content on both popular tradition and imagination, and conveyed, and certainly were believed to convey, a certain amount of historical material (1901: i, ET 2).

By 1917 Gunkel had totally revised his opinion on the matter of the oldest genre and now argued that "the myth…does not precede the folktale at all, but rather…it generally comes later", for "the genres of myth and saga (*Sage*) arose in their present form" from "the motifs originally deposited in folktales" (1917:7-8, ET 27). This reversal of opinion Gunkel credits to the discovery by Wilhelm Wundt, a German psychologist, that "primitive peoples" had stories that "resemble our folktales, where by and large therefore, the oldest kind of narrative can still be seen" (Gunkel 1917:7, ET 27).[10] Gunkel's views on the content of myth and the other three main prose genres – he had now added *Legende* to the list – remained more or less unchanged (1917:1-7, ET 22-7).

3.1.2. Gunkel's Genre Definition in Context: The Grimms as Pioneers of Oral Genres

Gunkel's choice of terminology – *Sage, Märchen, Mythus* – to describe the Old Testament narrative, as well as many of his fundamental notions concerning these genres and the "primitive people" that originated them, as will be seen below, link him firmly with nineteenth-century efforts to define folk traditions in terms of their literary types, to account for their origin and to assess their reliability.[11] Trailblazing work in the area of genre definition

---

10 Rogerson assigns Gunkel's views on myth, *Sage* and *Märchen* to two periods with the turning point around 1907, which more or less coincides with the time Gunkel credits Gressman for having drawn his attention to "folktale" (Rogerson 1974:57; 1987:13). For Gressmann's adoption of Wundt's ideas, see Gressman 1910; for Wundt's influence on Gunkel, see Klatt 134-6.

11 Perhaps somewhat surprisingly, the questions of biblical genre, particularly with reference to myth, had been extensively discussed by biblical scholars since the mid 1750's (Rogerson 1974:1). In his *Lectures on the Sacred Poetry of the Hebrews*, 1753 (ET 1787), Lowth had attempted to investigate the Bible on the basis of its style and had suggested that this investigation would be helped by insight gained from Latin and Greek poetry. Lowth also claimed that poetry was man's first language, with a distinction made between this kind of poetry derived from nature and poetry as a conscious art (Rogerson 1974:2). These ideas led the German classicist Heyne (1777, 1779) to argue, contra Lowth, that man's earliest speech was myth, not poetry, myth being man's attempt to understand his experiences by drawing analogues from nature

and origin had been done in Germany by Wilhelm and Jacob Grimm, and it is in fact their ideas that Gunkel most clearly echoes, particularly in the early part of his career.[12]

In their three major works, *Kinder- und Hausmärchen*, 2 vols, 1812-15, *Deutsche Sagen*, 2 vols, 1816-18, and *Deutsche Mythologie*, 1835, the Grimm brothers provided collections of, and definitions for, the three main prose genres relevant to folklore research.[13,14] The Grimm brothers saw

---

and to classify myths into two types, "historical" myths, which attempted to describe actual events, and "philosophical" myths, which were interested in the causes and origins of various phenomena (Rogerson 1974:2-3). Heyne's ideas were first applied to the Old Testament by J.G. Eichhorn, who interpreted Gen. 2-3 as historical myths, and the debate was then continued by Gabler (1793), who equated myth with *Sage* and distinguished it from both fable and *Märchen* (Rogerson 1974:3-4, 6-7). Through "the vicissitudes of the oral transmission process" both myth and *Sage* could undergo considerable change and might give rise to fables which, unlike myth or *Sage*, were fictional (*Dichtung*) (Rogerson 1974:7). With such a definition of myth considerable numbers of them could be found in the Bible. Herder (1782-3), too, employed a variety of genre terminology in his writings – *Fabel, Mythos, Poetische Sage, Sage des Ursprungs, Dichtung, Geschichte, Allegorie* – but his definitions remain somewhat confused (Rogerson 1974:12-14, esp. 13-4n68).

The most comprehensive reactions against these concepts of biblical genre and their presence in the Bible came from George and Ewald. George (1837) denied that myth was the same as *Sage* and criticised the "mythical school" for concentrating on the external aspects of events to the exclusion of their internal meaning, and then pursued the difference between the two genres on the basis that in myth the meaning of (*Idee*) of events predominated, in *Sage* their "external manifestations" (*Erscheinung*) (Rogerson 1974:24). Ewald, in turn, denied the existence of myth in the Old Testament, but addressed the issue of the *Sage* extensively. He defined *Sage* as "the story as it primarily arises and subsists without foreign aid, before the birth of the doubting or enquiring spirit" (Ewald 1867:14). He described the Hebrew *Sage* as having a "vivid sense for truth and fidelity, for sobriety and modesty, and an aversion to everything immoderate, vain, frivolous", and also contrasted it with *Geschichte* (ET "tradition"), a distinction which, he argued, was a prerequisite for understanding the Old Testament's relation to both (1867:13, 31).

What is most interesting here is that these endeavours seem to have made little (at least acknowledged!) impression on the subsequent form-critical work of Gunkel, despite the similarity of Gunkel's ideas, and even terminology, to those of Ewald. The role of Ewald's influence on form criticism is, however, as Rogerson points out, still largely unresearched (see Rogerson 1974:58-9). For a fuller discussion of the concept of myth and *Sage* in early biblical scholarship, see Rogerson 1974:1-32.

12   Kirkpatrick goes as far as to suggest that "the influence on folklore of form-critical method" as a whole "is best understood in the context of genre criticism and the work of the brothers Grimm" (23).

13   For earlier collections of tales and stories in German and their assumed folkloristic value, see W. Grimm's notes in *Kinder- und Hausmärchen,* 1856 III:285ff, ET 1884a II:447ff.

folklore as having originated in the most ancient times when man expressed spiritual things in a figurative manner (1884a II:579). Now fragments of these beliefs, the Grimms suggested, were still present in all stories like "small pieces of a shattered jewel...lying strewn on a ground all overgrown with grass and flowers", but could only be detected by the "most far-seeing eye" (1884a II:579). Thus the further one looked back in time, the more the mythical element expanded, having, the Grimms argued, "formed the only subject of the oldest fiction" (1884a II:579). The earliest stories were then myths, and as "divinities form the core of all mythology", they were stories about gods, god-myths, *Göttermythus*[15] – a definition of myth that remained operative at least till the end of the century[16] and, as we have seen, was espoused by Gunkel.

As for the origin of the prose genres, it was myth that the Grimms regarded as the basis for both *Sage* and *Märchen*: "Aller Sage Grund ist nun Mythus", the Grimms proposed, "ohne solche mysterische Unterlage lässt sich die Sage nicht fassen".[17] On the other hand it was "fairy-tales, not legends" that were similar to the myth in that they shared with them "a multitude of metamorphoses" such as the role of animals and the sense of the supernatural (Grimm 1883 III:xvi). Thus the *Märchen* could be seen as "broken-down myths".[18] The fairytale and the legend were, on the other hand, "with good reason distinguished" from each other, the fairytale being "looser, less fettered than legend (*Sage*)" and lacking "local habitation, which hampers legend, but makes it more home-like" (1884b III:xiii-xvii). The myth, on the other hand, shared some qualities with both.

The development from one type of a story to another seems, according to the Grimms, to have been prompted by changes in society. As "gentler and more humane manners" develop "the sensuous richness of fiction increases" and "the mythical element retires into the background and begins to shroud itself in the mists of distance" (1884a II:579). On the other hand "if the glamour of the heroic age takes possession of a nation and men's minds are stirred by great deeds, we have as a result a new transformation of the sagas" (1884a II:579). As for the transmission and diffusion of actual motifs or stories, or the similarities in tales and legends, the Grimms were less decided

---

14   It is obvious, however, that providing genre definitions was not the Grimms original
     intention as these are fairly casual and tentative at first and only tend to develop in
     subsequent editions, presumably as a response to the interest that had been aroused.
15   Grimm 1883 III:xvi-vii.
16   Kirkpatrick 77.
17   "Myth is the basis of all *Sage* and without such a mythical background the *Sage* cannot
     take shape."
18   See Thompson 1946:370.

and suggested two possibilities. It was possible for some stories or similar tradition-motifs that now resembled each other, to have sprung up independently as a response to basic social and cultural similarities that were common to people everywhere, i.e. institutions such as the family, religion, war, the use of artifacts such as the axe of the hoe (Grimm 1884a II:576). But the Grimm brothers insisted that no "chance agreement"[19] could explain striking and extended similarities in folklore, such as demanding a person in a story not just to perform a task but a certain unusual task, or series of tasks, for a fulfilment of a promise (1884a II:575). In such a case a common origin must be assumed.[20]

3.1.3. Müller and Lang: The Debate about the Development of Oral Genre

The ideas of the Grimm brothers were taken up by several, mainly German and British, scholars and developed in the second half of the nineteenth century into two opposing theories of the origin of folklore, and also to some extent its diffusion and transmission, and became most clearly juxtaposed in Max Müller's "solar-mythology" school[21] and Andrew Lang's "polygenesis" theory.[22] What is significant in this "battle of myths" from the point of view of subsequent oral narrative research, Gunkel's included, is that although both men took as their point of departure certain aspects of folklore which had been highlighted by the Grimm's publications,[23] they did so from very different perspectives. Thus while Müller's work represented a degenerative view of human culture, Lang built his theory on a model of evolutionary anthropology.

---

19 Cf. Wellhausen ET 296.
20 For the Grimms the common origin, or "the outermost lines of common property" lay in the time of the undivided Indo-German race (1884a II:580).
21 For the development of Müller's ideas, see Cox 1881. For a summary of the battle between Müller's and Lang's theories, see Dorson 1965, and Rogerson 1974:33-65. For the first applications of the solar-myth theory of the Old Testament, see Goldziher 1877, and Steinthal 1877.
22 For a summary and an assessment of Lang's work, see Dorson 1968:206-20.
23 These aspects, as summarized by Lang, were the distinct similarity of "the irrational, and unnatural character, answering to nothing in our experience", of the Household Tales, and the fact that parallels to Grimm's *Märchen* could also be found in "the higher mythologies of the ancient civilised races, in mediaeval romance and saintly legend" (Lang 1884b:xii).

According to Müller, then, myth was the original form of folklore,[24] and from myth *Märchen*, as well as *Sage*, were derived. Müller saw in the irrational elements of the *Märchen* relics of ancient, primitive man's anxieties about, and preoccupation with, natural phenomena, such as storms, sunrise and sunset, and change of seasons, and the inability to express himself except in a limited "mythopoeic" manner.[25] The change from myth to *Sage* and *Märchen* was due to both a long process of oral transmission during which the myths were diffused, and a period of linguistic "forgetfulness"[26] during which the original, metaphoric meaning of words was lost and they came to stand for deities. These "gods of ancient mythology" then evolved, or rather "degenerated", into "the demigods and heroes of ancient epic poetry", which in turn "became at a later age the principal characters in our nursery tales" (1868 I:243).

In Müller's view the recovery of the original myth was, however, possible and could be accomplished through comparative philology, i.e. a careful analysis of the names of key actors in folktales or legends to their earliest Aryan roots (Müller 1968 II:144, 200). For this the folktale was the starting point, "the modern *patois* of mythology", through which it was possible to "trace back each modern tale to some earlier legend, and each legend to some primitive mythe [sic]" (Müller 1968 II:201).

Lang's theory, which was an evolutionary model,[27] was almost the reversal of Müller's, and was also reached via a very different method, that of comparative anthropology.[28] Lang saw in the irrationalities of both myth and *Märchen* reflections of the "qualities of the savage imagination" – the things that now seemed unnatural to us, were not so to him, as his intellectual powers were not fully developed – and thus "survivals"[29] from the early man's culture and thought (1884b:xlii; 1887 I:32-3). The most original form of folklore in Lang's opinion were then the tales of the savage man which in

---

24   Müller went as far as to claim that "every one of the[se] common Aryan words" was "in a certain sense, a mythe [sic?]", that is, "mythology is only a dialect, an ancient form of language" (1868 II:54, 146).

25   That is, by using nouns for objects and verbs for qualities: Thus "the rainer", "the thunderer", instead of "the rain" and "the thunder", and "He rains", "He thunders", instead of "It rains", "It thunders" (Müller 1892:61, italics omitted).

26   For Müller's theory of "disease of language" language, see Rogerson 1974:34; Thompson 1946:372-3.

27   See Lang 1887 I:36.

28   For Lang's indebtedness to E. B. Tylor's anthropological thought, see Lang 1887 I:34, and Dorson 1986:207ff.

29   Lang compared the folklorist's study of the "surviving superstitions and stories" for the reconstruction of the earlier stages of human life and culture to the archaeologist's study of relics (1884a:11).

time "the civilised race... developed and elaborated into a localised myth", while among the largely "stationary and uneducated classes" a somewhat "advanced" version of the original savage story, a kind of a "civilised" *Märchen*, emerged (1884b:xlii; 1887 I:39ff). Grimm's Household Tales belonged to this latter category and thus were representatives of the intermediate stage between the savage story and the myth of early civilisations (1884b:xliii).

For evidence for his theory Lang turned to anthropology and its descriptions of peoples regarded as primitive in his time, such as American Indians, Maoris and Zulus, and the testimony of literature from the Bible and Greek philosophers to the accounts of early explorers (1884b:xlixff). Lang concluded that primitive men everywhere and at all times had a certain "state of mind", to which the occurrence of similar mythical motifs in vastly different places at vastly different times, could be credited (1884b:li).[30] As Lang's views eventually triumphed over Müller's, the primitive myth lost its position as the "mother-genre" to the polygenesis of folktale but perhaps more importantly, a notion of oral tradition as somehow more "reliable", or "accessible", had started to develop.

It is not our task here to establish the exact way nineteenth century folklore research influenced Gunkel's concept of the orality of the Old Testament narrative,[31] but rather to show the way his concept of the orality of Old Testament narratives is more generally indebted to, and continuous with, the contemporary ideas about traditional narratives, their composition, transmission and variant development. Looking at Gunkel's discussion of the main prose genres it would be impossible to ignore his affinity with the Grimms' genre definitions, obvious as much in the terminology used in *Genesis* and the issues addressed, as the direct references to Grimm in

---

30 The diffusion of the tales was for Lang, as it had been for Müller before him, the most difficult aspect of his theory to account for, as he was uncertain how far his concept of "polygenesis" could be applied to the structure of the stories – whether to the plots as well as motifs (1884b:lxx). Thus Lang could not exclude the possibility of borrowing of myths between different peoples (1884a:27).

31 Gunkel's indebtedness to the scholarship of the previous century, and on the other hand his possible original contribution to the development of folkloristic thought, has been discussed by several scholars over the last few decades, with some divergent results. Klatt credits Gunkel with an originality and independence of thought in his classification of Old Testament genres and thus runs counter to the commonly held view of Gunkel's indebtedness to the Grimm brothers, emphasized by Gibert and most recently articulated by Kirkpatrick, while Rogerson expresses surprise concerning Klatt's view and the general lack of treatment of Ewald's work in connection with Gunkel's oral narrative research (Klatt 110ff; Gibert; Kirkpatrick 23; Rogerson 1974:48)

Gunkel's works. The subsequent struggles over the origin of the various genres are also evident in Gunkel's work, not least in his change of heart concerning myth and its place in the chain of genre development and his espousal of Wundt's views, based on evolutionary anthropology, and very much akin to those of Lang. It is these concepts of genre and orality of traditional, orally transmitted narratives, that form the arena in which Gunkel's thesis of the Genesis narrative as *Sage* and the evidence of this in the presence of variants, can now be assessed.

3.2. Old Testament Narrative Genres as Oral Genres: A Reevaluation

3.2.1. Modern Genre Theory: Origin and Evolution versus Structure and Configuration

Gunkel's concept of certain Old Testament narratives as *Sage*, even *Märchen* and *Mythen*, not *Geschichte* – thence oral, not literary creations that developed according to certain universal principles, not haphazardly – was consistent with, and rooted in, the oral narrative scholarship of his time and therefore enabled as well as limited by its orientation and modes of expression. Thus when nineteenth-century genre studies have come under the scrutiny of twentieth-century folkloristics both strengths and weaknesses have emerged, which then inevitably also apply to Gunkel's work inasmuch he is a representative of the contemporary mode of thought.

What is most obvious in the more modern studies of oral narrative as compared to the early works in the area, is a widening of perspective, mirroring what Utley terms "in most fields of learning, from biology to literature, the established contrast between nineteenth and twentieth century...that of origin and evolution versus structure and configuration" (1969:91). In relation to the work of the Grimms and their successors what this shift to "structure and configuration" has meant is not the exposure of any basic "fault" in the original concept of genre, though inevitably this too has come under criticism from some quarters, but the realization of the inadequacy of a genre description based on "patterns of form, content, and context" and preoccupied with the issue of origin, such as the Grimms' model was,[32] to account comprehensively for the multiplicity of the issues and dimensions relevant to the study of folk narratives.

---

32   See Kirkpatrick 73.

In this widening of horizons what have proved to be perhaps the most pertinent, but also difficult, questions are the ones that concern the notion of genres in folklore as such, that is, on the one hand as labels for actual traditional material, on the other as the abstract relations between these materials, i.e. their classification into categories that can be studied analytically. Consequently the issue which is of particular interest to our current research, is the question whether, or to what extent, the traditional descriptions of myth, *Sage* and *Märchen* as perceptibly oral, as opposed to literary, genres, are born out by modern folklore scholarship.

Since the turn of the twentieth century several different approaches to the study of folklore have been undertaken by scholars, who have either developed the already existing models that emerged in the previous century, formulated new methodologies on the basis of the study of folklore material itself, or adopted approaches from other disciplines. A survey by Dorson of folklore scholarship over the last century enumerates eight major schools of thought, ranging from the historical-reconstructional and historical-geographical methods, originally attached to the names of Grimm and J. Krohn respectively, to the more recent structural, functional, oral-formulaic and contextual approaches and the more controversial psycho-analytic and ideological ones (1972a:7ff).[33] These approaches to the study of folklore could be categorized in a number of ways emphasizing, for instance, the kinds of critical assumptions involved[34] or types of material employed.[35] From the point of view of the reassessment of the nineteenth-century genre concepts the challenges that have come from structuralism (Propp, Lévi-Strauss), the oral-formulaic theory (Parry, Lord, Foley), and the contextual approach (Abrahams, Ben-Amos, Georges, Dundes) have been the most significant. With regard to the issues of variant development and diffusion, and the oral laws devised to unravel them, the discussion has centred on the historical-geographical approach.[36]

---

33   Dorson also mentions four less well established methods advocated only by a few proponents, namely those with cross-cultural, folk-cultural, mass-cultural or hemispheric orientation (1972a:40-4).

34   Cf. Ben-Amos, who points out the role "the continuous changes in theoretical perspectives" have in the attempts to (re)define genres (1976:xiii).

35   Any definition of genre would, however, have to take both of these realms into consideration to some extent, as Honko points out in relation to myth: "All attempts to define myth should...be based, on the one hand, on those traditions which are actually available and which are called myths and, on the other, on the kind of language which scholars have adopted when discussing myth" (1984:42).

36   The historical-geographical approach will then be the one most relevant to us, as we assess Gunkel's ideas on oral composition and transmission later in this chapter.

The amount of attention different types of narratives have received from these schools of thought has varied considerably, with some approaches originally dealing with only a very narrow segment of folklore – Propp, for instance, developed his structuralist approach solely in relation to the Russian wonder-tale (*skazki*) – and others being almost "constitutionally" predisposed to the study of certain kinds of material. On the whole the three "conventional" folklore genres of myth, *Sage* and *Märchen*[37] have stayed in the scholarly limelight. This has been particularly true of myth, the bone of contention of the nineteenth century controversies and still recently the subject of much debate,[38] but even more so of the *Märchen*, which as Dégh has somewhat exasperatedly pointed out, has had more than hundred years of folklore theory tailored for its study – to the neglect of such prose genres as fable, novella, riddle (Dégh 1972:59).

Consequently, the definitions of myth, legend and *Märchen*, so central also to Gunkel's work, have multiplied and manifested a spectrum of emphases depending on the approach and the perspective taken. The issue of origin of certain genres, myth in particular, has continued to vex folklorists, and the question of whether ordinary folktales can become myths in certain circumstances and vice versa, has never fully been laid to rest.[39] The question of the relationship of myth and ritual has occupied a central place in the myth studies of this century, while more recently issues such as "truth"[40] and "sacredness"[41] have been proposed as the determining factors for defining myth. Though some scholars, such as Gaster, have continued to press for "redefinition and a fresh approach" as he has found the concept of myth uncontainable within "the old categories",[42] many such recent redefinitions, such as Honko's "concise and descriptive" one have turned out to be

---

37 See Dundes (ed.) 1984:5. See also Clarke and Clarke for the difficulty of dealing with any of the genres, particularly myth and *Märchen*, in isolation (37).

38 See e.g. Sebeok (ed.) 1965; Dundes (ed.) 1984; and, for a summary of twelve "modern theories of myth", Honko 1984:46-8.

39 Thus as recently as 1965 Weisinger argued that myths emerged from "previous materials", which "for want of a better term" he called folklore (120). Others, on the other hand, still "so firmly believe in folklore as disintegrated myth" that they find it impossible to imagine "what any folklore preceding myth would look like" – except in terms of ritual or "dance and mime" (S. Hyman, cited in Weisinger 1965:120). See also Clarke and Clarke (34).

40 See Pettazzoni 1984.

41 Thus for Dundes "a myth is a sacred narrative explaining how the world and man came to be in their present form", "*sacred*" being the "critical adjective" that "distinguishes myth from other forms of narrative such as folktales, which are ordinarily secular and fictional" (Dundes [ed.] 1984:1).

42 Gaster 112.

remarkably reminiscent, if in more sophisticated and comprehensive terms, of the definition of the Grimms, as well as of Gunkel, with myth still basically being "a story of gods..."[43]

The most gargantuan effort on any genre must, however, be the Aarne-Thompson type index, The *Types of Folktale*, 1928,[44] listing some 2400 different folktale types for which variants are known, and Thompson's subsequent monograph, *The Folktale*, 1946, which deals with every aspect of *Märchen* research known by the time of the book's publication. These works are prime examples of the Finnish historical-geographical method, generally regarded as the best established of the schools of folklore, and its preoccupation with mapping the world of *Märchen* variants and perfecting the way of establishing their (hypothetical) original.[45] A rather different line of inquiry for the study of the *Märchen* has been dictated by the fact that *Märchen* studies have never quite been able to rid themselves of the Grimms' legacy of defining the *Märchen* as fragmentary myths (Clarke and Clarke 38). Consequently the questions of the genre's "self-identity", as well as its relationship to myth have formed a stable part of *Märchen* studies (Clarke and Clarke 38).

With the "hundred year domination"[46] of *Märchen* over in the 1960's, a "new epoch of legend research" dawned, focusing on such longstanding problems as the adequate description of the genre felt to "be so immense...that it touches upon the whole spectrum of folk culture" and at times seems to be "all content" without any fixable form at all.[47] Of the three conventional prose genres legends are indeed the most numerous, but with an "extremely variable" form, "reacting sensitively to local and immediate needs", it has also been the hardest to define (Dégh 1972:73).[48] The "belief

---

43   I.e. "Myth, a story of the gods, a religious account of the beginning of the world, the creation, fundamental events, the exemplary deeds of the gods as a result of which the world, nature and culture were created together with all the parts there of and given their order, which still obtains..." This definition, which eventually runs into 25 lines, is formulated on the four inbuilt criteria for the definition of myth: "form, content, function and context" (Honko 1984:49).

44   Revised and enlarged by Thompson, 1961.

45   See Dorson 1972a:7-12, for a description of the Finnish method.

46   See Dégh 1972:59.

47   Schmidt 1963 and 1965, cited in Dégh and Vázsonyi 1971:281. "Legend" here is seen as encompassing both *Sage* and *Legende*, though normally, particularly in older folklore research, "legend" corresponds to *Sage* only.

48   An international conference in 1963 suggested four tentative sub-categories, such as "etiological and eschatological legends" and "historical legends and legends of the history of civilization", based on existing materials to help to harness the issue of definition. See Dégh 1972:76 (italics omitted); and Hand 1965.

factor" has, however, emerged as one of the principal issues in legend scholarship, as "contacts with and attitudes toward reality" have traditionally been key criteria in defining the genre "legend", with the *Märchen* seen as expressing "the escape from reality", while "the legend faces the facts of reality" (Dégh and Vázsonyi 1971:282; Dégh 1972:59).

3.2.2. Genesis as *Sage*: A Reevaluation

To what extent, then, have the definitions of genre, established by the Grimm brothers and reflected by Gunkel, changed?   This question has potentially at least two different answers, depending on whether we look at the issue of genre in the more conventional sense of "origin and evolution", that is in terms of research that is methodologically continuous, no matter how far it has moved, with the early folklore studies of the Grimms *et al*, or whether we move into the realm of what Utley termed "structure and configuration".[49]

In one of the most influential reexaminations of the three main prose narrative genres conducted within the conventional approach, Bascom[50] defines myth, legend and tale in relation to one another by comparing them in terms of the six variables most commonly employed in modern genre debates, namely the presence of a "conventional opening", "told after dark" (transmission context), "belief", "setting" (time and place), "attitude" (sacred or secular), and "principal character" (human or non-human) (10-11). Consequently Bascom defines folktales as "prose narratives which are regarded as fiction", which are "not considered as dogma or history" and they "may or may not have happened" and "are not to be taken seriously" (8). Myths, on the other hand, emerge as "prose narratives which, in the society in which they are told, are considered to be truthful accounts of what happened in the remote past" (Bascom 9). Legends, for Bascom, "are prose narratives which, like myths, are regarded as true by the narrator and his audience, but they are set in a period considered less remote, when the world was much as it is today" (9).[51]

---

49   Utley 1969:91.
50   "The Forms of Folklore: Prose Narratives", 1984 (use of italics omitted). Bascom proposes the term "prose narrative" for "the wide-spread and important category of verbal art which includes myths, legends, and folktales" and thus distinguishes them from "proverbs, riddles, ballads, poems, tongue-twisters, and other forms of verbal art on the basis of strictly formal characteristics" (7).
51   Unlike myths and legends, folktales usually have conventional openings and are usually told after dark (Bascom 11). The audience's attitude to myth is sacred and its principal

In conclusion Bascom points to "how closely the three categories distinguished by the Grimm brothers correspond to the definitions offered here" and makes a passionate plea for folklorists to return to these categories, which he feels "the seeming conspiracy of later folklorists" has corrupted, so that "some basis of understanding in folklore" could be reached (29). Bascom's conclusion (if not the plea!) has been seconded by many others, such as Dundes, who affirms the fact that "since the days of the Grimm brothers" there has, in fact, been "general agreement among scholars as to generic distinctions between myth, folktale, and legend", as well as Dégh, who suggests that Jacob Grimm's statement "das *Märchen* ist poetischer, die *Sage* ist historischer" is still the basic reference point in genre definition (Dundes (ed.) 1984:5; Dégh 1972:58).

Yet despite all these efforts and harmonious remarks there has been an increasing amount of disquiet among folklorists concerning the adequacy of such definitions to deal with the genre of folklore. In 1964 Dundes famously remarked that "thus far in the illustrious history of the discipline, not so much as one genre has been completely defined"[52] – and to date that has not been contradicted. Several reasons have been cited for this lack of success.

The definition of folk genres presupposes the assumption that the material dealt with, here oral tradition or its presumed written representation, "is not a uniform mass as far as its nature and information value are concerned" and that it is possible "on the basis of various criteria to differentiate, at least in principle, clear-cut genres" (Honko 1968:50). One of the main hindrances to translating this into practice has been the sheer number of possible variables that would make up such criteria. Honko has suggested that at least nine factors should be used for comprehensive genre analysis, namely contents, form, style, structure, function, frequency, distribution, age and origin (1968:62). When each one of these variables has ambiguities or possible "unknowables" attached to it, such as the fluidity of form in conventional prose genres, each of which can potentially develop into either of the two others in certain circumstances,[53] the perennial frustrations caused by lack of standardization in genre related terminology,[54] and the difficulty in

---

character is non-human, while legends, with their human main characters, can be regarded as either sacred or secular, and folktales are secular, even though their principal characters can be either human or non-human (11).

52   Dundes 1978:24.
53   Georges has highlighted the problem that "one man's myth is another man's legend" (1971:13).
54   See e.g. Honko 1968:54-6.

categorizing anything objectively on the basis of style, the task becomes even more daunting.

Approaching the issue of comprehensive genre definition from another perspective Ben-Amos suggests that the blame for such a definition not having materialized lies not with the folklorists, but with "the very incongruity between ethnic[55] genres of oral literature", i.e. genres as cultural modes of communication, and "the analytic categories", i.e. models of organization of texts, constructed for the classification of ethnic materials – or even with the problem in defining "what kind of a category genre is"! (1969:275; 1976:xiv). Developing a configurational model that would synchronize these two categories and their differing functions and purposes – ethnic genres as communication systems each with their own "internal logical consistency", based on "distinct socio-historical experiences and cognitive categories", and analytic genres with their concerns for "the ontology of literary forms" in a context of scholarship – Ben-Amos sees as "methodologically, if not logically, impossible" (1969:275, 285).

Various solutions have been suggested as potential ways out of this impasse over definition.[56] The best hope, in Dundes' estimate, for an adequate genre definition as well as folklore being recognized "as a science", lies with the structuralist and formalist approaches – and indeed the "belatedly epoch making", as it has been called, structuralism of Propp and Lévi-Strauss, based on the more objectively definable types of action, has gained much following in genre research. Honko, however, feels that a genre definition which is "a simple by-product of style- or structure analysis" would be far too narrow to provide for the many tasks and functions that a genre definition needs to fulfil (1968:48). In the end the answer to genre definition may thus not be as much a theory of genres as a system of genres,[57] or a "theory of theory of genres",[58] that could accommodate different, ethnic as well as analytical, genre categories. Or maybe what is needed is simply an affirmation of the fact that there can be no absolutely comprehensive genre definitions, but simply "good enough" categories for the task at hand.

---

55   Or "native". See Bascom 10; and Dundes (ed.) 1984:5.
56   Including doing away with the concept of genre altogether!
57   Dealing with "text and context" of folklore, its "paradigmatical and syntagmatical units", "performance and competence" and the "factors of communication" (Voigt 1980:171, italics omitted).
58   See e.g. the "multi-leveled" approached of Voigt, which attempts to consider interpretative levels such as "general" and "native" terminologies of genres, the "synchronic" and "diachronic" systems of genres and the esthetic value of genres (Voigt 1976:490ff).

But where does all this leave us in wondering whether the stories of Genesis are indeed legends, *Sagen*, or history, *Geschichte*? The genre definitions of the Grimms or Gunkel looked at in these terms are, of course, found wanting. But this is not because they did not have any merit within the parameters they set out to work with, i.e. "form, context and content", but because the parameters are now regarded by some as inadequate in themselves. The desire for a new set of parameters does not, however, negate the validity or existence of the old ones (particularly in the absence of the new ones), which after all are based on questions that need consideration too! Thus while the new genre research holds out promise for a deeper understanding of the multiple variables that make up a traditional prose narrative, whether in the Old Testament or in folklore "proper", the conventional genre assessment provides confirmation of the validity of the work of the pioneers, Gunkel as well as the Grimms.

Within these attempts at genre definition, whether "conventional" or "configurational", the perception of *Sage*, myth and *Märchen* as oral traditional narratives has not been seriously disputed. Thus today, as in the time of the Grimms, the basic distinction of folklore genres and "literary" genres can be regarded as valid. Yet at the same time one can hardly claim that the issue of the level of orality, or "oralness", versus "literariness" in tradition that, after all, have mainly reached the folklorist in written form, has really been adequately debated. Yet for Old Testament scholarship, and for the issue of the phenomenon of double narratives in the Old Testament in particular, this question has been of great interest and has had a far higher profile than the level of discussion within folklore studies would suggest: after all, Gunkel's concept of double narratives as oral variants and Wellhausen's perception of them as literary variants can be seen, within the confines of the source-critical and form-critical methods used to establish these notions, as mutually exclusive – a situation compounded by the claims of scholars such as Van Seters and Koch that they can detect both oral and literary variants within the same doublet. To that extent we must also evaluate Gunkel's notion of the biblical *Sagen* as *oral* narratives, but ones that have, in fact, reached us in written form.

3.3. Oral Composition and Transmission: The Dynamics of Variant Development

3.3.1. Gunkel's Principles of Change

Perhaps the most influential aspects of Gunkel's study of the orality of Old Testament narrative, and certainly the most important ones in relation to the study of doublets, were his concepts that the original oral narrative contains some detectable characteristics by which it can be established as an oral, as opposed to a literary, composition, and that as the narratives developed they did so in accordance with a universal law of change (1901:xlv, ET 98).[59] This, conversely, meant that once these characteristics had been established the orality of a narrative could be "measured" by a set of literary criteria, or epic laws as they have come to be known, and the relative originality of variants of the same narrative could be established. In this respect, as in his work on genre definition and origins, Gunkel is clearly a product of his time, utilizing and developing contemporary thought on orality as he applies it to the biblical narrative. Thus again, in order to assess the validity of Gunkel's notion that double narratives in the Old Testament are oral variants, we should start by looking at his claims concerning orality, and their context in the scholarship of his day.

In the introduction to his Genesis commentary Gunkel makes a number of *a priori* statements concerning the characteristics of oral narrative, particularly with respect to Sage. Though he does not call these statements "laws" or draw up a list as some folklorists and even an occasional Old Testament scholar[60] have done, in essence these statements amount to as much. A scrutiny of the 1901 edition of his *Genesis* yields a set of some 27 "universals", some of which address several aspects of oral narrative composition or transmission. These statements represent most aspects of genre analysis (form, origin, content etc.) but can be divided, if somewhat arbitrarily, into two groups on the basis of whether their emphasis is on the form of the "early" legend or the development of its variants.

According to Gunkel the *Sage*-legend has the following characteristics:

---

59 "Der allgemeine Wechsel."
60 See Koch 141, ET 126-7; Nielsen 1954:36; cf. also B.W. Anderson xxiii-v.

1.   The original unit of oral tradition is an individual legend, *einzelne Sage.*   Only   later   are   these   units   construed   into   "greater   and   artistic compositions" (1901:xix-xx, ET 42-3).

2.   In its early form the legend is a complete unit in itself and has a clear beginning and a clear end.   Thus "the more independent (*selbständiger*) a story is, the more sure we may be that it is preserved in its original form". (1901:xx-i, ET 43, 45).

3.   The early legend is short, brevity being "a mark of the poverty of primitive literary art",[61] but also "condensed and effective" and "clear and synoptic (*übersichtlich*)".   Only later, in response to both the developing aesthetic faculties of man and the possibilities provided by writing, does the legend grow in length (1901:xxii, ET 47-8).

4.   In terms of the balance of its various parts the early legend is "outlined   with   extraordinary   sharpness"   thus   gaining   in   clearness   and "aesthetic charm" (1901:xxii, ET 48).

5.   The legend has only a few characters, two being the minimum, three or four more common.   If there are more characters they are not clearly distinguished but are treated as one, *als Einheit* (1901:xxiii, ET 49-50).

6.   The story-line of the legend is made up of a number of little scenes, *kleine Scenen.*   In each scene usually only two characters appear (1901:xxiii, ET 50).

7.   The leading and subordinate personages are distinctly separated.   The latter are treated with striking brevity and even the former are characterized remarkably briefly by only a few main traits (1901:xxiv-v, ET 52-3).

8.   The popular legend offers "a peculiar popular conception of man"[62] treating people as "types", *Typen,* in terms of their most essential traits and being unable to grasp or represent the many-sidedness of a person.   If different facets of a person need to be presented, this is achieved by legend cycles (1901:xxv-vi, ET 55-6).

9.   The art of the popular legend is unable to depict development in its characters and is also sparse on outward characteristics (e.g. a person's complexion, eyes or clothes) (1901:xxvi, ET 56-7).

10. In primitive legend characterisation of personages is subordinated to action, *Handlung* (1901:xxvii, ET 57).   The narrator cares above all for action, with even thoughts being expressed by action (e.g. "Joseph wept"). Sometimes the spiritual life of a person is expressed by "articulate speech", i.e. words spoken by the person in question (1901:xxviii-xxix, ET 61-3).

---

61   "Das Zeichen der Armut dieser alten Kunst."
62   "Volkstümliche Betrachtung des Menschen."

11. The popular legend was above all an oral art and the performance of the story-teller (tone of voice, gestures) had an essential role in conveying aspects of the story not otherwise made explicit (1901:xxix, ET 62).

12. The legend is on the whole extremely economical on circumstantial details, yet occasionally presents very minute descriptions of an element in the story (e.g. the meal Abraham serves to his three guests) (1901:xxxi-ii, ET 68).

13. The essential requirement for a story is its inner unity: each event in a series must depend on the preceding one (1901:xxxii, ET 69).

14. Many legends "are fond of varying a given motive [sic](*Motiv*)"[63] (1901:xxxiii, ET 71).

15. The course of action in a legend "must be probable, credible, even highly unavoidable",[64] as judged according to the standards of the time (1901:xxxiii, ET 72).

16. Out of the legend develops another, longer, more discursive and more detailed narrative type more akin to modern fiction, seen at its best in the Joseph-story. "Epic discursiveness (*epische Breite*)", i.e. repetition of popular detail to hold the interesting and attractive aspects of the story longer in front of its audience, is one of its main characteristics (1901:xxxvii-viii, ET 79-83).

17. The origin of legend "always eludes the eye...going back into prehistoric times" (1901:xl, ET 88).

Characteristics more specifically to do with the development of variants are as follows:

18. Poetic variants precede prose variants (1901:xvii, ET 38).

19. Legends change in transmission as change in oral tradition is inevitable. This change is at least at first unconscious; only "in the more recent modifications" can we speak of "conscious art (*bewusste Kunst*)" (1901:xviii, ET 39).

20. Often legend variants originate in the storyteller's need to answer different questions on the same subject matter. One variant then answers one question, a second one another (1901:xxxvi, ET 76-7).

21. It is characteristic of the legend, and oral tradition in general, that it exists in the form of variants. These variants show the adaptation of the legend "from place to place" and "age to age" according to the universal law of change (1901:xliv-v, ET 98).

---

63   E.g. the use of "nakedness" and "clothing of man" in the Eden story.
64   "Wahrscheinlich, höchst glaubwürdig, ja notwendig."

22. The features that typically get added in variant development are "relatively unconcrete" things, such as speeches, that are then out of place in the otherwise harmonious story (1901:xlv-vi, ET 100).

23. Typical omissions in the development of variants are features that are deemed objectionable (according to the current, but changing, standards of ethics and morality) (1901:xlvi, ET 101).

24. Details whose meaning or connection has been forgotten are replaced with known ones as variants develop (e.g. as it was forgotten who the king of Gerar was, he was replaced by the king of Egypt) (1901:xlvi, ET 102).

25. Sometimes narratives amalgamate by several personages growing together (1901:xliv, ET 97).[65]

26. In the religious sphere in younger variants theophany is modified. Older legends mingle profane and religious motives in a naive way, which later on is no longer tolerated (1901:xlvii, l, ET 104, 110).

27. The changes that develop as foreign themes are amalgamated into Israelite legends include the disappearance of polytheism and an "infilling with the spirit of a higher religion", while foreign personages are replaced with native ones (1901:xliii, ET 95).

There are four basic principles underlying these statements of Gunkel. First of all Gunkel sees the dynamic involved in these developments to be a universal force, or law, of change, operational in all oral traditions (1901:xlv, ET 98). Secondly, the actual changes are affected by historical and geographical influences as the *Sage* adapts as it wanders "from place to place" and "age to age" (1901:xliv, ET 98). Thirdly, Gunkel sees the composition of oral narrative as collective: the stories have a "common" authorship rather than an individual one (1901:xviii-ix, ET 41). Lastly, the transmission situation in which variants arise is the oral performance (1901:xxviii-xxix, ET 61-3).

3.3.2. Gunkel and Olrik: Olrik's Epic Laws

Before the publication of the third, revised edition of *Genesis* in 1910 Gunkel had become acquainted with the work of the Danish folklorist Axel Olrik, whose epic laws he consequently embraced in the new edition. Olrik had entertained the notion of epic laws governing the development of the folk

---

65   Gunkel argues that e.g. the "the figure of Noah...consists of three originally separate personages, the builder of the ark, the vintager, and the father of Shem, Ham and Japhet" (1901:xliv, ET 97).

traditions, *sagn*,[66] since the early 1890's[67] and set some in print by 1905.[68] In 1908 Olrik gave a lecture in Berlin which was subsequently published in an expanded version in German as "Epische Gesetze der Volksdichtung" in 1901.[69] Though Olrik worked on the laws until his death in 1917, it is in the 1909 German form that his ideas became best known among non-Scandinavian readers, whether folklorists or biblical scholars.[70]

Gunkel seems not to have become acquainted with Olrik's work until just before the publication of the third edition of his *Genesis*. A letter from him to Olrik survives, dated March 1, 1910, saying:

> I recently read your essay in *Zeitschrift* [sic] and I was pleasantly surprised to find an almost uncanny affinity between your research and mine, which I have presented especially in my Genesis commentary (first edition published in 1901). My Genesis commentary will appear in its third edition at Easter; I have been able to include some references to your essay at the last minute (in the introduction).[71]

However, even though Gunkel does not seem to have had sufficient time to consider fully the implications of Olrik's laws in relation to his own notions of change in oral tradition, as many as sixteen references to these laws appear

---

66   Although *sagn* is usually translated with the German "Sage" and the English "legend", Olrik saw the word term as an all-inclusive one encompasing "folktales, myths, folksongs, heroic sagas *(Heldensagen)*, local legends *(Ortsagen)*" (Olrik 1909:2). In the broadest sense of the term *sagn*, for Olrik, "designates a report of an event that is passed along by word of mouth without the informants' being able to check its origin or its previous authorities" (1992:1).

67   Already in his doctoral thesis (1892-4, 2 vols) Olrik suggested some principles according to which oral narratives developed. Thus "two *sagn* that are related, or just two *sagn* that resemble each other" will grow even more similar as "one borrows from the other, not just by one simple loan, but repeatedly over time" (Olrik 1894:107). On the other hand, certain episodes, such as battle scenes, "require a certain pattern of a few elements", as oral tradition cannot reliably transmit much detail concerning various "battles, people and lands", and this then results in all such scenes having a certain resemblance (1894:115).

68   In "Torden guden og hans Dreng" Olrik proposed the "law of opposites", *modsætnings-loven*, as the "simplest and yet strongest *(allermægtigste)* of the rules that govern folkliterature" (1905:146). Earlier on Olrik had already alluded to the "law of intro-duction" (1899:12) and "the natural law of the supernatural", *det overnaturliges naturlove* (1904:19).

69   In *Zeitschrift für Deutsches Altertum und Deutsche Literatur*, vol. 51, pp. 1-12, ET in Dundes (ed.) 1965:129-41.

70   The final, much expanded version of the laws was published posthumously in 1921, completed by one of Olrik's students, H. Ellekilde (ed.), as *Nogle Grundsætninger for Sagnforskning*. The ET of this, *Principles for Oral Narrative Research*, was not published until 1992.

71   Cited from Olrik 1992:156.

in the footnotes of his new edition of Genesis, receiving, it seems, Gunkel's unequivocal support.

The 1909 version[72] of Olrik's laws stipulates thirteen "epic laws":[73]

1. The Law of Opening and Closing. "The *Sage* does not begin with sudden action and does not end abruptly", rather it "begins by moving from calm to excitement, and...ends by moving from excitement to calm" (131-2).

2. The Law of Repetition. "In literature, there are many means of producing emphasis, means other than repetition" as "the dimensions and significance of something can be depicted by the degree and detail of the description of that particular object or event. In contrast, folk narrative lacks this full-bodied detail". Thus "for our traditional oral narrative, there is but one alternative: repetition" (132-3).

3. Law of Three. "The repetition is almost always tied to the number three" (133).[74]

4. The Law of Two to a Scene. "Two is the maximum number of characters who appear at one time." More characters is "a violation of tradition" (134-5).

5. The Law of Contrast. "The *Sage* is always polarized" and works "from the protagonist of the *Sage* out to the other individuals, whose characteristics and actions are determined by the requirement that they be antithetical to those of the protagonist" (135).

6. The Law of Twins. "Whenever two people appear in the same role, both are depicted as being small and weak." In this situation they can come under the Law of Twins instead of the Law of Contrast (135-6).

7. The Importance of Initial and Final Position. In a series of persons or events "the principal one will come first. Coming last, though, will be the person for whom the particular narrative arouses sympathy" (136).

8. The Law of the Single Strand. In contrast to literature, the folk narrative "does not go back in order to fill missing details" (137).

9. The Law of Patterning. "Two people and situations of the same sort are not as different as possible, but as similar as possible" (137).

10. The Use of Tableaux Scenes. These are scenes "where the actors draw near to each other" and the *Sage* rises to a peak (138).

---

72 References here are to the ET (1965).

73 Olrik subsequently elaborates on these laws in *Nogle Grundsætninger for Sagnforskning*, 1921, (ET 1992:41ff). However, Olrik does not draw up a list of the laws in his later work as he does in the 1909 article, and also uses the word "law" more sparingly, thus leaving some room for interpretation as to the difference between laws and possible supporting principles.

74 In the Indic stories the Law of Three is often replaced by the Law of Four (133).

11. The Logic of the *Sage*. "The themes which are presented must exert an influence upon the plot, and moreover, an influence in proportion to their extent and weight in the narrative" (138).

12. The Unity of Plot. "The presence of loose organization and uncertain action in the plot is the surest mark of cultivation" (138).[75]

13. Concentration on a Leading Character. This is "the greatest law of folk tradition." In case of two heroes "one is always the formal protagonist" (139).

Even a cursory comparison of these laws with the principles drawn above from Gunkel's *Genesis* shows some remarkable similarities in how oral composition is perceived. Gunkel's Principles 2 (clear beginning and end), 5 and 6 (few characters, two to a scene), 6 (many small scenes to a story), 7 (distinct leading personages), 13 (inner unity of story), and 15 (credibility of action), are virtually identical with Olrik's Laws 1 (opening and closing), 4 (two to a scene), 10 (use of tableaux scenes), 13 (concentration on a leading character), 12 (unity of plot), and 11 (law of logic), respectively. Gunkel's concept that the *Sage* treats men as types also corresponds closely to Olrik's Law of Contrast (5), while in addition both men emphasize the primacy of action in the story,[76] the single-strandedness of the story-line,[77] the scarcity of detail,[78] and repetition for the sake of effect.[79]

The only concepts that Gunkel does not in some way parallel are Olrik's Law of Twins (6), and Importance of Final Position (7). There are no obvious contradictions in the way the two men perceive oral tradition as having developed. In the 1909 article Olrik does not emphasize the distinction between the characteristics of oral narrative in general and their variants in the way Gunkel does, but he does address the matter in more detail in his later work.[80] We will return to the more specific issue of variant development below.

Gunkel's exposure to Olrik's work and Olrik's possible influence on Gunkel's own principles of oral composition and transmission have been a matter of some ambiguity, with later Old Testament scholarship sometimes treating Gunkel's original *Genesis* statements concerning the *Sage*-genre and its variants almost interchangeably with Olrik's epic laws.[81] However, on the

---

75   However, the unity of the plot of e.g. a myth, or a heroic saga, is less obvious than that of a *Märchen* or a local legend (138).
76   Gunkel (10); Olrik mentions this as a "general principle" (1965:137).
77   Gunkel 1901:xxxiii, ET 70-1; Olrik (8).
78   Gunkel (12); Olrik (9).
79   Gunkel (12); Olrik (2 and 3).
80   See Olrik 1992:95ff.

basis of this recently published correspondence it now seems clear that Olrik had no direct impact on Gunkel's thinking as he initially outlined his ideas about the orality of the Genesis *Sage*.[82] In fact Holbek, who has written perhaps more extensively on Olrik's work than anyone else, remarks, on the basis of Gunkel's correspondence with Olrik, that "by another of those quirks of history, virtually the same discovery [of epic laws] was made at the same time by Hermann Gunkel, the German theologian" (Holbek 1992:xxii-iii). It is perhaps not unreasonable to assume, then, that in terms of the ideas about orality of traditional narratives, the two men shared in, or drew from, a common background, and that this background was the late nineteenth century folklore scholarship and the disciplines folklore studies emerged from.

Because of the more decisive and "professionally" folkloristic way Olrik articulates the principles which Gunkel proposes in more descriptive terms, and also because of the widespread interest in Olrik's work even amongst biblical scholars, Olrik's epic laws form perhaps the best starting point for the study of the concepts of orality and variant development that undergird not only Olrik's work, but Gunkel's as well.

---

81 Warner (331) wonders "exactly to what extent Gunkel was influenced by Olrik", while Whybray (150) asserts that "Gunkel...relied heavily" on Olrik's laws, "especially" in the 1910 edition of *Genesis*, and Niditch (1996:2) assumes that Gunkel's perception of Israelite tradition as "poetic, repetitive, simple, and single-stranded in plot" was "influenced by Axel Olrik's 1908 study 'Epic Laws of Folklore'". On the other hand Culley (1986:33-4) argues that in Gunkel's work Olrik's laws "are clearly used to substantiate insights Gunkel had already arrived at", and Kirkpatrick (25) credits Gunkel with anticipating "many of the conclusions" of Olrik.

82 That the reverse is also true is apparent from comments in Olrik's later work (see 1992:116ff). The extent to which the two men's academic careers paralleled each other is, however, remarkable. Just as Gunkel was first trained in source-criticism as the prevailing method for the study of Old Testament narratives, so Olrik's earliest works, 1887 and 1892-4, dealt with the differentiation of the Icelandic and Danish sources in Saxo's *Gesta Danorum*, a task which Olrik felt was possible on the basis that the types of material each bore their own distinctive style (see Holbek 1971:264-8; 1992:xix). Olrik's realization that "the 'Danish' narrative style was actually the style of oral narrative art" then provided the impetus for his study of epic laws – a development not unlike Gunkel's claim that the whole style of the patriarchal narratives could only be understood "on the supposition of its having been oral tradition" (Holbek 1992:xx-xxi; Gunkel 1901:ii, ET 4).

3.3.3. The Making of Epic Laws

In his introduction to the English translation of the final, expanded version of Olrik's *Principles for Oral Narrative Research*, Holbek goes as far as to describe the work as "perhaps the most comprehensive methodology for research in oral verbal art ever devised by a single person" (1992:xv).[83] Although Olrik's individual contribution to folklore methodology can hardly be overestimated, what we, however, also have in his work is a culmination of efforts at systematization of folkloristic knowledge that have manifested themselves sporadically since the time of the Grimms and more consistently during the last decades of the nineteenth century. For Olrik was not the only, not even the first, person to entertain the idea that oral composition and transmission was governed by some universal principles. In this respect he was specifically indebted to two of his former teachers, the Danish folklorist Svend Grundtvig and the Norwegian Moltke Moe, who, from the 1840's to 1890's attempted to come to grips with the way Scandinavian folk traditions, in particular, had developed, and to some extent also to two Finnish scholars, Julius and Kaarle Krohn, who, in the wake of the collecting and publication of *Kalevala*, studied the ways folklore variants witnessed to a tradition's adjustment to changes in time and location. The approach that resulted from the efforts of these Finnish scholars, which Olrik concurred with, has come to be known as the historical-geographical, or the Finnish, method, now considered by many to be the "dominant force in folklore science".[84] It is this method and the work of its developers, preoccupied from the start with the study of variants and the laws that govern their development, that form the best context for the appraisal of Gunkel's ideas about the principles of change according to which he believed the Genesis *Sagen* had evolved.

3.3.3.1. *Svend Grundtvig*

As early as 1867, in a work on Scandinavian heroic *sagn*, Grundtvig had suggested that in oral tradition there were certain principles of change and adaptation at work that moulded the development of the tradition. These principles, which Olrik later summarized as Grundtvig's six "general laws", *almene love*, dealt with, or governed, the development of narratives in terms of their basic unit, birth, growth, death, susceptibility to political and

---

83   This view is echoed by Dundes (ed.) 1965:129-30.
84   Dorson 1972:8.

historical influences, and also helped in the detection of later additions.[85] Thus, for instance, the development of the heroic *sagn* was determined in its "construction and context by political considerations, rather than historical" (law 1), and would have "reached a late stage in its life" when "the hero-figures in the king's retinue" had grown "to such a stature as to overshadow the hero-kings themselves" (law 5).[86]

Before his work on the heroic *sagn*, since the 1840's, Grundtvig had studied vast numbers of variants, particularly of Danish ballads, and had come to realize the significance of these variations in reflecting not only the original form of a given tradition but the history of its development: "every item of tradition is an individuality", Grundtvig argued, and "the sum of them is something quite different from the individual texts in their independent existences".[87] Thus Grundtvig saw ballads as "a living organism" and their "life" in oral tradition as one of continuous change and adaptation to ever-new local and cultural environments (Holbek 1971:261; Piø 203).[88] Piø points out that although in his earlier work Grundtvig can be seen as advocating the ideas of Herder and Grimm, "the methodological basic thought" underlying this concept of oral tradition as a living organism is new and one that is taken up and developed by Olrik, as is Grundtvig's idea of general laws (Piø 196-7, 203).

3.3.3.2. *Moltke Moe*

The idea of "epic laws" as such Olrik borrowed form Moe,[89] who had already in 1889 used the term "fundamental epic laws", *episke grundlove*, for "the forces that shape the life of a narrative in oral tradition" (Holbek 1971:289-90).[90] Moe understood such forces to be either of psychological (general or individual) or of historical nature, and applicable to all epic, i.e. oral folklore, material (Moe 1914:1-2).[91] He categorized these forces as four laws. The first law governs the development of a single epic motif under the

---

85 Olrik 1903:336-7. The ET (1909) of the work omits this section.
86 Olrik 1903:336-7, cited in Holbek 1971:271.
87 Olrik describing Gruntvig's work (Olrik 1906:178-9, cited in Holbek 1971:261).
88 Interestingly Grundtvig, as Olrik as well as Gunkel after him, saw this variation as a sign of the fidelity of oral transmission, not of any kind of deterioration.
89 See Olrik 1915:51.
90 Moe's epic laws were published posthumously in four articles in *Edda*, 1914-17.
91 Moe uses the word "epic", *epik, episke*, in a very general sense, not for "fairytales alone" but in contrast to individual literary art (1914:3).

influences of a "shaping impulse" and a "sequalising impulse"[92] and explains how a motif would "develop to a greater copiousness and volume, either by a poetic expansion" of elements imbedded in the motif itself, "by absorption and adaptation" of related material, or addition of similar features (Moe 1914:1; Bødker 112-3, 234). The second law deals with changes to tradition as it comes into contact with other subject matters and groups of tradition (Moe 1914:1). Here two opposing sets of impulses are in evidence, working on the one hand toward the amalgamation and recasting of traditions,[93] on the other hand causing an expanded tradition to contract back to "its original volume, the simple foundation", or dissolving it to smaller units[94] (Moe 1914:1; Bødker 25, 224, 262-3). Both of these laws Moe attributed to "general psychological" factors (1914:1).

The third law, one that stems from "historical" factors, explains how a tradition's encounter with other cultural standpoints and changing historical circumstances moulds it in terms of both its "outer elements", i.e. form, scenery, actors, as well as its "inner attitudes", e.g. by changing the "fantastic wonders" of the myth and the fairytale "for the plain content and the simple, natural motivation of the story of everyday-life"[95] (Moe 1914:2; Bødker 222-3, 298-9). The last law deals with the effects of a narrator's personal faculties, – memory, talents, presentation – on his or her art and was accredited by Moe to "individual psychological" factors (Moe 1914:2).

3.3.3.3. *J. and K. Krohn*

The principles according to which variants develop also vexed Finnish folklorists in the second half of the nineteenth century. Nowhere in Europe had the interest in collecting national folk heritage, sparked off by the Grimm brothers in Germany, been carried out with more fervour than in Finland. Decades of field work had produced not only the national epic, *Kalevala*, its lyric counterpart, *Kanteletar*, and volumes of folktales, incantations, riddles, etc., but had also raised the question of how to relate to the numerous variants, sometimes running to hundreds, of the same folk tradition, that had also emerged in the collecting process. *Kalevala* itself was a case in point.

---

92 "Plastisk utformningsdrift og fortsættelsdrift." Besides "impulse" the word "*drift*" could also be translated as "instinct" or "epic instinct" (Bødker 234; see also Olrik 1915:51).

93 "Sammensmeltningsdrift, analogiseringsdrift."

94 "Sammendragnigsdrift, opløsningsdrift."

95 "Tillempningsdrift, omsmeltningsdrift."

While the 1849 definitive edition, the so-called new *Kalevala*, was made up of 50 cantos in 22795 lines, another 400000 lines stood on record by the 1883.[96] Much the same situation existed with other types of folklore.[97]

The first person to confront this problem of variation was J. Krohn. While puzzling over the question of the origins of the *Kalevala* material, he came up with the realization that the key to the issue of original form, time and location of the traditions lay not in the material itself, but in its variants (J. Krohn 1885:379). In most cases, Krohn argued, "enlightenment for the past was available in those numerous variants," which, "when grouped together according to the location where they were found and compared with one another" revealed "a completely new world of overlapping formations and developments" from which the birth process of *Kalevala* could be read (J. Krohn 1885:379). Thus it was the method of comparing variants on a regional and historical basis that, Krohn felt, would show "which forms are incidental, which come later, which features originally entered an alien context etc., until we can really lay our hands on the original forms".[98] These forms were, in Krohn's view, simple and plain "primal cells", *alkusoluja*.[99]

In the process of implementing this method Krohn made what came to be regarded as the fundamental discovery of the now emerging historical-geographical method,[100] namely that variants "differ more the further they are separated geographically".[101] Thus poems in one region would resemble one another more than those from another region, the differences becoming the greater the more the areas were separated, the poems thus forming "a geographical chain", *maantieteellisen sarjan*, of development that the folklorist could then observe.[102]

---

96   See Hautala 1954:199.
97   The holdings of the Finnish Folklore Archives increased from 43000 items in 1877 to over 200000 in 1900. The number of folktales, *Märchen* alone in the collection jumped from 1200 to 24000 in the period (Hautala 1954:215).
98   J. Krohn 1885, cited in Pentikäinen 1971:16.
99   See Hautala 1954:192; 1969:72.
100   Some, particularly Finnish, folklorists call J. Krohn's prototype of the method "regional-historical", applying the term "historical-geographical" (or "geographico-historical") to the method from K. Krohn onward (see e.g. Pentikäinen 1971:15).
101   J. Krohn, cited in K. Krohn 1918:39. As implied in the term "historical-geographical" J. Krohn also took into account the fact that traditions changed as they were passed on from one generation to the next. However, he never laid as much emphasis on historical variation as on geographical, mainly because as in his day *Kalevala* poems had only been collected for just over a century, he felt historical aspects were difficult to establish (see K. Krohn 1918:39).
102   J. Krohn, cited in K. Krohn 1918:39.

J. Krohn also discussed the issue of cycle formation. He pointed out that although "good singers indeed know all or almost all the songs now collected in the *Kalevala*", the order in which they performed the poems was generally "altogether haphazard" varying from day to day (J. Krohn 1885:380). However, he also observed that some singers had attempted to "melt" several poems into a unity, but that a complete "organic" unity was finally a literary feature accomplished by collecting and editing, even if some formation of "poetical cycles, miniature epics"[103] already took place at the oral stage (J. Krohn 1885:380, 582).[104]

The historical-geographical method was taken up and developed by J. Krohn's son, K. Krohn, and became most clearly articulated in, and exemplified by, K. Krohn's first major work on the *Kalevala*, *Kalevalan Runojen Historia*, 1903-10. For K. Krohn, as for his father, the history of the *Kalevala* tradition, i.e. the process that "shows how the folk poems have acquired the form in which Lönnrot found them and used in his compilation", was evident in the many variants of the poems.[105] K. Krohn pointed out that while "the poems in their variants display such a variety that at a superficial glance one could suspect that they never had a permanent form", on a closer examination "one will soon see that the variants are not accidental either, but that they have their particular geographical areas".[106] An even closer examination would reveal that "the forms in the areas nearer each other are also in closer inter-relation" and that "where several formations of the same poem regularly presuppose each other, their areas also appear in a corresponding geographical order".[107] This method, K. Krohn argued, would not only demonstrate that "poems travelled" – a fact he already regarded as self-evident – but would help the folklorist towards the solution of a much trickier a problem, namely "how they travelled" and provide a kind of "life history" of the poem in question as well (K. Krohn 1903:24.)

It was also by K. Krohn, in his thesis, 1888, that the method was for the first time applied to non-epic material, this time the fairytale. Here the

---

103 This life-history, for J. Krohn, would reach from "simple, insignificant primal motifs" through additions, loss of original motifs and development of new ones, to the formation of "poetical cycles, miniature epics" (J. Krohn 1903, cited in Hautala 1969:104.)

104 Here J. Krohn makes reference to Steinthal's article "Das Epos", 1868, and the idea that "epic works in their entirety, not only in terms of their material, are folklore", which he rejects, yet conceding that some, even fairly advanced oral formations develop at the oral stage (J. Krohn 1885:576). Gunkel's ideas concerning cycle development in Genesis bear a significant similarity to Steinthal's.

105 K. Krohn 1903:20-21, cited in Hautala 1969:102.

106 K. Krohn 1903:21, cited in Hautala 1969:102.

107 K. Krohn 1903:21, cited in Hautala 1969:102.

starting point for scientific study, K. Krohn argued, should be exactly the same as it had been with epic poetry, namely the publication and study of all known variants.[108] According to K. Krohn some of the "original form" of the tales was "evident everywhere in greater or lesser degree" in the tales despite their long migrations, and thus the comparison of variants would reveal "the original form restored from all later additions, omissions and other changes" (K. Krohn 1888:38-9). Eventually, when "a sufficiently large, complete and organized series" of such original forms had been obtained, this method could answer even the much debated question concerning fairytales, namely "what thoughts and incidents" had in the first place "instigated their birth" (K. Krohn 1888:39).[109]

While the merits of the historical-geographical method were obviously in K. Krohn's estimate many and great, he was nevertheless realistic about the method's limitations. The main one of these was the fact the method could only really operate where the variants were very numerous, no matter what type of folklore was in question.[110] Krohn also warned against any mechanical application of the method, pointing out the significance of judging each variant and each case on its individual merits.[111]

3.3.3.4. *Psychological Laws; Laws of Thought and Metre*

Both J. and K. Krohn regarded the composition and transmission process of oral tradition as subjected to certain principles, which J. Krohn outlined in terms of "psychological laws".[112] The earliest forms of tradition, the "primal cells", *alkusolut*, J. Krohn argued, were living, self-contained organisms, independent of any singer, so much so that "much of the making of an epic took place so subconsciously that the process was almost machine-like" (J. Krohn 1885:584). The laws that governed this subconscious process J. Krohn named as "memory", "desire to assimilate",[113] and "desire to

---

108 K. Krohn's comment in the Minutes of the meeting of the Finnish Literature Society, 9th April, 1885, cited in Hautala 1969:90-1.
109 K. Krohn rejected the Grimms' theory of folktales being broken up myths, as well as Lang's theory of polygenesis of myths based on common psychological properties. (See Hautala 1954:216-7).
110 See Hautala 1954:228.
111 See e.g. K. Krohn 1888:39.
112 See Hautala 1954:193.
113 "Yhtäläistämistaipumus". Hautala translates this as "tendency towards conformity" (1969:73), Pentikäinen as "desire for similarity" (1971:16).

continue"[114] (J. Krohn 1885:584-5). Memory, J. Krohn argued, was an important factor on two accounts: On the one hand its accuracy made the preservation of even long poems possible, on the other hand its "momentary lapses" were "a powerful developer of poems" (1885:584). For, J. Krohn maintained, the singers generally wanted to pass on the poems faithfully, as they had heard them, and had no intention of changing anything, but as sometimes poems got mixed up in the singer's mind elements were transferred from one poem to another (J. Krohn 1885:584).

The "desire to assimilate" also worked, in J. Krohn's view, subconsciously, and was the major force for the amalgamation of poems. This tendency often manifested itself "when a hero has become particularly dear to the people" and resulted in the "accumulation all on its own accord under his name of all sorts of things that originally had nothing to do with him" (J. Krohn 1885:584). The rationale here was, J. Krohn explains, that since the hero "has done so much, the singer thinks even without noticing it that he must also have done this and that" (J. Krohn 1885:584). Closely related to this law, but already working more consciously, was the "desire to continue". This took effect when a particularly pleasant feature was found in a poem and the singer was tempted to "make its effect greater by the addition of one, even two similar features" (J. Krohn 1885:585).

Later K. Krohn developed these laws on similar lines and also pointed out that it was the understanding of these laws that enabled a folklorist, by the means of a comparative study of variants, to recover the original form of the poem. He divided the laws into two categories: "the laws of thought" and "the laws of metre" (K. Krohn 1918:51ff, 67ff). The laws of thought were represented by "the law of fading memory" in its manifold forms, such as omission, substitution, generalization and simplification, while its opposite, "the law of addition", explained how poems accrued new material either through borrowing or the singer's creativity, sparked off by, for instance, association of a common hero or place, or simply by forgetfulness, resulting in "repetition, duplication or multiplication of certain elements" (K. Krohn 1918:55, 58, 64; 1971:65ff, 71ff). Working together with both of the preceding was the more ambiguous "law of change", which Krohn compares to "analogous forms in language" (1918:54).[115] The "laws of metre",[116] on

---

114 "Jatkamishalu." Pentikäinen translates this as "desire for continuity" (1971:16).
115 The Law of Change takes effect when a word is misunderstood or misheard or is unfamiliar to the storyteller and is then "mutated" into a more meaningful form (see K. Krohn 1918:54; 1971:78ff).
116 By "metre" K. Krohn means "all matters concerning the form of the poems" (Hautala 1969:122).

the other hand, exercised themselves when, for instance, a poem adapted to another dialectical area (K. Krohn 1918:69).

K. Krohn pointed out, however, that these laws should not be applied mechanically and indiscriminately (1918:80). For instance the law of fading memory might indicate that the fuller variant was the more original, while from the law of addition one could draw the opposite conclusion (K. Krohn 1918:81). Thus all viewpoints must be taken into consideration and each case judged individually and in detail. "The chief rule for the student of folklore" was, according to K. Krohn, "the principle of naturalness, the axiom that each folkpoem has been born a sound and unforced whole".[117]

It was in the work of A. Aarne that the historical-geographical method finally received its proper theoretical presentation and became well known outside Finland and Scandinavia (Rausmaa 39).[118] Although Aarne is now perhaps best known for the "type-index" he developed, he also pursued the issue of the criteria by which variants could be analyzed, utilizing work done by both Olrik and the Krohns in so doing. Aarne, too, maintained that variation developed according to certain "laws of thought and imagination", *Gesetz der Umgestaltung*, and introduced the concept of *Ur*-form, or archetype, for the "original" form which, he suggested, could be recovered through the application of criteria that reflected these laws of thought.[119] Aarne suggested eight such criteria[120] and a further sixteen "principles" of oral tradition[121] that would help in their application.[122]

Just as we found that Gunkel's principles of oral composition bear a striking resemblance to Olrik's Epic laws, so we can see a strong similarity between Gunkel's ideas of oral transmission and variant development and the

---

117 K. Krohn 1918:82, cited in Hautala 1969:122.

118 See particularly Aarne's *Leitfaden der vergleichenden Märchenforschung*, 1913, which has been described as the method's "textbook".

119 See Bødker 34-7, 125-6.

120 Thus according to Aarne, for instance, "the form that has the greatest frequency of occurrence will more often be original than the form that occurs more rarely", and "such *details* as captivate the audience by their telling or entertaining character...will keep better, and become more generally diffused, than others" (Aarne 1913:46ff, cited in Bødker 35).

121 These concern the circumstances of changes in folktale, e.g. forgetting a detail, amplification, multiplication, repetition, substitution (see Bødker 36-7, or Thompson 1946:436, for a summary).

122 Later, within the historical-geographical school, two more "laws" that arose from Aarne's 1913 work, were more fully articulated and debated: the "law of self-correction" (W. Anderson 1923) and the "law of automigration" (see von Sydow 1935). Von Sydow, however, regarded the laws "unacceptable" (Bødker 35, 38-9, 124-5; see also Thompson 1946:437ff).

historical-geographical notions underlining the laws of change and transmission. Nowhere is this similarity more obvious than in the area of the basic dynamics both Gunkel and these architects of the historical-geographical method see as governing the process of folklore transmission and diffusion. Gunkel's statement that the *Sage* adapts as it wanders "from place to place and age to age" echoes the very term "historical-geographical" method, while his concept of this adaptation taking place according to a universal law of change matches the Nordic efforts to unravel oral transmission and variant development. Gunkel's other key concepts of the collective, rather than individual, authorship of the narratives, which are transmitted by the means of an oral performance, are also widely attested in the writings of the two Krohns and Olrik.[123] However, similarities can also be found on the level of detail. Thus, for instance, Gunkel's principle of amalgamation (number 25), i.e. several personages growing together in the course of transmission, is very much like the first of J. Krohn's psychological laws, "the desire to assimilate", while Gunkel's notion of "epic discursiveness" (number 16), corresponds to J. Krohn's "desire to continue". Both Gunkel and the Krohn's emphasize the role of "forgetfulness" in the development of details (Gunkel, number 24, and K. Krohn's "law of fading memory").

3.4. Gunkel's Concept of Oral Variants: An Evaluation

As we attempt to re-evaluate the validity of Gunkel's concepts of oral composition and transmissions, evident in the form of certain biblical narratives and, in particular, the phenomenon of variants, our task is twofold. First of all we need to reassess in the light of current research the claims first made by Gunkel and then developed by form and tradition-historical critics concerning the detectability of orality in biblical narratives. Here we need to take into consideration both the criticism expressed by biblical scholars concerning the methodology involved in the detection of orality, as well as the current consensus of folklore scholarship on the validity of such endeavours. Secondly, we need to attempt to identify the salient principles involved in Gunkel's claims and thus pinpoint the scholarly arena in which a further, and perhaps a conclusive, re-evaluation of the issues involved could take place.

---

123 See Gunkel 1901:xviii, xlv, ET 39, 98; Olrik 1992:7; J. Krohn 1885:584.

What has emerged from the above chapter is the remarkable similarity Gunkel's ideas bear to those of such contemporary folklorists as Olrik and J. and K. Krohn, in particular. As observed before, this similarity extends to both the underlying dynamics involved in oral composition, transmission and variant development – the concept of oral tradition adapting, according to a universal law of change, as it encounters new circumstances – and some of the specific details of these dynamics, articulated in the various "laws" of composition and transmission, outlined above. Much more could be said about the way Gunkel's ideas on formation of *Sage*-cycles and collecting of traditions, alluded to above, reflect those of his contemporaries, as well as the respective views on the context of composition and transmission.

On the basis of these similarities I would like to suggest that what we have in Gunkel's work is the working out within another tradition, namely the Old Testament, of the same kind of folklore methods and principles as we find in the Fenno-Scandinavian scholarship, where the various Nordic traditions and, more generally, European folktales, are discussed. Inasmuch as the two approaches then stem from or reflect the same conceptual basis, the criticisms, as well as affirmations, that are made concerning the latter apply, at least to an extent, also to the former.[124]

In the past Gunkel's concept of the composition and transmission of Old Testament narrative, particularly with reference to the notion of epic laws, has been criticised on two main accounts. First of all, Gunkel's concept of the universal law of change from which the "principles of change", listed above, seem to arise, has been equated with Olrik's epic laws, which then have been used to "test" the orality of Old Testament narratives. Here the criticism has concentrated on the ambiguity of the articulation of the laws, i.e. Olrik's own "unclear and inconsistent" presentation of them (Whybray 145). Thus there has been uncertainty as to the actual number of the laws involved, with as few as ten and as many as twenty cited,[125] as well as to how many of the laws should be detected in a given narrative for it to be deemed "oral" (Whybray 145; Warner 332-3). The integrity of particular laws has also been a cause for confusion and Olrik has been accused of leaving

---

124 For criticisms of the historical-geographical method, see the works of A. Wesselski and C. von Sydow, and for a summary Dorson 1972a:8ff. Some of the criticisms expressed by these scholars have been commented on in the Old Testament context by Kirkpatrick, but on the whole they await for biblical critical application.

125 Whybray quotes R. McTurk, who lists twenty laws, while Van Seters only uses ten (Whybray 145; Van Seters 1975:160).

"loopholes" in some of the laws as, for instance, the Law of Three becomes the Law of Four in the Indic stories (Warner 333).[126]

Secondly, the appropriateness of the application of such laws to Old Testament tradition has been questioned, both on the grounds that Olrik's work is based on the study of only Scandinavian, at best European, traditions, which from biblical perspective can be regarded as remote, and on the basis of these traditions being "faulty texts", i.e. written, already possibly heavily edited texts, rather than proper oral traditions as such.[127] Thus Warner argues that the fact that "Olrik based a great deal of his evidence, not only upon small *Märchen*, but upon the very much longer Icelandic and Danish epic Sagas proper," makes "a mockery" of Gunkel's "distinction between *Sage* and *Geschichte*, the starting point of his whole analysis", as Gunkel, whom Warner sees as dependent on Olrik, should have realized that "the same type of criteria are to be found in both long and short orally composed stories" (Warner 332). Kirkpatrick goes even further and not only questions the applicability of Olrik's laws to biblical narratives for reasons such as their Europeanness, but also challenges the very validity of the laws as indicators of orality, claiming them to have "since been proved to be untenable" on the basis that they were based on material which "had itself been edited in the process of transcription", and on the basis that they "have recently been seen to apply to both oral and written texts" (Kirkpatrick 56, 63).[128]

It should perhaps first of all be pointed out that the wholesale importation of Olrik's laws to Old Testament studies as a kind of literary litmus test has been ill-advised, as these laws were never meant to be applied in isolation from the larger methodological framework in which they were devised.[129] The main problem with the application of Olrik's laws to Old Testament narrative, or anything else for that matter, is not the uncertainty as to how many laws there are or how many are needed to prove orality, but the perception of these laws as detectors or "measurements" whose mechanical application produces absolute and conclusive "either oral" "or literary" results.

Ben-Amos in his foreword to Olrik's *Principles for Oral Narrative Research* points out that Olrik used the term "law" "in the spirit of the time,

---

126 Warner finds three other laws with which, he argues, Olrik makes similar "exceptions" (333).

127 See e.g. Kirkpatrick 56; Warner 332; Whybray 149.

128 For the latter criticism Kirkpatrick (57) cites as evidence a single study by L. Danielson, which applied eight of the thirteen epic laws to 143 narratives in "oral and popular print sources" (Danielson 130), and found that seven of the laws "functioned in both kinds of narrative at 'roughly the same intensity'".

129 See e.g. Olrik 1992:42.

as an application of scientific principles in physics to a humanistic field" (1992:vii-viii).[130] Although Olrik is undeniably seeking "in oral tradition the same type of regulatory mechanism" as is found in nature, and obviously believes in its existence, the laws as we have them in his work are not that mechanism yet. They are, as Ben-Amos puts it, "propositions for research and an invitation for exploration of their universal or conditional applicability", i.e. they are "not a doctrine but an agenda" (1992:vii-viii).[131]

In practice Olrik saw the epic laws very much as "diagnostic tools" for the recognition of orality in written texts, but only so in the hands of "a trained person" and as a part of a comprehensive diagnostic endeavour (Ben-Amos 1992:ix). Olrik not only recognized that his laws had been based on "faulty texts", it was the purpose of these laws to detect orality in just such, sometimes long since recorded and edited traditions. Historically, the epic laws emerged from Olrik's attempt to differentiate between Danish and Icelandic sources and styles in Saxo's *Gesta Danorum*: the epic laws are the description of the Danish style, which Olrik came to regard as oral in its origin.[132] In this respect at least, Gunkel's and Olrik's methods are comparable, since they are both based on "faulty texts" and, in fact, both start from the premise that there are differences in "styles" in parts of the respective, now written sources.[133] Thus Olrik both repeatedly emphasized and, in his own work, exemplified the importance of looking at the quality of the written text, recognizing the incomplete and fragmentary nature of many texts, resulting from imperfections in recording, transmission, preservation of manuscripts or, in fact, even in the original oral performance.[134]

On the other hand Olrik, and the other practitioners of the historical-geographical school, had a vast amount of experience in dealing with various kinds of folk traditions and had developed a certain "feel" for them. Thus although Olrik was looking for scientific principles for detection of orality, there is a way in which, as K. Krohn pointed out, the application of these

---

130 Cf. Olrik: "We call these principles 'laws' because they limit the freedom of composition of oral literature in a much different and more rigid way than in our written literature" (1909:2, ET 165:131).

131 A fact that, Ben-Amos surmises, also explains the existence of "several sets of theoretical propositional statements" in Olrik's work, and thus the difficulty of arriving at an authoritative list (1992:viii).

132 See Olrik 1892, 1894; Holbek 1971:261-7; 1992:ixx-xx.

133 We should, however, remember that the Finnish scholarship was based on more properly "oral" texts, i.e. ones where either all editorial work was scrupulously documented, as in the case of *Kalevala*, or texts that were recorded specifically for study purposes. See K. Krohn 1971:47.

134 See Ben Amos 1992:ix.

principles "was more a matter of art than that of science" (1903:30). There was general recognition that because of the many imperfections endemic to the materials under scrutiny, subjective decisions would often have to be made. Thus neither Olrik nor his Finnish colleagues always expected to arrive at a watertight conclusion concerning the oral characteristics of a given narrative.[135]

The issue of the applicability of epic laws to both oral and literary texts is an intriguing one, and highlights what could be seen as the problem of unnecessary polarization of "pure orality" and "pure literariness", both in the results expected from the application of the laws and in the concept of narrative composition as such. The practitioners of the historical-geographical school readily acknowledged the oral and literary interaction in the transmission of traditions, not ruling out, for instance, the return of a literary version to orality,[136] while on the other hand it would be highly unusual to think that literary composition is totally discontinuous with oral composition, which is generally acknowledged to have historical precedence. A comparison Ben-Amos makes between the formulation of Olrik's laws and Aristotle's *Poetics* is in this respect a revealing one, underlining this time not the differences but the similarities in all literary composition, whether oral or written.[137]

3.4.1. Van Seters versus Olrik: Wife-sister Stories

An instructive illustration of the application of the epic laws is provided by the treatment of the Wife-sister stories, as presented by Van Seters in his *Abraham in History and Tradition*, reviewed in some detail in Chapter 1 above, and Olrik's own discussion of the stories, which he wrote in 1915-16, after his acquaintance with Gunkel's work.[138] While Van Seters' application of Olrik's laws to the three Wife-sister variants resulted in his recognition of

---

135 See e.g. Olrik's discussion of the Wife-sister stories below.

136 See e.g. K. Krohn 1888:39, 1971:47; Olrik 1992:32-4.

137 Thus according to Olrik "there is no sharp distinction between folklore and the products of a higher culture" (1992:9). Interestingly, the study by Danielson, quoted by Kirkpatrick above as she argues against the validity of Olrik's laws, could be equally used here in support of this more integrating approach to literary form: Danielson's narratives "in oral and popular print sources" were represented by "fabulates and memorates" of supernatural experiences, i.e. types of "vernacular forms of personal experience story" – surely a "literary" genre that is very similar to its oral counterpart? (131-2).

138 See Olrik 1992:180ff.

oral compositional characteristics in only the ch. 12 version, which he also recognized as corresponding "rather closely to a folktale model", Olrik regarded "the entire narrative" as "a typical collection of the peculiarities of folk tradition", with a plot that is "simple, and reminiscent of the structure of the folk narrative" (Van Seters 1975:170; Olrik 1992:130-1).

Of the remaining two variants Van Seters labelled ch. 20 as "a deliberate literary recasting of the story for quite different purposes" than story telling, namely for dealing with the theological and moral issues the story of Abraham's visit to Pharaoh's court had raised, and the ch. 26 version as "a literary conflation of both of the other stories" and one in which the "literary reworking has completely destroyed the clear oral pattern of the earlier story" (1975:173, 179, 183). Olrik, on the other hand, saw the main difference in the versions not in terms of literary as opposed to oral variation, but in terms of "a declining value in the quality" of the oral motifs (1992:131). Thus, according to him, the plot was the "best" in the Gen. 12 variant, and "weakest" in ch. 26, where "no single character appears who will take possession of the wife of the patriarch" (Olrik 1992:129). In the ch. 20 variant, Olrik argues, the plot is "in itself...well-rounded and powerful", but obscured by elements that move "outside the mentality that is otherwise associated with the ancestor", such as God punishing the entire royal household for the crime of one, i.e. the king (1992:129-30).

As for the detection of epic laws more specifically, Van Seters saw the ch. 12 variant as an outstanding illustration of Olrik's laws, while in ch. 20 the laws that "work so well" in the earlier variant "break down in almost every case" (1975:170, 172-3). In ch. 26 the epic laws are not very well observed, instead, in Van Seters' opinion, the evidence of literary borrowing is compelling (1975:176-7). Olrik, in turn, finds in the basic structure of the narrative the Law of Two to a Scene "conspicuous", evident in "dialogues *tête-à-tête*" of the "patriarch and his spouse, the foreign servants and their master, the king and the patriarch" (1992:130). The Law of Closing and the Law of Opening, in turn, are present in "very pronounced forms", the latter in the famine that "forces the starving Israelites to go down to Goshen" in ch. 12, the former in all the variants, "not only" in the handing over of the wife but also because "a large number of cattle are added as a gift" (Olrik 1992:130).

The difference in the conclusions arrived at by Van Seters and Olrik concerns not so much the form expected from a typical oral narrative, as both agree on this, but the extent to which the meaning of the features not deemed typical can be interpreted. Van Seters strives for definite, clear-cut categories labelling them as *either* oral *or* literary, and does not, unlike Olrik, allow for the existence of less than typical oral forms.[139] Thus while for Olrik a folktale remains a folktale, and therefore essentially oral in form, despite the decline in the quality of its motifs,[140] Van Seters is compelled to judge, sometimes it seems by default, the non-oral characteristics as literary.

Although some of the differences in the two men's conclusions can be catered for on the basis of the emphases of their respective agendas as they scrutinize the three variants, Van Seters' method manifests two major weaknesses. The criteria which Van Seters uses, besides Olrik's laws, to determine the oral versus literary distinction in the variant development, are at best rudimentary and have not been established to any degree in folklore scholarship. Van Seters uses three criteria to establish oral development (this in contrast to, for instance, Aarne's 16), with none of Van Seters' criteria overlapping with Aarne's. The four guidelines Van Seters uses for literary development have not been tested in any significant measure in folklore scholarship.

The main problem with Van Seters' designation of the variants in chs 20 and 26 as literary is, however, the fact that such a decisive description is arrived at on the basis of such a small amount of comparative material. Within the historical-geographical method a large number of variants is deemed necessary for the establishment of a measure of certainty within simply the direction of variation.[141] Van Seters regards a sample of three sufficient to establish not only the type of variation, whether oral or literary, but the direction of dependency as well! Thus although Van Seters' reasoning concerning the way the variants might have developed has some

---

139 Olrik sees chs 20 and 26 as "conflations".

140 Interestingly, Olrik regards the patriarchal histories on the whole as being "on the borderline of folklore or on the periphery of its domain" and singles out two features that make them distinct from most other folklore, namely "the immense power of the religious" which "breaks the palpability of the narratives", and "the extraordinary role of localization" (1992:116, 118-9). This does not, however, in Olrik's opinion by any means obliterate the epic laws. In his discussion of the patriarchal narratives Olrik gives examples of eleven of the thirteen laws tabulated in his 1909 article, and further-more, he sees some of them as operative not only in individual narratives, but also on the level of the patriarchal cycle as a whole. Thus e.g. the Law of Closing can be seen not only in the concluding episode of "the courtship scene with Rebeccah", but also in Isaac going to meet his bride, which brings closure to the Abraham story as a whole (Olrik 1992:124, 127). Similarly, the Law of Contrast manifests itself in the relationship of Abraham and Isaac throughout the cycle, besides being operative in occasions such as when "Agar [sic] taunts the childless Sarah" and "Ishmael plays with younger Isaac" (Olrik 1992:125).

141 For his famous study *Kaiser und Abt* W. Anderson has some 480 variants at his disposal (see Thompson 1946:433).

convincing elements in it, his conclusions must be described at best as conjectural.

On the question of the applicability of Olrik's laws to Old Testament material on the basis of their Europeanness, we should again observe the similarity of Gunkel's "principles", based on the study of Genesis, and Olrik's laws, based on European texts. Thus to the extent that the two sets of laws are descriptive, rather than prescriptive, the question of Europeanness does not arise. However, this issue hides another far more fundamental question, namely that of the universality of epic laws. It is here that we really encounter the concept and force of a law, in that, although the lists of laws themselves may be descriptive, both Gunkel and Olrik assumed that the literary characteristics the laws are descriptive of are a result of a fundamental principle operational in the human mind and culture: they are indicators of a compositional and transmissional dynamic valid on a universal level. Thus it is the principle of how these laws are seen as operating, rather than any uniform or comprehensive articulation of the laws themselves, that makes the epic laws "laws", and it is this principle that should then also be the primary focus of any assessment of their validity.

3.4.2. Superorganic Evolution

The overriding principle operational in the concept of epic laws has been recognized as "analogous to what anthropologists term a superorganic conception of culture" (Dundes 1965:129).[142] The term superorganic, first coined by Herbert Spencer as "superorganic evolution",[143] has been used by anthropologists to describe culture as "an autonomous abstract process, *sui generis*, which requires no reference to other orders of phenomena for an

---

142 So far the concept of the superorganic has been raised mainly in connection with Olrik's laws (Dundes 1965:129-30; Pentikäinen 1978:17), but also Anderson's "law of self-correction" (Dundes 1965:130). Holbek, however, points out that the notion is already present in the Grimms' famous 1816 statement "Das Märchen ist poetischer, die Sage historischer" (Holbek 1987:24). I would suggest that the similarity of Gunkel's "universal law of change" to the principles of Olrik's laws extends the application of the term to Gunkel's method as well.

143 H. Spencer 1876 I:4; see Bidney 34. Since then the term has been used in somewhat different ways (Bidney 329-333). The way the concept has been used in folklore studies is dependent on the work of A. Kroeber, particulary his article "The Superorganic", 1917, which defines "superorganic" as designating the "non-organic, or that which transcends the organic" (Bidney 36, citing Kroeber; see also Hultkrantz 221; Pentikäinen 1972:132).

explanation of its origin, development, and operation" (Dundes 1965:129). Thus while the "organic level" is seen as denoting man, the superorganic is "above" man, describing a sphere of activity which is independent of, and not reducible to, purely human terms (Dundes 1965:129). The rationale here then is that "just as man himself is considered to be more than the sum of inorganic (chemical) elements of which he is composed, so the superorganic is assumed to be more than the organic elements which underlie it" (Dundes 1965:129-30).

Applied to folklore in general and epic laws in particular, what this means is that certain superorganically operating forces or laws are conceived of as "actively controlling individual narrators", who have no alternative but to obey these laws or, perhaps more accurately, are "programmed" to do so as the process is generally regarded as subconscious (Dundes 1965:130) It is this controlling and subconscious nature of the laws man is subjected to that then "renders his behaviour consistent",[144] which in turn produces the consistent features in folklore that caught the eye of Olrik, the Finns, even the Grimms, as well as Gunkel, and led to the "discovery" of the epic laws.[145] Gunkel's statement that oral tradition is subjected to a "universal law of change" typifies this position.[146]

The notion of the superorganic is fundamentally an evolutionary one – as already suggested by Spencer's "superorganic evolution" – and as such assumes that "everything that happens in the world", and folklore is no exception, "is a factor in a vast, uniform, strictly ordered process of evolution" (Hautala 1954:174). The concept became prominent in both cultural studies in general and folklore studies in particular, in the wake of the publication of Darwin's *The Origin of Species*, 1859, as the evolutionary hypothesis was applied to culture. However, the application of the idea of evolution to folklore was not uniform; rather, two juxtaposed models emerged: the "devolutionary" model, one of negative evolution, and the more properly "evolutionary" model, one of progress.[147]

According to the devolutionary view the "best days" of folklore are in the past – "in most cases", as Dundes observes, "specifically in the far distant past" – as the tradition decays and degenerates in its transmission (Dundes

---

144 Pentikäinen 1978:17.
145 Dundes goes as far as to suggest that Olrik's laws are "one of the strongest arguments in favor of a formal, superorganic approach to folklore" and that such a formal approach to folklore can in turn help in the discovery of "principles controlling human culture generally" (1965:128, 130).
146 Gunkel 1901:xlv, ET 98; see p. 134ff above.
147 See Dundes 1969:5ff.

1969:5). What is left for the folklorist to observe are the relics of the early tradition. This concept is already evident in the Grimms' definition of *Märchen* as "the detritus of myth", and conspicuously so in Müller's theory of the "disease of language". In this sense, as Dundes has pointed out, the evolution is not "*of* folklore", but "*out* of folklore", as the increasingly civilised man leaves behind the crudeness of his early traditions (Dundes 1969:12). The clearest and most systematic presentation of the devolutionary view appears, however, in the concept of the *Ur*-form, developed by the later historical-geographical scholars, Aarne and Thompson in particular. The *Ur*-form is the "reconstructed" form of a folklore item, the form from which all variants and versions descend, and typifies the premise which is intrinsic to (this type of) devolutionary model, namely that the original version must have been "the best, fullest or most complete one" (Bødker 34; Dundes 1969:8).

The positive form of evolution applies the idea of progress to folklore, i.e. the "cultural product" itself, rather than the man, nation or culture that fosters it, and was espoused in particular by the pioneers of the geographical-historical school (see Hautala 1969:63). Thus J. Krohn's method has sometimes been called "Darwinism adapted to folklore, even as regards to detail".[148] J. Krohn's concept of folk traditions originating as "primal cells" which, like "living organisms",[149] grow fuller and more perfect as they diffuse, illustrates this model (Hautala 1969:70, 72).[150] Similarly, Olrik writes about "a 'struggle for existence' among narratives" and how "defective forms" will "most often soon die out" as "*selection*" will "constantly take place" (1992:62-3). Thus the tradition that the folklorist observes can be regarded as the "endpoint of a development leading upwards",[151] rather than any "relics" of devolution, and this upward development, "from the simple to the complex"[152] may have involved a "(usually slow) raising of the entire spiritual level of the narrative world".[153]

From the point of view of folklore studies several concerns regarding the perception of epic laws as superorganic have been raised. The foremost of these is the way adherence to such a concept "might lead one to

---

148 Hautala 1969:70, citing Haavio 1931:58. Besides Darwin Hautala lists Comte, Spencer and H. T. Buckle as J. Krohn's influences, while Holbek contrasts Olrik's "Darwinism" with Grundtvig's Hegelian views (Hautala 1969:63; Holbek 1992:xvii).
149 See also Holbek 1971:266.
150 See also Olrik's "original form", which "means the common basic form of the extant variants" (1992:91).
151 Hautala 1969:63.
152 Olrik 1992:101.
153 Olrik 1992:63. See also Dundes 1969:11.

underestimate the individual and social component" in folklore composition and transmission, and in extreme cases make the tradition bearers "talking automats" (Pentikäinen 1978:14, 17). Other concerns include issues such as the role of cognitive elements in the process, i.e. that is the extent to which the narrators are aware of the laws.[154] As the concept of the superorganic has been adopted to folklore studies from the social sciences, most accurately from social anthropology, it is ultimately in that realm, or in conjunction with that discipline, that the validity of the concept should be assessed.[155] What is more important for our present study is that, having identified the wider intellectual and cultural context of Gunkel's concept of oral composition and transmission, we can see more clearly the basic assumptions operative in it. We can see that in all oral laws surveyed at least an element of the notion of the "superorganic" is involved. This will therefore also apply to Gunkel's principles of composition and change.

3.5. Summary

In Gunkel's work there is no theoretical consideration of the principles of orality in relation to his concept of the oral origins and development of biblical narrative. We have also seen that he wavered significantly during his career on certain issues and particularly so in relation to his understanding of the myth-*Sage-Märchen* complex. However, when it comes to Gunkel's key concepts of the dynamics of change they are in obvious harmony with the historical-geographical school of folklore studies, perhaps particularly its more strictly Darwinistic side of evolutionism. In a sense Gunkel, too, was a folklorist, and a pioneering one, developing the ideas of orality in the context of biblical traditions, while some of his contemporaries did so with regard to European folklore.

Being able to establish such a close affinity with the methodological basis of form and tradition-historical criticism on the one hand, and folklore studies on the other, is not without considerable significance for biblical studies. First of all, it makes it possible to assess biblical critical notions with the help of another well-established discipline, if not for positive proof for the validity of an idea, at least for awareness of the balance of the probabilities in the current debate on it. Thus, for instance, we have seen

---

154 See Pentikäinen 1978:17-8; Holbek 1987:18.

155 See Pentikäinen, 1978, as an attempt to test the nature of the epic laws through the method of repertoire analysis.

Gunkel's notion of *Sage* as an oral genre largely affirmed by modern folkloristics. Similarly his concepts of principles of change of composition and transmission are in harmony with the oral laws of well established folklorists. At the same time it has to be pointed out that the methodology to assess the validity of the notion of the "superorganic" operative in these laws is still, at best, in its infancy.

Biblical criticism sharing methodology with folkloristics has also brought the study of biblical narrative into the wider realm of oral narrative research and its engagement with the oral-written interface. This may yet prove significant not only to the debate about oral versus literary variants, but to the discussion of how biblical traditions developed on the whole – an issue at the centre of all biblical critical endeavour. Perhaps above all Gunkel's link with the early folklore scholarship helps biblical studies to realize more of its indebtedness to the nineteenth-century intellectual context out of which it grew. This, in turn, would help biblical studies to assess and advance its own methodology with the help of advaces in disciplines it is already indebted to through common origin.

Chapter 4: Double Narratives: Towards a Definition

One of the main problems in attempting to study double narratives is the lack of adequate, agreed terminology for the phenomenon. "Double narrative",[1] though readily recognized by anyone acquainted with Old Testament scholarship, is not a well-established technical term that would ensure that it is only used and understood in one way. Nor is there agreement whether double narrative means the same as "doublet", "variant" or "duplicate stories", or how these relate to "type-scenes", "conflation" or "embellishment" or, simply "repetitions", all terms used by scholars to denote similarity and/or suggest interdependence in two or more narratives.

The consequences of this terminological ambivalence are twofold: on the one hand the same narrative pair is labelled in various ways, on the other hand the same term can be used by different – and sometimes even the same! – scholars to denote narrative relationships that are in fact quite different in nature. Furthermore there is the question, which none of the terms listed above addresses, namely what amount of repetition, and of what kind, is needed for an occurrence of repetition to be called a "double narrative"? It is not surprising, then, that in Old Testament scholarship there is no appreciation of double narratives as a general phenomenon: that is, of the variety or the extent of the duplication in biblical narrative traditions, which, after all, has served as the very cornerstone of biblical criticism!

The purpose of this final chapter is to seek to establish such terminology as would enable us to distinguish the various facets of double narratives as well as to comprehend the extent and complexity of the phenomenon as a whole. This will put us in a better position to assess the way double narratives have been used, and could be used, in the development of Old Testament methodology. To accomplish this we will first look at the kind of terms that have been associated with double narratives in the past and how they have been used, as well as some actual attempts at definition. Secondly,

---

1   I have chosen to use "double narrative" as the "umbrella term" in this research for the main reason that, being less common than, for instance, "variant" or "doublet", it is more neutral and not readily associated with any particular kind of duplication in narrative pairs or any particular theory concerning their origin.

I would like to demonstrate by means of a double narrative "chart" the extent and complexity of the double narrative phenomenon in the Old Testament, as well as the difficulty of arriving at truly exclusive and technical terminology, before finally making some terminological proposals of my own.

In the second part of this chapter another, related issue of definition is explored, this time on the interface of textual and literary criticism. Here the issues that are addressed are the distinction between literary and textual variants and the question how much variance is needed to constitute a doublet, i.e. how much, or what kind of, duplication determines whether variants are textual or literary.

4.1.   Double Narrative Terminology in Old Testament Scholarship

When the fact that certain narratives and narrative elements tended to recur in the Old Testament first attracted the critical eye of scholars, such as Simon and Astruc, they simply labelled these recurrences as "repetitions".[2] As the early interest centred on the reasons for these recurrences rather than on the phenomenon itself, the term was at first used to cover any kind of repetition, from the two accounts of the creation of man and woman in Gen. 1 and 2, to Shem's two genealogies, and to Abraham addressing God in Gen. 8:27 and then again in vs. 30. Simon also used the term "recapitulations".[3] Eichhorn, in turn, talked about "twice-telling",[4] pointed to "the double biography"[5] of David, and used the term "double(d) narrative",[6] of which the Flood "was the most detailed but not the only example", as, for instance, "also the flight of Sodom and rescue of Lot" were "twice notified" and "traces of a doubled narrative" could be found in several other places, such as the story of Laban.[7] Eichhorn also added "recensions",[8] "editions"[9] and "parallel passages"[10] to the terminological list, all of which were later also

---

2   "Répetitions" (e.g. Simon Preface ** 1, ET Preface a 6; Astruc 10).   See also pp. 6ff above.
3   "Recapitulation" (I:38, ET I:39).
4   "Einerlei wird zuweilen *doppelt erzählt*" (II:264, emphasis mine).
5   "Doppelte Lebensbeschreibung" (II:451).
6   "Doppelte[n] Erzählung" (II:270).
7   II:270.
8   "Recension" (I:180).
9   "Ausgabe" (I:180).
10   "Parallelstelle" (I:276).

taken up by de Wette. Kuenen, on the other hand, used "doublets"[11] and Wellhausen extended the discussion to "parallel histories" and "traditions", while also using the term "variant", soon to be popularized by Gunkel. More innovation was brought along by Cassuto who preferred "duplications" and "repetitions", besides using "recapitulation" in a sense different from Simon's,[12] while most recently Alter has muddied the waters even further by introducing the concepts of "type-scene" and "convention"[13] into the discussion.

The problem is obvious: the Hagar stories, for instance, one of the most often referred to double narratives, are "repetitions" for Astruc and Cassuto, "variants" for Gunkel, "doublets" for the Wellhausen generation and a "type-scene" for Alter. On the other hand the two Creation stories, the Flood narrative and the three Wife-sister stories, all very different in the type of duplication they contain, are all at times simply called variants, doublets and duplicate narratives. In other words, there is multiplicity of labelling for one and the same story or narrative pair, while little distinction is made between one type of duplication and another.

A kind of definition of double narratives was attempted as early as in Kuenen's *Hexateuch*, where "doublets",[14] were seen as "diverse renderings of a single tradition, or as variations on a single theme" (42, ET 39). Another concise definition was offered, only much later, by Noth, who described "duplications" as "the *repeated occurrence* of the same narrative materials or narrative elements in *different versions*" (1948:21-2, ET 21-2). However, more comprehensive attempts to clarify the issue have been made only by Cassuto and Whybray, as they have suggested definitions that make explicit the dualism in the phenomenon implied already by Kuenen.

Cassuto,[15] in his *Documentary Hypothesis*, observes how a closer examination of Old Testament narrative reveals two different types amongst the stories told twice (or more times). These types he labels "duplications" and "repetitions". When "parallel sections appertain...entirely to one subject, which is depicted in each of them in a different form and with variation in detail", Cassuto uses the term "duplication" (1961:69). When, on the other hand, "parallel sections are concerned with events that are unrelated to each other, but yet are so similar in their principal motifs that one may conjecture

---

11   "Doubletten" (42, ET 39).
12   Cassuto 1961:69, 83.
13   In the sense of a "repetitive compositional pattern" (Alter 1981:50). See also pp. 63ff above.
14   "Doubletten."
15   See pp. 55ff above.

that they are simply divergent developments of a single narrative", the term "repetition", Cassuto suggests, should be applied (1961:69). As a "classic instance of repetition" Cassuto mentions the Wife-sister stories, of duplication, the Creation stories (1961:69). Cassuto also has a further category, "recapitulation", for parallelism which he sees in less obvious, but nevertheless interrelated passages, such as the aforementioned journey of Sarah and Abraham to Egypt, and a later one by the children of Israel in Gen. 47ff, to the same place (1961:78-83).

Similarly Whybray,[16] in his *The Making of the Pentateuch*, attempts a definition of double narratives by using a shared narrative-base as a criterion. He surveys a number of narrative pairs, mentioning particularly some of the ones that were significant for the formation of the Documentary Hypothesis, namely the Creation stories of Gen. 1 and 2, the Hagar stories of Gen. 16 and 21, the Wife-sister stories of Gen. 12, 20 and 26, the two dreams of Joseph in Gen. 37:5-11, and the manna and quails stories of Ex. 16 and Num. 11 (Whybray 76-9). Out of these stories, Whybray suggests, "doublets in the strict sense of that term" are the ones "based on a common narrative source", i.e. instances of "*the same story* told twice with variations" (75, 79). The Hagar and Wife-sister stories would then be genuine doublets, as they appear to stem from the same traditions. The Creation stories, on the other hand, being, in Whybray's estimate, complementary and deriving originally from two separate story-traditions, would not qualify as genuine doublets (74-6).

Cassuto and Whybray use very different terminology, yet they have both identified one of the most obvious, yet difficult, problems in attempting to define double narratives: the fact that, historically, the word "doublet", and related terms, have been used to describe two very different kinds of narrative parallelism. In one of these there is a common story-base, that is, one is dealing with variants of the same story, where it is, or should be, possible to establish literary dependence (oral or written); in the other the common element is only the depicted event itself. In this second case the story-bases are different, though they must share a connecting element, such as a key figure. The event described will naturally have to be unique, or at least unusual enough, for the assumption to be made that the narratives address the same incident.[17]

---

16   See pp. 61ff above.
17   Sometimes this is quite obvious, as in the case of the creation of the world or even when David is introduced to Saul. But our lack of knowledge of the contemporary circumstances often leaves room for ambiguity: for instance, in 1-2 Samuel and 1 Chronicles, how many giants or "Goliaths" were killed by how many heroes?

Cassuto solves this problem by labelling the different types of duplication differently, Whybray by making one type, the variants of one story-base, the true doublet and excluding the other, stories deriving from separate story-traditions, from his definition. That the two different types are really quite distinct as literary phenomena, is obvious; that a definition of doublets should be achieved by the exclusion of one type, is problematic, particularly as one remembers that it was from the twice-told Creation story that much of the double narrative issue arose in the first place!

The definitions of Whybray and Cassuto cater well for the "classic cases" of double narratives, such as both of them are also eager to cite as examples. But they do not explain the status of narratives such as the Flood story, used from the earliest times by critics as an example of duplication, but of a type – often termed "conflation" – that does not apparently fit into the limits of either Cassuto's or Whybray's terminology. Neither do they reflect on the wider spectrum of narrative relationships, such as are suggested by Cassuto's concept of "recapitulations", or Alter's "type-scenes", where some literary dependence is seen as occurring, but more on a structural, thematic or "conventional",[18] rather than verbal, level.

The fact that the definitions Cassuto and Whybray offer have been useful and effective in their place reflects graphically on the way double narratives have been treated in Old Testament scholarship. Thus attention has been given to some *aspects* of the phenomenon, usually as a part of the "greater cause" of formulating compositional theories of the Pentateuch. Any definition that was used only needed to be adequate for that particular task. However, whether the definition of the whole would validate the definitions of the parts, has never as yet been tested.

4.2. Towards a Definition

A comprehensive definition of double narratives[19] faces many challenges. It would have to distinguish between any genuinely distinct elements in the phenomenon, yet also generalize enough to keep these elements related to one another, as parts of a larger whole, for there is a sense in which no two doublets "duplicate" in quite the same way and one could have as many

---

18   That is, resulting from the use of a literary convention.

19   Early last century the term "double narrative" even appeared in a title of a book, namely in Alfors Schulz's *Doppelberichte im Pentateuch*, 1908. The work discusses the Documentary Hypothesis and offers no definition of "Doppelberichte".

labels as there are double narratives. Furthermore, this definition should also be continuous, at least to some extent, with the way double narratives have been understood in the history of critical scholarship on which they have had such a crucial impact. Thus both the Creation stories and the Hagar stories should be able to be included in it.

In attempting to define double narratives clarification is first of all needed on the relationship of the classic types of doublets, the "Hagar-type" variants of the same story-base and the "Creation-type" accounts of the same event, to the wider, more abstract, network of perceived narrative relationships in the Old Testament, where the connections that are seen are more structural, symbolic, typological or conventional in nature, rather than obviously verbal, or connected by reference to the same event. There is a danger in pursuing an inclusive definition in this direction as well: where will the search for such parallels end? Is it not conceivable that one could make the phenomenon so comprehensive that everything in the Old Testament becomes "related" – as the links become more and more tenuous – and in a way, the phenomenon ceases to exist?

Another, somewhat different dimension is added to the problem of definition by the fact that Old Testament scholarship has always been interdisciplinary by its very nature, overlapping with disciplines such as folklore studies, literary criticism and poetics, as we saw in Chapters 2 and 3. Ideally Old Testament terminology should be accessible to scholars from these fields as well. Such is indeed the case with the form-critical use of the term "variant",[20] the standard term in folkloristics for a "single literary or oral record" of an item of folklore (legend, ballad, folktale etc.) of which more than one exist.[21] "Double narrative", on the other hand, is not a term used in folklore studies or poetics – although "doublet"[22] can sometimes be found - and would thus require an explanation.

---

20   "'Varians lectio', different reading" (Bødker 310). In folklore studies, where large numbers of variants of the same "item of folklore" exist, more specific terminology is often employed to distinguish between their various developmental stages as well as to refer to particular theories of such developments: see e.g. "archetype", "type", "version", "oikotype", "mutation" (Bødker); See also Olrik 1992:95-8;   Finnegan points out that there is not total unanimity in folklore studies even in the use of the term "variant", most problematic being its relationship to "version" (162).

21   Bødker 310.

22   Olrik 1992:25-6, 95-8. Olrik uses "doublet" in a more specific way than is customary in biblical studies: "'doublets' are variants within the same narrative", they are sections within an account that "appear as different events but are close to each other", and normally occur "because the narrator did not realize the identity of the two narratives" (1992:96).

The challenge of defining double narrative is thus mainly twofold. On the one hand there is a need for distinction, on the other for comprehensiveness. As it may be difficult to deal with this question in the abstract, I would like to suggest that "mapping" the territory is the first, and perhaps the most crucial, step towards a definition. The following chart therefore attempts to tabulate at least the great majority of the narratives that have either previously come under the double narrative rubric, or could do so, and to suggest a possible categorization of these narratives under a manageable amount of types. This will then leave us better placed to appraise the adequacy of previous terminology and, if needed, suggest some new terminological directions.

4.2.1. The Chart

The chart distributes double narratives along a spectrum consisting of four major groups (A, B, C, D) which, in turn, divide into 15 sub-categories (A1-6, B1-6, C1-2, D). Four other groups (E, F, G, H) are included for the sake of illustration (and perhaps future potential), although they fall outside the traditional, historical understanding of double narratives.

The implication of the chart is that narratives in each main group have some significant element in common, which also distinguishes them from narratives in other groups, and that the progression from group to group is along a continuum: groups standing closest to each other have the most in common. There is also considerable variety within each group, particularly in group A, so much so that, at the point of the shift (in this case, from A6 to B1), one may in fact have to ask whether A6 might not have more in common with B1 than the other extreme of its own main group, A1. The chart thus illustrates how, looking at the opposite ends of the spectrum, A1 and D, it is easy to see the fundamental difference in the narratives in terms of their "double element", but moving along the spectrum the matter becomes much more gradual, more subtle, even controversial. Doublets in categories B and C have not been recognized as types of their own by previous definitions, although some of the stories in them have been recognized as examples of doublets in general.

What is also striking about the chart is the unequal amount of doublets that fall within the various categories, especially the first of them, A1, the "Hagar-type". This is of particular interest as at the opposite end of the spectrum, D, "the Creation-type", has very few stories in it, but has historically been as important for biblical criticism as its numerous opposite.

Inevitably there is some overlap between the categories and thus at times difficulty in deciding where an individual narrative pair should fall.

Group A

Narratives in group A are perceived basically as variants of the same story, i.e. the same story-base, with literary dependence as the crucial, uniting factor. This is particularly easy to see in the beginning of the group (A1-A3), but does become more of a matter of judgement when we reach sub-group A6.

A1. "Variant." Narratives in this category are straightforward variants of one story-base/tradition: e.g. the Hagar stories, Gen. 16:1-6 and 21:1-21.

A2. "Variant, different person." Same as above, but the significant parts in the narratives are attributed to different persons: e.g. two of the Wife-sister stories feature Abraham and Sarah, Gen. 12:10-20 and 20: 1-18, while the third features Isaac and Rebekah, Gen. 26:1-13. The Wife-sister stories are a good example of a doublet/triplet that would naturally belong to more than one category, A1 and A2.

A3. "Variant, part of a story in common." There is an unmistakable similarity between parts of two stories, but the larger narrative units, in which these elements are embedded, differ significantly: e.g. Gen. 19:1-29 and Judg. 19:1-30.

A4. "Variant, one aspect in common." A striking story-element is repeated, again, as a part of a larger narrative unit. The nature of the "one aspect" is such that literary dependence may be suggested: e.g. the punishment with leprosy in Num. 12:1-15 and 2 Kgs 5:1-27.

A5. "Conflation." A narrative manifests one or several repetitive elements, which suggest that in the past variants of the same story-base (or possibly of even other types of doublets) may have been conflated to form a narrative that now appears independent: e.g. the Flood story, Gen. 6:9-8:22. The existence of "past variants" is traditionally thought to be betrayed by the presence of (often contradictory) repetition in the narrative.

A6. "Frame." A type of a variant that suggests that one narrative reflects another in terms of its plot, story-line or other structural features, rather than the amount of verbal similarity: e.g. the Golden calf stories, Ex. 32:1-35 and 1 Kgs 12:20-23.

Group B

B1-B2. "Symbolic or typical duplication." The narratives in this group are linked to each other on the basis of a theme (B1), or on symbolic or typical grounds (B2). For instance, Abraham's journey to Egypt, Gen. 12:10-20, could be seen as the "type" of other significant journeys to Egypt, particularly that of Israel (the person or the nation), whose "father" Abraham is, Gen. 46:1-34. This type of duplication is frequently highlighted in more theologically orientated approaches to biblical narratives.

Group C
C1. "Similar incidents." These are narratives or incidents so striking that they are easily perceived as linked together, and indeed a use of a convention may be involved. However, it is difficult to establish a relationship of dependence between them as they may have been recorded simply because of their newsworthiness and the similarity may be accidental:[23] e.g. the incidents of ecstasy in Israel in Num. 11:24-30 and 1-2 Samuel.
C2. "Convention or type-scene." The linking element here is a perceived literary convention, such as a meeting at a well as a prelude to a prominent marriage, Gen. 24:1-67, 29:1-14 and Ex. 2:11-22.

Group D
D. "Same event differently reported." This group implies that the same event has been reported in two, normally mutually exclusive, ways. The events that fall into this category will then have to be such as could happen only once: e.g. David's introduction to Saul, 1 Sam. 16:14-23 and 17:1-18:5, or the Creation of the world Gen. 1:1-2:4a and 2:4b-25. Without this element of uniqueness it may be impossible to determine that two stories actually report the same incident.

Other Possible Groups, E, F, G, H
These types are included to show how the spectrum of duplication and repetition could be widened even further.
Group E. "Intentional repetition." The assumption here is that the repetition in the narrative exists for the sake of literary effect and is not indicative of, for instance, conflation of sources: e.g. Joseph's dreams in Gen. 37:5-11. This category is fairly controversial, as the history of Old Testament scholarship would testify.
Group F. "Reported story." A category where the judgement is made that two similar stories are the event and its report (as they are purported to be) and not two variants camouflaged as such: e.g. the institution of Passover and its first celebration, Ex. 12:1-20 and 12:21-50.
Group G. "Parallel histories." The repetition of whole cycles of traditions or chronicles, instead of individual narratives: e.g. 1-2 Samuel and 1-2 Kings, and 1-2 Chronicles.

---

23 In which case they should not really be classified as doublets.

Group H. "Verbatim repetition." The incidence of verbatim repetition of certain passages in different parts of the Old Testament: e.g. Josh. 15:16-19 and Judg. 1:12-15.

Even more categories are possible. For instance, one could be suggested for variants that exist in both narrative and poetical form, such as the Death of Sisera, reported in Judg. 4 and in Deborah's song in Judg. 5.

A₁ Variant

Man's sin and corruption
Gen 6:5-8 vs* 6:11-13

Promise of son to Abraham
(cf. E) Gen 12:1-9 vs 15:1-
21 vs 17:1-22 vs 18:9-15 vs
22:1-22

Wife-sister stories (cf. A₂)
Gen 12:10-20 vs 20:1-18 vs
26:1-13

Covenant with Abraham
Gen 15:1-21 vs 17:1-22

Hagar's flight
Gen 16:1-16 vs 21:1-21

Esau's wives
Gen 26:34-35 vs 28:6-9

God appears to Jacob at
Bethel
Gen 28:1-22 vs 35:1-15

Jacob tricks Laban
Gen 30:25-43 vs 31:1-45

Jacob's name changed to
Israel Gen 32:28 vs 35:10

Jacob meets an angel
Gen 32:1-2 vs 32:22-32

Joseph's brothers offer to be
his slaves Gen 44:16 vs
50:15-22

God calls Moses
Ex 3:1-4:23 vs 6:2-7

Israel's "jewellery"
Ex 3:20-22 vs 11:1-3 vs
12:35-36

Institution of Passover
Ex 12:1-20 vs 13:3-16

Mannah and Quails
Ex 16:1-36 vs Num 11:1-35

A₁ Variant continued

Water from a rock
Ex 17:1-7 vs Num 20:2-13

Not going with Moses
Ex 18:1-27 vs Num 11:14-
16, 24-30

Where the law was given
Ex 19:1-20:26 vs Ex 15-25

Punishment by fire (cf. A₂)
Lev 10:1-2 vs Num 11:1-3

Death of Joshua (A₅)
Josh 24:29-31 vs Judg 2:6-9

God will not drive out
Caananites Judg 2:1-5 vs
2:20-23 vs 3:1-6

Victory over Sisera
Judg 4:1-24 vs 5:1-31

Judges with 30 sons
Judg 10:1-5 vs 12:8-15

Saul chosen/confirmed as
King 1 Sam 10:17-27 vs
11:1-15

David anointed king
2 Sam 2:1-4 vs 2 Sam 5:1-17

Saul attempts to kill David
with spear
1 Sam 18:6-16 vs 19:9-10

David becomes Saul's son-
in-law 1 Sam 18:17-19 vs
18:20-28

David spares Saul's life
1 Sam 24:1-23 vs 26:1-23

Census in Israel
2 Sam 24:1-25 vs 1 Chr
21:1-30

God appears to Solomon
1 Kgs 3:4-15 vs 9:1-9

A₂ Variant, different person

Relatives separate
Gen 13:2-18 vs 36:6-7

Offering hospitality to divine
beings
Gen 18:1-16 vs 19:1-29

Treaty concerning well with
King of Gerar
Gen 21:22-34 vs 26:14-33

Bearing twins
Gen 21:22-34 vs 41:50-52

Jacob gets blessed / blesses
Ephraim
Gen 27:1-45 vs 48:1-22

Struggling with an angel
Gen 32:22-32 vs Ex 4:24-26

Holy Ground
Ex 3:5 vs Josh 5:13-15

Call to obedience and life
Deut 29:1-30:20 vs Josh
23:1-24

The ark that kills (cf. C₁)
1 Sam 6:19-21 vs 2 Sam 6:
11

Who killed the giant? (cf. C
1 Sam 17:1-18:5 vs 2 Sam
21:19 vs 2 Sam 21:20-21 vs
Chr 11:22-24

Disobedience of man of God
1 Kgs 13:11-32 vs 20:35-43

Living water / food
2 Kgs 2:15-22 vs 4:38-44

* vs = versus, or compare

A₃ Variant, Part of story	**A₄ Variant, One aspect**	**A₅ Conflation**
Sodom-like incident Gen 19:1-29 vs Judg 19:1-30	Lifting hand/spear for victory Ex 17:8-16 vs Josh 8:18-29	The Flood Gen 6:9-8:22
Jacob gets blessing Gen 27:1-45 vs 27:46-28:9	Punishment with leprosy Num 12:1-15 vs 2 Kgs 5:1-27	Jacob and Laban name stones Gen 31:45-48; 31:49
Idols called to revenge Judg 6:25-32 vs 1 Kgs 18:1-46	"Chopping" / sending pieces to call a war Judg 19:1-29 vs 20:1-21:25 vs 1 Sam 11:1-11	Joseph sold to Egpyt Gen 37:12-36
		Joseph's brothers journey to Egypt (cf. A₁) Gen 42:1-38; 43:1-43
		Plagues 1-9 (cf. E) Ex 7-10
		10th Plague (cf. A₁, E, F) Ex 11:1-13:16
		Giving the law (cf. A₁) Ex 19:1-20:26 vs 31:18 vs 34:1-35
		Crossing of Jordan with dry feet / passing before the Ark Josh 3:1-17; 4:1-5

A₆ Frame	B₁ Thematic	B₂ Symbolic/ Typical	C₁ Similar Incidents
Five kings beaten by God's man Gen 14:1-24 vs Josh 10:1-22	Conspiracy 1 Kgs 12:33-13:34 vs Amos 7:10-17	One family spared from catastrophe (cf. C₂) Gen 6:9-8:32 vs Gen 19:1-30 vs Josh 2 and 6	Ecstasy Num 11:24-30 vs 1 Sam 9:1-10:16 vs 1 Sam 19:18-27 vs 2 Sam 6:1-23
Circumcision as preparation Ex 4:24-26 vs Josh 5:2-9		Going to Egypt Gen 12:10-20 Abraham Gen 37:36 Joseph Gen 42-43 Joseph's brothers Gen 46:1-34 Jacob Ex 4:9-23 Moses	Representation of disease for healing Num 21:4-9 vs 1 Sam 6:1-18 Not destroying plund Judg 7:1-26 vs 1 Sam 15:1-35
Crossing water with dry feet Ex 13:17-14:31 vs Josh 3:1-4:24 vs 2 Kgs 2:1-14			
Golden Calf Ex 32:1-35 vs 1 Kgs 12:20-33			
Gathering coins, making an idol Ex 32:1-35 vs Judg 8:22-27 vs Judg 17:1-13			
Moses/Elijah and Mt. of God Ex 3:1-10 vs 1 Kgs 19:1-18			
Living water Ex 15:22-25 vs 2 Kgs 2:15-22			

C₂ Type-Scene, Literary Convention

Call narratives
Gen 6:9 Noah
Gen 11:28-12:9 Abraham
Gen 26:23-25 Isaac
Gen 28:10-22 Jacob
Gen 31:11-13 Jacob
Num 27:12-23 Joshua
Josh 1:1-9 Joshua
Judg 6:11-40 Gideon
1 Sam 3:1-41 Samuel
1 Sam 9:1-10:16; 10:17-22 Saul
1 Sam 16:1-13 David
1 Kings 3:4-15 Solomon

Barren woman becomes mother of hero
Gen 21:1-13 Sarah
Gen 25:21-28 Rebekah
Gen 30:14-24 Rachel
Judg 13:1-25 Manoah
2 Sam 1:1-28 Hanna

C₂ Type-Scene... continued

Meeting at a well results in marriage
Gen 24:1-67 Rebekah
Gen 29:1-14 Rachel
Ex 2:11-22 Zipporah

Trials of great men
Gen 22:1-22 Abraham
Gen 32:22-32 Jacob
Gen 39:7-23 Joseph

Last words
Gen 48:1-7, 8-22 (cf. A₁) Jacob
Gen 50:25 Joseph
Deut 33 Moses
Josh 23-24:1 Joshua
1 Sam 12:1-25 Samuel
2 Sam 23:1-7 David
1 Kgs 2:1-12 David

D Same Event Differently Recorded

Creation
Gen 1:1-2:4a vs 2:4b-25

Younger brother gets seniority by deception (cf. A₂ & A₃)
Gen 25:29-34 vs 27:1-45

Call of Joshua
Josh 1:1-9 vs Num 27:12-23

David's introduction to Saul
1 Sam 16:14-23 vs 17:1-18:5

Saul's death
1 Sam 31:1-13 vs 2 Sam 1:1-27

David's last words
2 Sam 23:1-7 vs 1 Kgs 2:1-12

E Intentional Repetition

Dreams in Joseph's life
Gen 37:5-11 vs 40:5-19 vs 41:1-32

Elevation of Joseph
Gen 39:1-6 vs 29:21-23 vs 41:37-57

Disputing Moses' leadership
Num 12:1-15 vs 16:1-50 vs 17:1-13

Atrocity / civil war
Judg 19-21

Elijah brings down fire
1 Kgs 1:3-16

F Reported Story

Passover, institution and celebration
Ex 12:1-20 vs 12:21-50

Tabernacle, building instruction and construction
Ex 25-31 vs 35-40

G Parallel History

See 1-2 Samuel, 1-2 Kings and 1-2 Chronicles

H Verbatim Repetition

Daughter promised
Josh 15:15-19 vs Judg 1:11-15

Water brought to David
2 Sam 23:13-17 vs 1 Chr 11:15-19

4.2.2. Suggested Definition

The difficulty in suggesting a concise, but comprehensive, definition for double narratives lies in the fact that, as illustrated in the chart, Old Testament narratives do not duplicate in clear-cut ways, but in various degrees and kinds. However, among these shades three main "manners" of duplication can be seen in terms of the type of dependence the narratives manifest on each other. Thus the relationship of stories in group A is one of literary dependence, albeit in various degrees, and it should be assumed that some kind of knowledge of one story existed for the other to be created, whether this knowledge be in oral or written form.

Stories in groups B and C have a symbolic or thematic link and, where authorial intention is an issue, as it has been in the critical approaches discussed in this research, it is important that the fact that this link has been intentionally fashioned and exploited is, if not established, at least strongly suspected. However, the kind of link that is found in narratives in these categories can also very easily emerge with hindsight, or be accidental. The recognition of duplication here is more subjective than in the previous category A where, in contrast, literary dependence could be shown to exist actually and objectively. In any case it is important to notice that the story is not used in its own right but as a "stepping stone" or a symbol, the link having been established through the use of a convention of some kind. Thus a "genetic" difference always exists between A-type duplication and types B and C.

Stories in group D are related by their reported connection to the same, unique event, and as a rule the stories themselves are verbally independent. Their recognition as doublets has perhaps as much to do with the fact that they fall within the same literary corpus, where they have been seen as creating contradiction, as with the actual duplication.

However, in terms of the history of Old Testament criticism, it is the narrative relationships that prevail in groups A and D that have been perceived as doublets. So these are in a sense the "original" double narratives, and the term should probably always be used with the historical connection in mind. B and C can be included under the double narrative rubric where intentionality of usage is at least a strong likelihood.[24]

---

24   That is, with approaches that regard this aspect as important.

Of all the groups, group A has the widest spectrum of types of variation within it. Some of these may seem quite remote, such as is the case of the "frame", and care should be taken to establish literary dependence. This is the type of duplication that is properly "variant" in the technical sense of the term and coincides with what is usually meant by duplication in other related disciplines, such as folklore studies. The term "variant" for this group is my preferred term, where no connection with the history of scholarship needs to be made.

The introduction of the "type-scene" concept has been one of the major innovations into double narrative studies in the past century, and one that offers much potential for further research. However, my use of the term differs from Alter's, who uses it not as an exclusive designation for a form of conventional duplication, as it was in Homeric studies where the term was adopted from, but as an inclusive, even alternative term for many types of duplication, including what the chart designates as A1 types. I see the use of the term in its "Homeric" sense of a "convention" as the legitimate one and, consequently, Alter's usage as confusing. For instance, an occurrence of "meeting at the well leading to a prominent marriage", a story-type recognized by Alter as a "type-scene" and a compositional convention, would only form a double narrative if it also shared a story-base with another narrative, or gave a second, different report of a unique meeting at the well. Thus for stories to form double narratives something *more* than a conventional link is needed, namely substantial literary dependence or reference to a unique event.

What is perhaps most needed in biblical scholarship when narrative duplication is being discussed is more specificity as what is being duplicated and by what means. The term "variant" denotes actual literary dependence, but as this exists in various degrees in biblical narratives, "grading" the dependence along terminology, such as is suggested in the chart, may be helpful.

Duplication in groups B and C has an element of literary dependence in it, yet this does not amount to much in terms of "quantity", as the duplication consists more of the reuse of an idea, pattern, type or symbol, rather than of "so many words". The link is established through some kind of pattern or convention, external to the stories themselves. It is the use of such an convention that is most characteristic of duplication here, and should perhaps then be the operative word, again, with specification as to what the convention is, i.e. whether a type, symbol or a type-scene.

4.3. Literary and Textual Variants

The "charting" of double narratives above has, I hope, demonstrated the complexity and the multifarious character of the phenomenon, hopefully suggesting dimensions not previously thought of. What have traditionally been regarded as doublets, such as the Creation or Wife-sister stories, represent but the extremes of a spectrum of repetitions and patterns of variation, which encompasses much of the narrative material in the Old Testament. The variants at the end of the spectrum may stand out because the duplication is so obvious, but they are really only what meets the eye: a great mass of undifferentiated duplication lies between the poles. One purpose of this chapter has therefore been to try to bring to the surface the kinds of narrative variants that do exist in the Old Testament but have so far escaped with little or no scholarly attention: the other, to try to explore the nature of the phenomenon as a continuum, rather than as neatly definable, isolated categories.

In this section of the chapter the discussion will be extended in another direction: towards textual studies. The study of narrative variants and textual variants has usually been conducted separately under different branches of Old Testament scholarship. Textual criticism has long been regarded almost as an "exact science",[25] particularly when compared to the more hypothetical literary study of narrative variants. Some recent textual work does, however, raise questions as to whether this polarization is justifiable: might the two realms of variants – textual and literary – in fact be closer together than previously realized, sometimes even overlapping?[26] And if so, what implications would that have for the study of double narratives?

The textual work under scrutiny here is mainly that of Shemaryahu Talmon. Reviewing his classification of different types of textual variants in the Old Testament, their origin and underlying literary processes, will hopefully help us to explore, if not answer, three central questions relating to the juxtaposition of literary and textual variants:

1. Is there an intrinsic difference between textual variants and literary ones (i.e. double narratives)? Could areas of overlap be found?

---

25 See e.g. Weingreen 25.
26 Natalio Fernandéz Marcos calls for combining the efforts of textual and literary criticism to "bring us to a frontier zone of the history of the biblical text", the study of which has so far been barely outlined (82-3).

2. In what way are the origins of the two types of variants and the processes involved in their development different/similar?

3. Could the study of double narratives benefit from research into textual variants, and if so, how?

4.3.1. "Variant", "Synonymous" and "Double" Readings

In a series of articles, the most comprehensive of which is "Double Readings in the Massoretic Text", 1960,[27] Talmon endeavours to stretch the traditionally perceived boundaries of textual variants. He points out that the study of textual variants has usually been conducted "vertically": each extra-masoretic tradition compared individually with the Masoretic Text (MT) (1960:144-5). Consequently, types of variants are then often seen as unique to that textual tradition. Widening the scope "horizontally", studying all the textual variants of various traditions "synoptically", will, Talmon contends, reveal patterns of variation transcending recensional lines, and give us new insight into the origins and development of textual variants (1960:145). To facilitate such cross-recensional explorations Talmon complements the traditional division of textual variants (i.e. variant readings) into three basic types with a further one, which he subdivides into two and labels "synonymous readings" and "double readings".

4.3.1.1. *Variant Readings*

The first category, variant readings, represents the traditional classification of textual variations by Old Testament scholars. It has resulted mainly from the comparison of the MT with the Septuagint (LXX), the Samaritan Pentateuch (SP), and more recently the Dead Sea Scrolls (1960:144). Variant readings are usually divided into three "archetypes" (1960:144):

a) Deliberate corrections and emendations of the text.
b) Variants arising from the scribal routine.
c) Textual corruptions resulting from visual (graphic) and aural mistakes, or from faulty memories of scribes and copyists.

The axiom underlying the analysis of variant readings is the existence of an *Urtext*[28] from which these variants derive. Thus the existence of a single

---

27   See also Talmon 1961; 1962; 1964; 1975; 1976; 1986.

Hebrew version is assumed, from which the variant readings of the SP and the extra-Masoretic MSS deviate and (a form of ?) which would have served as the prototype for the LXX. The reconstruction of the *Urtext* is then assumed to be possible through the comparison of these variants. Variant readings are therefore either freaks resulting from scribal errors, or deliberate, often sectarian, alterations to the text (1960:144).

Talmon, however, argues that these traditional types of variant readings, though legitimate in their place, are inadequate to explain all the kinds of divergence found in the Old Testament text. They have catered for the vertical comparison of one version at a time with the MT (1960:145). Talmon therefore proposes categories of "synonymous readings" and "double readings" to explain a pattern of variation present in the Old Testament textual tradition but excluded by the above definition of variant readings (1960:146, 150).

4.3.1.2. *Synonymous readings*

Synonymous readings – so labelled on the analogy of synonymous parallelism[29] – are alternative readings that now appear, besides the versions, in the parallel traditions[30] in the Old Testament, as well as different traditions of Kethib and Qere.[31] For readings to be "synonymous", Talmon argues, they have to display four characteristics (1960:146):

a) They result from the substitution of words and phrases by others which are used interchangeably and synonymously with them in the literature of the O. T.
b) They do not affect adversely the structure of the verse, nor do they disturb either its meaning or its rhythm. Hence they cannot be explained as scribal errors.

---

28   Talmon points out that the axiom of the *Urtext* and its reconstruction has been mainly utilized in the LXX studies, where it is usually associated – if not entirely justifiably – with the name of P. de Lagarde (see Talmon 1960:144). For a more detailed discussion on the classification of textual variants and their relationship to various theories of the origin of the Hebrew text as well as the early versions, see the work of E. Tov.
29   For the potential origin of synonymous readings in the Old Testament literary feature of "parallelism of members", see Talmon 1961.
30   Most notably the Former Prophets, the Chronicles, some repeated prophetic utterances and psalms. Thus, for instance, the alternation between כף and יד in 2 Sam. 22:1 and Ps. 18:1 (Talmon 1960:149; Tov 1992:260).
31   Cf. Tov's definition of synonymous readings as words in variants which "serve a similar or identical function on the literary level although their meaning is not necessarily identical" (1992:260).

c) No sign of systematic or tendentious emendation can be discovered in them. They are to be taken at their face value. Synonymous readings cannot be explained as variants with a clearly defined ideological purpose. They are characterized by the absence of any difference between them in content or meaning.

d) ...[T]hey are not, as far as we can tell, the product of different chronologically or geographically distinct literary strata.

Synonymous readings do not, therefore, have a direct bearing on the emendations of the text in the way variant readings do: by definition "it is impossible to decide that any of them is intrinsically preferable to the others" (Talmon 1960:146). Thus to call these readings "variants" or "substitutes" in any technical sense would be a misnomer: as they arose there was no *textus receptus* from which they could have accidentally diverged (Talmon 1960:149).

While variant readings are seen as derivations from an *Urtext*, Talmon suggests that synonymous readings originated at the more ancient level of textual development when the material was in more inchoate form, "pentateuchal literature"[32] rather than the Pentateuch, which preceded the assessment of the different literary traditions and the establishment of a "clear-cut, authoritative text of the national lore" (Talmon 1960:147-8; 1976:170). They preserve ancient traditions often initiated by scribes of various groups but belonging to the common Jewish heritage before the emergence of exclusive sectarian boundaries (Talmon 1960:145, 147). However, due to the more stringent editing of Scriptures in normative Judaism, these readings are now more evident in the literature of "dissident groups" (1960:145). This, Talmon suggests,[33] explains why the Samaritan text sometimes represents a tradition which, while different from that in the MT of the Pentateuch "is nevertheless identical with the parallel reading presented in the MT of the Chronicles" (1960:145). Or why the text of 4Q Sam[a] tallies much more closely with the Chronicles than the Samuel of the MT (1960:145-6).

The moves towards an authoritative text Talmon sees as precipitated by socio-political forces: amid sectarian rivalry and "heterodox opinions and

---

32 Perhaps even at the oral stage (Talmon 1976:170; similarly Tov 1992:260).

33 Talmon apparently reflects here G. Gerleman's work, which, in line with P. Kahle's text-development theory, argues that the SP is a more vulgar text than the MT, though the latter, due to the Masoretes' critical restoration of the text, gives the impression of being more ancient. A similar situation, Gerleman contends, is reflected within the MT, where the text of the Chronicles, being part of the "less sacred" Hagiographa, has undergone less revision than the Samuel-Kings of the Prophets, which now appears as the older text. See Gerleman 1948.

doctrines" clear lines of demarcation were needed as "authority was sought in the oral and still more in the written tradition" (1960:148). Parts of tradition that were normative for a given community – i.e. had "proof-text" value – got consolidated first, and equally, others were rejected if they carried that value for a rival group (1960:148).

As a rule, Talmon contends, synonymous readings did not have such ideological significance and other factors had to be considered as the editors came to choose between them. The main factor would have been the preservation of a reading in "a number of codices that were regarded as particularly holy" (1960:148). But left without any such guidance – "when the variants in question were purely stylistic, without any ideological significance, and the number of books supporting each of the parallel readings was equal" – the editors faced a "recensional dilemma" (1960:148).[34] The solution to this dilemma led to the preservation of synonymous readings in one of two ways: they could be preserved in parallel literary units, such as appear in the Former Prophets and the Chronicles, or different traditions of Kethib and Qere, for the editors of the unified text felt no burden for "imposing linguistic unity" on such passages (Talmon 1960:149). But when only a single text was available another measure was resorted to: conflating the synonymous readings into a "double reading", which enabled the preservation of alternative wordings in a single tradition/verse (Talmon 1960:149-50).

The motivation for such efforts of text preservation came, Talmon suggests, from reverence for the Scriptures – both readings were regarded "'the words of the living God'" (Talmon 1960:148). This is an interesting point and, it seems, a central one in any discussion trying to understand the puzzling literary form of the Old Testament as we now have it and the rationale for its codification. However, it is also a highly problematic one, since, as seen above, this reverence did not reach the rival groups' proof-texts or readings in codices that were not regarded as "particularly holy".[35]

---

34 Talmon points to some often quoted references in Jewish tradition as evidence that such a process of determining the wording of the text did in fact take place: P.T. Ta'anith 4:2 (68a); *Sifre* Deut. 33:27; *Soferim* 6:4; *Aboth de Rabbi Nathan*, version B:46, (1960:146). Whether, however, they refer to the time and process of Talmon's synonymous/double readings development, is not entirely clear (1960:146). For a more detailed treatment of these texts, see Talmon 1962.

35 Exactly the same arguments are used in source criticism, where the presence of doublets is argued for on the basis of "respect for the tradition", yet the editorial work necessary to smooth out the resulting contradictions is allowed despite that respect.

4.3.1.3. *Double Readings*

The practice of double readings,[36] Talmon points out, is best known from the versions, particularly the late redactions of the LXX[37] (1960:150). However, he argues that the practice originated with ancient Hebrew traditions and was only taken over by the versions (1960:151). This, Talmon suggests, can be demonstrated by a careful analysis of the types of double readings found in the LXX (1960:151). According to Talmon, three types can be detected (1960:151):

a)   Double translations.   These are usually the work of copyists who combined alternative renderings of a single Hebrew word or a single Hebrew expression found in the different MSS of the version in question...[38]

b)   Conflate translations of synonymous readings.   In these cases the translator had recourse to a doublet to preserve two alternative Hebrew traditions which he found in different MSS of the original, because he would not presume to prefer one to the other.[39]

c)   Translations of double readings which had already been incorporated as such in the Hebrew MS used by the translator and whose conflate character escaped his notice; or if he noticed them, he did not presume to correct them.[40]

The origins of the double readings in the first two categories (a and b) Talmon sees in the versional tradition itself, i.e. the process of translating the Hebrew text and then transmitting the translation: the work of copyists and translators. Double readings of the third type (c) Talmon sees as having been derived "from the Hebrew original", to which he also attributes the textual

---

36   "Conflate readings", "alternative readings" and "doublets" in the text-critical sense are all at times used as synonyms to "double readings" (Talmon 1976:170; Janzen 434).

37   Most notably the Lucianic revision.

38   For instance, איש בחור (שבע מאות) לבד מישבי הגבעה התפקדו) of Judg. 20:15 MT is translated ἄνδρες νεανίσκοι ἐκλέκτοι in LXX (A), ἄνδρες ἐκλεκτοὶ in LXX (B). Talmon regards νεανίσκοι as "pleonastic" and "undoubtedly parallel" to ἄνδρες, which he sees as already translating the Hebrew בחור (Talmon 1960:150 [where LXX A and B are, it seems, accidentally reversed] ; 1976:171).

39   For instance, two different meanings of בעבים, "cave" and "thicket", in Jer. 4:29 MT are rendered separately in the LXX: εἰς τὰ σπήλαια καὶ εἰς τὰ ἄλση (Talmon 1976:171).

40   For instance, Joel 3:1 (MT 4:1) already has a doublet in בימים ההמה ובעת ההיא, which the LXX faithfully renders ἐν ταῖς ἡμέραις ἐκείναις καὶ ἐν τῷ καιρῷ ἐκείνῳ (Talmon 1976:171).

phenomenon on which the second type, "conflate translations", is based. Both types b and c, therefore, as textual phenomena "go back to an ancient Hebrew tradition or traditions" (1960:152).

Talmon admits that proving the origin of the phenomenon in the Hebrew text is, as yet, difficult, but this, he argues, is only because of the "paucity of extra-massoretic Biblical MSS" (1960:152). Against some scholars, who regard the double readings phenomenon as a versional one, Talmon insists that in fact the translator's primary task was to translate and it was only fairly late in the versional process that the translator started to base his work on more than one MS at a time (Talmon 1960:152). Thus, he argues, many of the doublets found in translations are in fact derived from a double reading in the Hebrew original, rather than the result of a translator combining readings from more than one MS. As more Hebrew MSS come to light, this, Talmon contends, will be born out.

4.3.2. Double Readings: Three Dimensions

Talmon's main interest in "Double Readings", having established his terminology and types of variants, is to analyse the phenomenon of double readings in the MT, which he does with an impressive array of examples. In mapping out his examples Talmon uses three aspects of double readings as organizing criteria. Firstly, "types of synonymity", i.e. "the sources of double readings"; secondly, "the extent of the duplication"; and thirdly "the methods of conflating alternative readings and the location of doublets in the sentence" (Talmon 1960:158-60). As these criteria seem to echo various important issues in the study of double narratives, we will look at them in some detail and endeavour to point out the implications.

In discussing the types of synonymity and the sources of double readings Talmon illustrates the versatility of the double reading phenomenon by pointing out how each of the different parts of speech – verbs, nouns, adjectives, particles – may give rise to a doublet. Many textual doublets originate simply in linking of two more or less synonymous words. Sometimes even different spellings of the same word, or an abbreviated spelling of the word recorded side by side with its full form, form double readings (Talmon 1960:158-9).[41]   On the other hand, however, Talmon

---

41   For instance, האָרֶב הֶרֶב in the MT of Judg. 20:38, הֶרֶב being the defective form of האָרֶב (Talmon 1960:161).

points out, at the much more complex end of the spectrum, a doublet may be made of a shortened form of a verse and a more elaborate one, both of which have been preserved in parallel sources (1960:159). One of the examples[42] Talmon uses of such a case, Judges 19:9, has particularly interesting implications for double narratives (1960:181).

The MT for Judges 19:9 reads: הנה נא רפה היום לערב לינו נא הנה חנות היום לין. פה Talmon suggests that the two alternative readings found here were not preserved in the MT in their entirety, but can be constructed from the LXX, where A and B read:

A: Ἰδοὺ δὴ εἰς ἑσπέραν κέκλινεν ἡ ἡμέρα

B: Ἰδοὺ δὴ ἠσθένησεν ἡ ἡμέρα εἰς τὴν ἑσπέραν

Talmon thus conjectures the two original Hebrew readings as:

a. הנה נא רפה היום לערוב לינו נא (פה)

b. הנה (נא) נח(ו)ת היום (לערוב) לין (ו) (?) פה

What is remarkable here, however, is, that precisely this difference has been used by some scholars, such as Nowack,[43] to separate two sources in the verse. The question then is: how do we distinguish between literary variants and simple textual ones – "just" synonyms or alternatives – as it has often been precisely such use of synonyms[44] that has enabled source critics to delineate their documents with great authority and precision?

Another example that Talmon offers, almost in passing, for double readings derived from parallel historical traditions, also turns out to have much more significance than at first meets the eye, 2 Sam. 15:24 (Talmon 1960:156-7): והנה גם צדוק וכל הלוים אתו נשאים את ארון ברית האלהים ויצקו את ארון האלהים (ויעל אביתר) עד תם כל העם לעבור מן העיר. Here the carrying of the Ark is attributed to Zadok the Priest, while Abiathar offered sacrifices (or "went up", as in the LXX καὶ ἀνέβη ʾΑβιαθάρ – a reading preferred by many translations). But Abiathar, too, officiated to David as a priest, for instance in 1 Sam. 22:21-23; 23:9. Talmon argues that the redactor must have had two traditions available to him: in one Zadok carried the Ark, in the other Abiathar did. He then "blended" them by inserting into the text the words

---

42 This, according to Talmon, is an example of "alternative readings distinguished by some additional word(s) found in only one of them without affecting the meaning of the passage" (1960:180-1, italics omitted).

43 Talmon 1960:181. Nowack argues that in Judg. 19:9 "treten beide Quellen [J and E] deutlich zu Tage", obvious in the two repetitious phares under discussion here (161).

44 For instance, אמה/שפחה in Genesis, to quote one of the most famous examples.

ויעל אביתר, which served as parallel reading to והנה גם צדוק. Talmon therefore offers a reconstruction of the verse as two original parallel reading as follows:

והנה גם צדוק

וכל הלוים אתו וגו'

ויעל אביתר

What is interesting is the kind of synonyms we are dealing with here – for Talmon treats them as no more than such – namely, proper nouns.   In tradition-historical scholarship this would be a significant variation, not unlike the change from Abraham to Isaac in the last of the Wife-sister stories! If no reference to Abiathar's dealings with David existed elsewhere, how would this "synonym" be looked upon?   It seems to me that in historical-critical scholarship lesser evidence than this has been used to vindicate the existence of parallel sources or rival traditions concerning the patriarchs.

The second of Talmon's organizational criteria is the extent of the duplication (1960:159).   Firstly, as just seen above, the extent of the alternative reading may vary anywhere from a one-letter spelling difference to, Talmon suggests, a whole sentence that is a word-for-word equivalent of the first (1960:159).   But secondly, Talmon observes, the technique of preserving synonymous readings in the frame of a doublet is not uniform either; rather, various methods of conflation are employed, affecting the extent of the resulting doublet (1960:159).   Thus, although there are many cases where the alternative reading is simply copied or recorded in full, at the other extreme, Talmon suggests, sometimes a part, even only a mere hint, of the variant may have been preserved "in the form of a single word or two, or in a hybrid reading which is a conflation of two synonymous grammatical forms" (1960:159).   Such word(s) would perform the function of a *custos*, a reminder, i.e. "preserve the memory of a reading which the scribe knew of, but which he did not copy out in full" (Talmon 1960:159).

Talmon provides an example of the use of *custos* from the wider literary and structural context of the book of Judges.[45]   Talmon argues, on various socio-religious and linguistic-literary grounds, that the "appendices" to the book of Judges, chs 17-18 and 19-21, which relate the stories of the Danite migration and Micah's sanctuary, and the concubine of Gibeah and the ensuing war against Benjamin, originally belonged together with the material in ch. 1 (1986:45-6). But since the traditions concerning the rest of the tribes and their wars in ch. 1 were only "relatively short notes" and the traditions now in the appendix were lengthy – chs 17-18 alone expanding to "what

---

45   See Talmon's article "'In Those Days There was no מלך in Israel' – Judges 18-21", 1986.

amounts to a novella" – Talmon argues that the "arranger", מסדר, of the book transferred the longer traditions to the end of the book, leaving only a brief reference, i.e. a *custos*, to remind of them in their original location (1986:46).

According to Talmon, then, "the Amorites pressed the Danites back into the hill country, for they did not allow them to come down to the plain" (Judg. 1:24), serves as a *custos* for the Danite migration, elaborated on in the "novella" of chs 17-18 (1986:46). Similarly, הבכים in Judg. 2:1 is left as a reminder of the story of the concubine and the Benjamite war, particularly ch. 20, where "the people of Israel...wept (יבכו)" (20:23), and where "the children of Israel, and all the people...wept (יבכו)" (20:26) (1986:46).[46]

Thus the extent of the doublet, Talmon contends, would not depend solely on the extent of the variant or considerations of the subject-matter, but, in fact, decisively on the inclinations and methods – scribal conventions – of the scribe recording the text.

As for the relative antiquity of these methods of conflation, Talmon pleads that lack of information on scribal techniques and the history of alternative readings prevents him from tracing their development step by step. He nevertheless surmises that "the recording of the alternative in full" was likely to have preceded "the systematic abbreviation of it to a single key-word", as the latter obviously called for "careful deliberation and weighing of possibilities" (1960:159). Talmon also suggests that the use of a *custos* is indicative of scribal technique that has developed well beyond the purely mechanical combination of readings and has become an "intellectual accomplishment" – a literary one? – a trend also seen in hybrid readings (1960:159-160).

The third and last of Talmon's criteria for charting out double readings comprises the methods of conflating and locating doublets in the sentence. This criterion has already been touched upon above. However, Talmon's observations have a pertinent further implication for the study of double narratives. Talmon points out that sometimes the readings are placed side by side without any attempt to join them syntactically. In other cases, however, disturbances in the grammatical structure are ironed out, while in yet others the double reading is placed outside the syntactical context of the sentence (1960:159). Could an analogy be found with variant narratives that are presented as separate incidents, such as the Wife-sister stories, and the ones, on the other hand, where great pains have been taken to harmonize the stories, as in the case of David's introductions to Saul's court?

---

46   See also Judg. 21:2

4.4. Appraisal

Talmon's work raises several interesting issues with regard to the study of double narratives. The most intriguing ones deal with the definitions and relationships of textual and literary variants, and the status of some of his exemplary doublets. As Talmon is looking at variants primarily from a textual point of view it would be unfair to criticize him for not saying more about double narratives as such. However, as on his own admission he is pushing back the boundaries of the definition of variants, it is only reasonable to look at his ideas from the point of view of our current research.

By adding the category of synonymous readings, and its conflate, double readings, to the traditional three (arche)types of textual variants, Talmon is not only stretching the conventional limits of text criticism, but in fact, stepping beyond them. Admittedly his main interest is in mapping out this fourth type of variant, not in investigating its relationship to literary criticism – though he does make a plea for someone else to do so! Yet it seems that his definition of synonymous variants does create the need for the negative point to be explained: why are the doublets he is dealing with not literary variants, and what would be the difference if they were? This, of course, is not as much a fault in Talmon's work as a tantalizing incompleteness, yet one that does raise questions with regard to the variant status of some of his examples.

Talmon's classification of possible doublet-types is scrupulously thorough, as is his scrutiny of variants, which sometimes deals with differences as minute as variations in spelling or half words. Yet when it comes to dealing with large and complex units of variants, the lack of wider literary definition does expose an obvious weakness in biblical critical methodology, now widened to include textual criticism as well: there is no common language, or overall theory, which would make it possible to address the issue of variation in both of its dimension, textual and literary, at the same time. The incident of Carrying the Ark, 2 Sam. 15:24ff, discussed above, is a case in point. One wonders how the proposed conflation here differs from that found in such traditional literary examples as the Flood narrative or the Journeys of Joseph's brothers. Why should one be credited to a scribe, the other to a (much earlier) literary editor – or even an oral former of a *Sagen*-cycle? And how extensive and complex can a variant become and still be regarded as a "textual" one?

Another issue is raised by Talmon's treatment of the Ark narrative as an example of a double reading "derived from parallel historical traditions" and the reconstruction that he subsequently offers (1960:156). The interesting question here from the point of view of double narratives is that if there had indeed been two traditions of different priests carrying the Ark, why were they conflated and not, for instance, presented as separate incidents in the style of the stories about David sparing Saul's life? The logic Talmon offers in his reconstruction is much (exactly?) the same as is employed by source critics in disentangling conflate narratives, such as the Flood.

Perhaps the most intriguing and controversial point Talmon raises is the idea of the use of a *custos* to preserve the memory of a wider reading. This suggests a kind of process of doublet (double narrative?) reduction for doublets as scribal skills improved and these duplications might have been perceived as repetitious and redundant. The problem with this idea is that it seems to militate directly against the very rationale of double readings that Talmon outlines elsewhere, namely that these constructions were resorted to because of the reverence felt for the most minute details of the text and wish for their consequent preservation. However, Talmon's *custos* argument is very persuasive when one comes across such strange – it seems, intriguingly incomplete – passages in the Old Testament as the "Bridegroom of Blood" text of Moses' circumcision, Ex. 4:24-26. One is tempted to think that maybe originally what is in the text stood for something more, something that is now lost.

4.5. Textual Variants and Double Narratives - An Interface?

In the beginning of this chapter we set out with three questions in mind relating to the origin and development of the variant phenomenon, textual as well as literary. Where has our study of Talmon's work on synonymous and double readings taken us, and what are the implications for our understanding of double narratives?

As to the first question of whether there is an intrinsic difference between textual and literary variants, the answer seems to be both yes and no. By our traditional understanding of the two phenomena, they are distinct. And looking at "typical" examples of either, say the Hagar stories on the one hand, a difference in spelling between the MT and 1QIs on the other, it is easy to recognize them as separate and distinct. But as Talmon introduces some of his complex or hybrid double readings and as we, on the other hand, think of double narratives that may now be only partially extant in the Old Testament, such as the above mentioned Bridegroom of blood -incident, we rightly start to hesitate. This is probably because we usually think of either phenomenon only in terms of its typical examples, not in terms of its essential definition. Then what exactly makes a variant literary or textual? Is it something in their "physical" appearance, such as length or extensiveness? Or rather something in the intentionality or unintentionality of their origin? Or should we look for the answer in the wider context of text development that gave rise to them?

It is interesting that though stereotypically we tend to associate the differences between the two types of variants with such issues as extensiveness and (un)intentionality (scribal errors!), neither of these seems to be a fundamental difference. A little application of Talmon's definition of textual variants to literary variants may be helpful here, and also go some way in answering the second question on the respective dynamics of the two different types of variants:

Talmon points out, as seen above, that the three traditional archetypes of text variants are: a) deliberate emendations. b) variants rising from scribal routine. c) corruptions (1960:144).

It seems that what is essential about the way variants originated in these categories is matched by similar perceived dynamics in literary variants. Thus, the intentionality of type "a" can also be found in what is often regarded as deliberately rewritten or retold narratives,[47] such as the Wife-sister stories. The variants rising from scribal practice could, in turn, be compared to doublets originating in assumed, perhaps later, editorial practices. As for the element of error or corruption that also arises with, for instance, the faulty memory of a storyteller, or the ascribing of the killing of Goliath to David, instead of Elhanan. The real difference in the traditional definitions of textual and literary variants must then be how we envisage their origins in relation to the larger body of Old Testament literature. Talmon points to this difference when he contrasts synonymous readings which, he suggests, arose at a relatively early, inchoate stage of text development – when literary variants are also thought to have originated – to the traditional textual variants, which are seen as deviations from an *Urtext*.

The point Talmon thus makes reflects on a long-standing dichotomy in Old Testament scholarship, where literary and textual variants (and all related issues) have been assigned to two different phases in the text development, occurring at different historical periods, and dealt with by different – and discontinuous? – branches of scholarship. The innovation he makes is to breach this traditional understanding of the two phenomena by proposing this definition of synonymous readings, i.e. a type of variant that is, by conventional terms, textual and literary at the same time.

---

47 The type of dependence – whether written or oral – is not the issue here, but the fact of dependence.

The question whether there is an overlap between textual and literary variants is therefore also a question of whether this long-respected division can still be upheld. Talmon's definition of synonymous and double readings, which are more like literary variants in some aspects, yet more like textual variants in others, challenges the conventional dichotomy. I would suggest that what we have seen in the first part of this chapter, in the definition of double narratives in terms of a continuum, rather than clear, easily distinguishable categories, also calls for the abolition of the old, too restrictive and simplifying, boundaries and the recognition of at least some common ground.

This is not to say that there exist no such things as unequivocally textual or literary variants, only that we may not be able to take the inherent separateness of what we have traditionally held as such variants for granted, and that there also exists an area of overlap which needs to be explored much more.

Conclusion

Double narratives have arguably been the single most important feature of the biblical text for the development of Old Testament methodology. The survey of the role of double narratives in the rise and development of Old Testament criticism in Chapter 1 demonstrated the extraordinary extent to which each successive critical approach based its argument for its particular understanding of biblical composition, and consequently of Israel's history and theological development as well, on its perception of the double narrative phenomenon. The implications of the study of the doublet phenomenon, formative for methodology, have thus reached far beyond the issues of composition and authorship to other realms of biblical studies.

Although all the approaches surveyed in Chapter 1 are individual and distinct in many respects, collectively they make only three basic claims concerning the significance of double narratives to the understanding of biblical composition: namely that doublets indicate the use of literary documents in the composition of the Bible (source criticism); that they witness to the oral origin and transmission of biblical tradition (form and tradition-historical criticism); or that they are evidence of literary artistry or theological intention in biblical composition (holistic approaches).

The first two of these claims are contradicted by the third on the level of how authorial control is perceived, i.e. whether authorship is heterogeneous or homogenous. This contradiction is no great surprise as the holistic approaches tend to be openly critical of the basic premises of the classical documentary theory or regard the attempt to reconstruct the development of traditions as irrelevant to their own task. That there might be methodological incompatibility between the first two approaches, represented by source criticism on the one hand, form and tradition-historical criticism on the other, has so far rarely been recognized. This research has, however, argued that such an incompatibility does exist and that it does so on the level of how compositional characteristics of narratives are perceived: that is, whether they are seen as literary features and indicators of the hallmark of the author and his time – even if the author employed oral sources in his work – or whether they are thought of as witnesses to the anonymous oral composition and lengthy oral transmission of the narrative – even if these narratives are now in written form.

It has not been the aim of this research to rule in favour of any particular approach to double narratives to the exclusion of others, nor to propose a new theory for their existence in the Old Testament. However, this current research strongly suggests that, were such a new theory to be attempted, a more satisfactory solution to the doublet problem, and a way out of the impasse of incompatible approaches might be found in a synthesis of the existing theories. This new theory would have to recognize far greater differentiation in the double narrative phenomenon than has so far been the case and pursue the possibility that double narratives may actually have originated in several different ways and therefore, in effect, witness to several different modes of composition and transmission. However, what has also emerged from this research is the inescapable observation that, post-Wellhausen, all critical theories concerning the composition of Old Testament narrative materials with doublets in them, those within the Pentateuch in particular, have assumed at least a measure of compositional heterogeneity in the process. At the same time, for instance, the fairly clearly defined Four Document hypothesis seems untenable from the point of view of the present research.

The validity of the methodological claims raised by the study of double narratives has traditionally been exceedingly difficult to assess, a fact that has often resulted in scholars holding and working with what now seem to me to be contradictory methodological notions, or the kind of biblical critical "excommunications" of previous views by every new approach, that was alluded to by Barton. In the second chapter of this book I have attempted not so much to validate or invalidate biblical critical methodologies as to find ways of understanding some of the main claims they make concerning double narratives in terms of the basic underlying assumptions that are attached to these claims. I have thus argued that the role of conceptual models and the wider intellectual framework and context of the time in which these models have arisen is pivotal in trying to understand, let alone evaluate, the methodological claims made by these approaches.

Three main models were identified. Spinoza and the early biblical criticism were looked at in terms of the "naturalist" model arising from the context of Spinoza's rationalistic philosophy and the dawning scientific consciousness of the early Enlightenment; Wellhausen and the fully "mature" source criticism, on the other hand, were seen to reflect the model of a "historian" and the context of nineteenth-century German historiography, its organic understanding of historical periods and institutions, and emphasis on the *Zeitgeist*; and finally, the "literary artist" model of Alter and the new literary critics was seen to be indebted to the "Bible as literature" approach and modern literary criticism in their, as yet, somewhat undifferentiated views of what constitutes literature.

The recognition of these models showed the impossibility of evaluating methodological claims in the abstract and emphasized the need of interdisciplinary research to provide new perspectives in this area of biblical studies. One of the contributions of this present work is indeed the recognition of the fact that any further methodological study of the Old Testament is difficult, if not indeed impossible, in biblical critical isolation: basic premises in biblical criticism have to a large degree been adopted, consciously or unconsciously, from sister disciplines, which carry with them their own intellectual contexts and assumed premises. It is the recognition and incorporation of this wider context in biblical studies that suggests the most promising directions for research in biblical methodology, double narratives in particular. Such work could be undertaken, for instance, in any of the related fields surveyed above: for instance poetics and narratology offer large potential for understanding duplication and repetition as a wider phenomenon in narrative discourse, as is the case with folklore studies, while research into the philosophical background of biblical criticism and its place in the history of ideas is of paramount importance for the clarification and strengthening of the role of biblical criticism in the world of scientific debate.

Chapter 3 addressed the issue of double narratives as indicators of oral composition and transmission of the biblical tradition, pioneered by Gunkel and fostered since by approaches as diverse as the Scandinavian concept of fixed, reliable oral tradition and the preoccupation of Koch and Van Seters with epic laws. This notion of biblical narrative as oral in origin and subject to a "universal law of change" in its transmission, such as Olrik's laws crystallize, was discussed in the context of folklore research, both contemporary to early biblical critics and modern. I have argued that Gunkel did not simply adopt "epic laws" or even the concept of such laws, from Olrik, but was indebted to the intellectual ethos of the time in which such ideas were current, if not yet always completely formulated. The type of folkloristic thought that Gunkel reflects most clearly is that of the historical-geographical school of the Nordic scholars, J. and K. Krohn, M. Moe and Axel Olrik. Gunkel's form-critical and tradition-historical notions of the orality of biblical narratives can be seen as a pioneering application of these basic principles to the realm of the Bible.

The role of epic laws in biblical scholarship has been contentious and their validity much argued about. Although folklorists, many recent ones included, are confident that some kind of formalisation of the oral compositional process is possible, i.e. that there are some inherent "laws" operational in oral transmission, what our discussion in Chapter 3 has shown is that the circumstances in which such optimism is shown, i.e. in terms of the sheer number of variants available, are vastly different from those experienced in Old Testament studies. Perhaps the mistake of Old Testament scholars has not been the application of epic laws to biblical narrative, but the fact that the limitations posed by the paucity of variants (in folkloristic terms) in the Bible have not been taken into account, and the extremely tentative nature of any conclusions thereby arrived at has not been fully appreciated.

It is also the conclusion of this present study that the concept, pioneered by Gunkel, of some Old Testament narratives being oral in origin, is a sound and realistic one, supported by modern folklore studies. Much further research, not only on the specific issue of double narratives as possible oral variants, but on the nature and development of narratives of potential oral origin as such, could thus be undertaken with the help of folkloristic methodology. One such area, and perhaps the most pressing one, is the oral-written interface, embryonic in the work of Olrik and the Krohns, but more recently in an innovating way pursued by the oral-formulaic approach pioneered by Milman Parry, attempting to determine the nature and extent of orality in now written texts.

In this present work, perhaps unusually, the definition comes last! The reason for this is that the issues that necessitated such an elaborate "definition" arose from the previous three chapters. Perhaps the main hindrance for double narrative studies has been lack of adequate definition for, as well as comprehension of, the phenomenon. The purpose of Chapter 4 is not to suggest any one term for the various forms of doublets found in the Old Testament, but almost the opposite: what is needed is to be able to appreciate the complexity of the phenomenon and thus feel less of a need to prescribe uniform solutions.

The charting of double narratives in Chapter 4 does indeed suggest that either a single definition or a single methodological solution for the breath and complexity of the double narrative phenomenon in the Old Testament is hardly realistic: future research may well, I believe, reveal the double narrative phenomenon as many, rather than one, encompassing duplication originating from several distinct causes. This conclusion is further strengthened by our recourse to the textual work of Talmon and his discovery of the overlap between what textual critics have traditionally regarded as textual variants and literary critics as literary variants. The pursuit of this potential interface between textual and literary criticism offers, I believe, one of the potentially most fruitful avenues for future double narrative research.

What has also become clear in this research is the pivotal importance of the earliest critical observations concerning doublets as indicators of the use of sources, i.e. heterogeneity of origin, in the composition of Scripture. Thus even though the idea that the sources were literary documents was soon challenged by the form-critical and tradition-historical concept of double narratives as oral variants, and eventually contradicted by the "holistic" approaches crediting the presence of doublets to literary artistry or authorial intention of a more theological kind, it is of no small significance that in none of the approaches to biblical criticism that involve the dimension of authorial intention in their equation is the presence of some kind of heterogeneity in biblical composition totally refuted. This concept of heterogeneity of composition is then perhaps the most lasting heritage bequeathed by the critical study of double narratives to Old Testament studies as a whole, and despite the controversies concerning the interpretation of doublets themselves, no critical approach has so far provided a credible alternative to the hypothesis of heterogeneity and progression in the authorship of biblical texts.

Perhaps another observation of great importance that has emerged from this research is the complexity of the double narrative phenomenon and its unique role in the Old Testament. Our discussion of the last of the conceptual models in Chapter 2, that of the "literary artist", and the accompanying disciplines of literary criticism and poetics, demonstrated the enormous possibilities that there are for understanding biblical repetition with the help of interdisciplinary concepts and methods. The phenomenon of double narratives in the Old Testament has, however, emerged as a distinct one, not easily containable by classifications made in other fields. Double narratives are thus not a unique, but a highly unusual literary phenomenon, and they must not simply be absorbed into the larger, more general category of repetition and duplication of literature.

Bibliography

Aarne, A.
   1913   *Leitfaden der vergleichenden Märchenforschung*, Hamina.
Aarne, A. and Thompson, S.
   1928   *The Types of the Folk-Tale. A Classification and Bibliography*,
   Helsinki (revised and enlarged by S. Thompson, Helsinki, 1961).
Abrahams, R. D.
   1969   "The Complex Relations of Simple Forms", *Genre* 2: 104-28.
Alonso-Schökel, L.
   1975   "Hermeneutical Problems of a Literary Study of the Bible", VTS
   28: 1-15.
   1985   "Of Methods and Models", VTS 36: 3-13.
Alphandéry, P.
   1924   "Jean Astruc (1684-1766)", *RHPR* 4: 54-72.
Alt, A.
   1929   "Der Gott der Väter", BWANT 3/12, Munich (ET 1966 "The God
   of the Fathers", in *Essays on Old Testament History and Religion*, Oxford:
   1-66).
Alter, R.
   1981   *The Art of Biblical Narrative*, London.
   1983   "How Convention Helps Us Read: The Case of the Bible's
   Annunciation Type-Scene", *Prooftexts* 3: 115-30.
Alter, R. and Kermode, F. (eds)
   1987   *The Literary Guide to the Bible*, Cambridge, MA.
Anderson, B. W.
   1981   "Martin Noth's Traditio-Historical Approach in the Context of
   Twentieth-Century Biblical Research", Introduction to: M. Noth, *A
   History of Pentateuchal Traditions*, Chico, California: xiii-xxxii (1st edn
   1971).
Anderson, W.
   1923   *Kaiser und Abt*, Helsinki.
Arend, W.
   1933   *Die typischen Szenen bei Homer*, Berlin.
Armogathe, J-R. (ed.)
   1989   *Le Grand Siècle et la Bible*, Paris.

Astruc, J.
1753 *Conjectures sur les Mémoires originaux dont il paroit que Moyse s'est servi pour composer le Livre de la Genèse*, Brussels.
Auerbach, E.
1946 *Mimesis. Dargestellte Wirklichkeit in der abendländischen Literatur*, Bern (ET 1953, *Mimesis. The Representation of Reality in Western Literature*, Princeton).
Auvray, P.
Richard Simon (1638-1712), Paris.

Baentsch, B.
1903 *Exodus-Leviticus-Numeri*, Handkommentar zum Alten Testament 1/2-4, Göttingen.
Bakhtin, M. M.
1973 *Problems of Dostoevsky's Poetics*, Ann Arbor.
Barbour, I. G.
1974 *Myths, Models and Paradigms*, London.
Barr, J.
1981 *Fundamentalism*, London. (1st edn 1977)
1990 *The Bible in the Modern World*, London (1st edn 1973).
Barton, J.
1984a *Reading the Old Testament: Method in Biblical Study*, London (new edn 1966).
1984b "Classifying Biblical Criticism", *JSOT* 29: 19-35.
Bascom,W. R.
1983 "The Forms of Folklore: Prose Narratives", in A. Dundes (ed.), 1984: 5-29.
Ben-Amos, D.
1969 "Analytic Categories and Ethnic Genres", *Genre* 2: 275-301.
1976 "Introduction", in D. Ben-Amos (ed.), 1976:ix-xlv.
Ben-Amos, D. (ed.)
1976 *Folklore Genres*, Austin and London.
Berlin, A.
1983 *Poetics and Interpretation of Biblical Narrative*, Sheffield.
Berlin, I.
1979 "The Divorce between the Sciences and the Humanities", in I. Berlin and H. Hardy (ed.), *Against the Current*, Oxford.
Bidney, D.
1953 *Theoretical Anthropology*, New York.
1965 "Myth, Symbolism, and Truth", T. A. Sebeok (ed.), 1965: 3-24.

Blenkinsopp, J.
  1992   *The Pentateuch. An Introduction to the First Five Books of the Bible,* London.
Bloom, H.
  1990   *The Book of J*, London.
Bødker, L.
  1965   *Folk Literature (Germanic)*, Copenhagen.
Bray, G.
  1996   *Biblical Interpretation: Past and Present*, Leicester.
Brenner, A.
  1997   "Female Social Behaviour: Two Descriptive Patterns within the 'Birth of the Hero' Paradigm", in A. Brenner (ed.), *A Feminist Companion to Genesis*, Sheffield: 204-21.
Brooks, P.
  1981   "Introduction", in T. Todorov, 1981:vii-xix.
Budde, K.
  1883   *Die Biblische Urgeschichte*, Giessen.

Carr, E. H.
  1982   *What Is History?*, London.
Cassuto, U.
  1934   *La Questione della Genesi*, Florence.
  1961   *The Documentary Hypothesis and the Composition of the Pentateuch*, Jerusalem (Hebrew original 1941).
  1964   *A Commentary on the Book of Genesis. Part II: From Noah to Abraham*, Jerusalem (Hebrew original 1949).
  1967   *A Commentary on the Book of Exodus*, London (Hebrew original 1951).
Clarke, K. W. and Clarke, M. W.
  1963   *Introducing Folklore*, London.
Cooper, A.
  1987   "On Reading the Bible Critically and Otherwise", in R.E. Friedman and H.G.M. Williamson (eds), 1987: 61-79.
Cox, G. W.
  1870   *The Mythology of the Aryan Nations*, 2 vols, London.
  1881   *An Introduction to the Science of Comparative Mythology and Folklore*, London.
Craigie, P. C.
  1978   "The Influence of Spinoza in the Higher Criticism of the Old Testament", *Evangelical Quarterly* 50: 23-32.

Culley, R. C.
    1974 "Structural Analysis: Is it Done with Mirrors?" *Interpreter* 28:
    165-81.
    1976 *Studies in the Structure of Hebrew Narrative*, Philadelphia and
    Missoula, Montana.
    1985 "Exploring New Directions", in D. A. Knight and G. M. Tucker
    (eds), 1985: 167-200.
    1986 "Oral Tradition and Biblical Studies", *Oral Tradition* 1: 30-65.
Curley, E.
    1994 "Notes on a Neglected Masterpiece: Spinoza and the Science of
    Hermeneutics", in G. Hunter (ed.), *Spinoza: The Enduring Questions*,
    Toronto: 64-99.

Damrosch, D.
    1987 *The Narrative Covenant. Transformations of Genre in the Growth
    of Biblical Literature*, San Francisco.
Danielson, L.
    1979 "Toward the Analysis of Vernacular Texts: The Supernatural
    Narrative in Oral and Popular Written Sources", *JFI* 16: 130-54.
Dégh, L.
    1972 "Folk Narrative", in R. M. Dorson (ed.), 1972: 53-83.
Dégh, L. and Vázsonyi, A.
    1971 "Legend and Belief", *Genre* 4: 281-304.
Dorson, R. M.
    1965 "The Eclipse of Solar Mythology", in A. Dundes (ed.), 1965:
    57-83.
    1968 *The British Folklorists: A History*, London.
    1972a "Concepts of Folklore and Folklife Studies", in R. M. Dorson
    (ed.), 1972:1-50.
    1972b "The Use of Printed Sources", in Dorson (ed.), 1972: 465-477.
    1983 *Handbook of American Folklore*, Bloomington, Indiana.
Dorson, R. M. (ed.)
    1972 *Folklore and Folklife: An Introduction*, Chicago and London.
Driver, S. R.
    1913 *An Introduction to the Literature of the Old Testament*, Edinburgh
    (9th edn, 1st edn 1891).
Dundes, A.
    1969 "The Devolutionary Premise in Folklore Theory", *JFI* 6: 5-19.
    1978 "Texture, Text and Context", in *Essays in Folkloristics*, New Delhi
    1984 Editorials in A. Dundes (ed.), 1984.

Dundes, A. (ed.)

1965 *The Study of Folklore*, Englewood Cliffs, N. J.

1979 *Analytic Essays in Folklore*, The Hague.

1984 *Sacred Narrative: Readings in the Theory of Myth*, Berkeley and London.

Eichhorn, J. G.

1780-3 *Einleitung ins Alte Testament*, 3 vols, Leipzig (2nd, enlarged edn 1987).

Eissfeldt, O.

1922 *Hexateuch-Synopse*, Leipzig.

1965 *The Old Testament: An Introduction*, Oxford.

Engnell, I.

1945 *Gamla Testamentet. En traditionshistorisk inledning, I*, Stockholm.

1960 "Methodological Aspects of Old Testament Study", VTS 7: 13-30.

1962 Articles in *Svenskt Bibliskt Uppslagsverk*, Stockholm

1970 *Critical Essays on the Old Testament*, London (ET of articles published in *Svenskt Bibliskt Uppslagsverk*, Stockholm, 1962).

Ewald, H.

1864 *Geschichte des Volkes Israel*, I, Göttingen (ET 1867, *The History of Israel*, I, London).

Exum, J Cheryl,

1993 "Who's Afraid of 'The Endangered Ancestress'", *The New Literary Criticism and the Hebrew Bible*, Sheffield.

Fernandéz Marcos, N.

2000 *The Septuagint in Context*, Leiden.

Finnegan, R.

1992 *Oral Tradition and Verbal Arts*, London.

Fohrer, G.

1986 *Introduction to the Old Testament*, London (German original 1965, 1st Eng. edn 1968).

Foley, J. M.

1988 *The Theory of Oral Composition: History and Methodology*, Bloomington and Indianapolis.

Frei, H. W.

1974 *The Eclipse of the Biblical Narrative*, London.

Friedman, R. E. and Williamson, H. G. M. (eds)

1987 *The Future of Biblical Studies: The Hebrew Scriptures*, Atlanta.

Frye, N.

1982 *The Great Code. The Bible and Literature*, London.

Gabel, J. B., Wheeler, C. B. and York, A. D.
1996   *The Bible as Literature: An Introduction*, Oxford.
Garrett, D. (ed.)
1996   *The Cambridge Companion to Spinoza*, Cambridge.
Gaster, T. H.
1984   "Myth and Story", in A. Dundes (ed.), 1984: 110-36.
George, J. F. L.
1837   *Mythus und Sage. Versuch einer wissenschaftlichen Entwicklung dieser Begriffe und ihres Verhältnisses zum christlichen Glauben*, Berlin.
Georges, R. A.
1971   "The General Concept of Legend: Some Assumptions to be Reexamined and Reassessed", in W. E. Hand (ed.), 1971: 1-19.
Gerleman, G.
1948   "Synoptic Studies in the O.T.", *Lunds Universitets Årsskrift*, 5: 1-32.
Gibert, P.
1979   *Une théorie de la Légende*, Paris.
Goldziher, I.
1877   *Mythology among the Hebrews and its Historical Development*, London.
Goshen-Gottstein, M.
1989   "Bible et judaïsme", in J-R. Armogathe (ed.), 1989: 33-38.
Gottcent, J. H.
1986   *The Bible: A Literary Study*, Boston.
Greenstein, E. L.
1989   "Theory and Argument in Biblical Criticism", in *Essays on Biblical Method and Translation*, Atlanta: 53-68.
1990   "Biblical Studies in a State", in S. J. D. Cohen and E. L. Greenstein
(eds), *The State of Jewish Studies*, Detroit: 23-46.
Grene, M. and Nails, D. (eds)
1983   *Spinoza and the Sciences*, Dordrecht.
Gressmann, H.
1910   "Sage und Geschichte in den Patriarchenerzählungen", *ZAW* 30: 1-34.
1913   *Mose und seine Zeit. Ein Kommentar zu den Mose-Sagen*, FRLANT 18, Göttingen.

1921   *Die älteste Geschichtsschreibung und Prophetie Israels*, in H.
Gunkel *et al*, SAT, II.1, Göttingen (ET 1991 "The Oldest History Writing
in Israel", in D. M. Gunn (ed.), *Narrative and Novella in Samuel*,
Sheffield: 9-58).
1922   *Die Anfänge Israels (Vol. 2. Mose bis Richter und Ruth)*, SAT 1/2,
Göttingen.
Grimm, J. L. C. and W. C.
1812-15 *Kinder- und Hausmärchen*, 2 vols, Berlin (ET 1884a, tr. and ed.
by M. Hunt, *Grimm's Household Tales*, 2 vols, London).
1816-18 *Deutsche Sagen*, 2 vols, Berlin.
1835   *Deutsche Mythologie*, Göttingen (ET 1883-85 tr. by J.S.
Stalybrass, *Teutonic Mythology*, 4 vols, from the 4th edn, 1875-8, 4 vols.,
Berlin)
Grundtvig, S. (ed.)
1853-76 *Danmarks gamle Folkeviser*, 8 vols, Copenhagen.
Gunkel, H.
1895   *Schöpfung und Chaos in Urzeit und Endzeit*. Göttingen.
1901   *Genesis übersetzt und erklärt*, Göttingen (2nd edn 1902; 3rd edn
1910) (ET of Introduction., 1901 [2nd edn 1964] *The Legends of Genesis*,
New York; ET of the whole work, 1997 *Genesis*, Macon, Georgia).
1917   *Das Märchen im Alten Testament*, Tübingen (ET 1987 *The
Folktale in the Old Testament*, Sheffield).

Hamilton, J.
1849   *The Literary Attractions of the Bible*, London.
Hand, W. D.
1965   "The Status of European and American Legend Study", *Current
Anthropology* 6: 439-46.
Hand, W. D. (ed.)
1971   *American Folk Legend: A Symposium*, Berkeley and London.
Hautala, J.
1954   *Suomalainen kansanrunoudentutkimus*, Helsinki.
1969   *Finnish Folklore Research, 1828-1918*, Helsinki.
Heyne, C. G.
1777   *De origine et causis fabularum Homericarum, Commentationis
Societatis Regiae scientiarum Gottingensis*, NF 8.
1779   *Opuscula Academica*, I. III.
Holbek, B.
1971   "Axel Olrik (1864-1917)", in D. Strömbäck (ed.), 1971: 259-96.
1987   *Interpretation of Fairytales*, Helsinki.
1992   "Introduction", in A. Olrik 1992:xiv-xxviii.

Honko, L.
   1968   "Genre Analysis in Folkloristics and Comparative Religion",
   Temenos 3: 48-66.
   1984   "The Problem of Defining Myth", in A. Dundes (ed.),
   1984: 41-52.
Hultkrantz, Å.
   1960   *General Ethnological Concepts*, Copenhagen
Hurvitz, A.
   1974   "Dating the Priestly Code", *RB* 81: 24-56.
   1983   "Dating the Priestly Source in the Light of the Historical Study of
   Biblical Hebrew a Century after Wellhausen", *ZAW* 100: 88-100.

Iggers, G. G.
   1968   *The German Conception of History*, Middletown, Connecticut.
   1973   "Historicism", in P. P. Wiener (ed. in chief), *Dictionary of the
   History of Ideas*, II, New York: 456-64.

Janzen, J. G.
   1967   "Double Readings in the Text of Jeremiah", *HTR* 60: 433-47.
Josipovici, G.
   1988   *The Book of God. A Response to the Bible*, London.

Kalevala
   1849   E. Lönnrot (ed.), 2nd edn, Helsinki.
Kirkpatrick, P.
   1988   *The Old Testament and Folklore Study*, Sheffield.
Klatt, W.
   1969   *Hermann Gunkel*, Göttingen.
Klever, W. N. A.
   1996   "Spinoza's Life and Works", in D. Garrett (ed.), 1996: 13-60.
Knierim, R.
   1985   "Criticism of Literary Features, Form, Tradition, and Redaction",
   in D. A. Knight and G. M. Tucker (eds), 1985: 123-65.
Knight, D. A.
   1975   *Rediscovering the Traditions of Israel*, Missoula, Montana.
   1982   "Wellhausen and the Interpretation of Israel's Literature",
   Semeia 25: 21-36.
Knight, D. A. and Tucker, G. M. (eds)
   1985   *The Hebrew Bible and its Modern Interpreters*, Chico, California.

Koch, K.
1964 *Was ist Formgeschichte? Neue Wege der Bibelexegese,* Neukirchen. (ET 1969 *The Growth of the Biblical Tradition. The Form-Critical Method,* London).

Kraus, H-J.
1969 *Geschichte der historisch-kritischen Erforschung des Alten Testaments,* Neukirchen-Vluyn.

Krohn, J.
1885 *Suomalaisen kirjallisuuden historia I. Kalevala i. Kauno-tieteellinen katsahdus Kalevalaan,* Helsinki.
1888 *Kalevalan toisinnot (Les Variantes de Kalevala). Suomen kansallis-epoksen ainekset,* Helsinki.

Krohn, K.
1888 *Tutkimuksia suomalaisten kansansatujen alalta. I. Viekkaamman suhde väkevämpäänsä, ketunseikoissa kuvattuna,* Helsinki.
1903-10 *Kalevalan runojen historia,* 7 vols, Helsinki.
1918 *Kalevalan kysymyksiä,* I, Helsinki.
1969 *Folklore Methodology,* Austin (tr. from 1926, *Die folkloristische Arbeitsmethode,* Oslo).

Kuenen, A.
1885 *An Historico-critical Inquiry into the Origin and Composition of the Hexateuch,* London.

Kugel, J.
1981 "On the Bible and Literary Criticism", *Prooftexts* 1: 217-36.
1982 "James Kugel Responds", *Prooftexts* 2: 328-332.

Kuhn, T. S.
1969 *The Structure of Scientific Revolutions,* Chicago (2nd, enlarged edn).

Kroeber, A. L.
1917 "The Superorganic", *American Anthropologist* 19: 163-213.

Kutsch, E.
1977 "Die Paradieserzählung Genesis 2-3 und ihre Verfasser", in G. Braulik (ed.), *Studien zum Pentateuch,* Vienna: 9-24.

La Peyrére, I.
1656 *Men Before Adam,* London.

Lagrée, J.
1992 "Irrationality With or Without Reason", in J. E. Force and R. H. Popkin (eds), *The Books of Nature and Scripture,* Dordrecht: 25-38.

Lang, A.
    1884a *Custom and Myth*, London.
    1884b "Introduction", in J. and W. Grimm 1884a:xi-lxx.
    1887 *Myth, Ritual and Religion*, 2 vols, London.
Liestøl, K.
    1930 *The Origin of the Icelandic Family Sagas* (tr. from 1929, *Upphavet til den islandske ættesaga.*)
Lods, A.
    1924a "Astruc et la critique biblique de son temps", *RHPR* 4: 109-39
    1924b "Astruc et la critique biblique de son temps", *RHPR* 4: 201-27
Longman, T.
    1987 *Literary Approaches to Biblical Interpretation*, Leicester.
Lowth, R.
    1787 *Lectures on the Sacred Poetry of the Hebrews*, 2 vols, London (Tr. from 1753, *De Sacra Poesi Hebraeorum Praelectiones*, Oxford).

Mandelbaum, M.
    1971 *History, Man, & Reason*, Baltimore and London.
Maull, N.
    1986 "Spinoza in the Century of Science", in M. Grene and D. Nails (eds), 1986: 3-13.
Miller, J. H.
    1982 *Fiction and Repetition: Seven English Novels*, Oxford.
Moe, M.
    1914 "Episke Grundlove", *Edda* 2: 1-16, 233-49.
    1915 "Episke Grundlove", *Edda* 4: 85-126.
    1917 "Episke Grundlove", *Edda* 7: 72-88.
Moreau, P-R.
    1994 "Spinoza's Reception and Influence", in D. Garrett (ed.), 1996: 408-33.
Morgenstern, J.
    1927 "The Oldest Document of the Hexateuch", *HUCA* 4: 1-138.
Moulton, R. G. *et al*
    1899 *The Bible as Literature*, London.
Mowinckel, S.
    1916 *Statholderen Nehemia. Studier til den jödiske menighets historie og litteratur*, Kristiania (Oslo).
    1937 *The Two Sources of the Predeuteronomic Primeval History (JE) in Gen. 1-11*, Oslo.
    1946 *Prophecy and Tradition. The Prophetic Books in the Light of the Study of the Growth and History of the Tradition*, Oslo.

Müller, F. M.
　1868　*Chips from a German Workshop*, 2 vols, London.
　1892　*Anthropological Religion*, London.
Myres, J. L.
　1958　*Homer and His Critics*, London.

Nicholson, E. W.
　1967　*Deuteronomy and Tradition*, Oxford.
　1998　*The Pentateuch in the Twentieth Century*, Oxford.
Niditch, S.
　1993　*Folklore and the Hebrew Bible*, Minneapolis.
　1996　*Oral World and Written Word*, Louisville.
Nielsen, E.
　1954　*Oral Tradition. A Modern Problem in Old Testament Introduction*, London.
　1983　*Law, History and Tradition; Selected Essays*, Copenhagen.
North, C. R.
　1961　"Pentateuchal Criticism", in H. H. Rowley (ed.), *The Old Testament and Modern Study*, Oxford: 48-83.
Norton, D.
　1993　*A History of the Bible as Literature*, 2 vols, Cambridge.
Noth, M.
　1948　*Überlieferungsgeschichte des Pentateuch*, Stuttgart (ET 1981, *A History of Pentateuchal Traditions*, Chico, California).
Nowack, W.
　1902　*Richter, Ruth und Bücher Samuelis*, Göttingen.
Nyberg, H. S.
　1935　*Studien zum Hoseabuche. Zugleich ein Beitrag zur Klärung des Problem der alttestamentlichen Textkritik*, UUÅ 1935:6.
　1947　"Korah's uppror (Num. 16f.). Ett bidrag till frågan om traditionshistorisk metod", *SEÅ* 12: 230-52.

Oden, R. A.
　1987a　*The Bible without Theology*, San Fransisco.
　1987b　"Intellectual History and the Study of the Bible" in R. E. Friedman and H. G. M. Williamson (eds), 1987: 1-18.
O'Doherty, E.
　1953　"The *Conjectures* of Jean Astruc, 1753", *CBQ* 15:300-304.
Olrik, A.
　1892-4　*Kilderne til Sakses Oldhistorie*, 2 vols, Copenhagen.

1903 *Danmarks heltedigtning. En oltidsstudie*, I, Copenhagen (ET 1919, *The Heroic Legends of Denmark*, New York).
1904 "Kong Lindorm", *Danske Studier* 1:1-34.
1905 "Tordenguden og hans Dreng", Danske Studier 2:129-46.
1909 "Epische Gesetze der Volksdichtung", *Zeitschrift für Deutsches Altertum und Deutsche Literatur* 51:1-12 (ET 1965, "Epic Laws of Folk Narrative", in A. Dundes [ed.], 1965:129-41).
1915 *Personal Impressions of Moltke Moe*, Helsinki.
1992 *Principles for Oral Narrative Research*, Bloomington, Indiana (Tr. from 1921, *Nogle Grundsætninger for Sagnforskning*, Copenhagen).
Olrik, A. (ed.)
1899 *Danske Folkeviser i Udvalg*, I, Copenhagen.

Parry, M. and Parry, A. (ed).
1971 *The Making of Homeric Verse*, Oxford.
Parry, A.
1971 "Introduction", in M. Parry and A. Parry (ed.), 1971:ix-lxii.
Pedersen, J.
1931 "Die Auffassung vom Alten Testament", *ZAW* 49:161-81.
1940 *Israel: Its Life and Culture*, London.
Pentikäinen, J.
1971 "Julius and Kaarle Krohn (1835-1888 resp. 1863-1933)", in D. Strömbäck (ed.), 1971:11-33.
1972 "Depth Research", *AEASH* 21:127-151.
1978 *Oral Repertoire and World View: An Anthropological Study of Marina Takalo's Life History*, Helsinki.
Pettazzoni, R.
1984 "The Truth of Myth", in A. Dundes (ed.), 1984:98-109.
Perlitt, L.
1965 *Vatke und Wellhausen. Geschichtsphilosophische Voraussetzungen und historiographische Motive für die Darstellung der Religion und Geschichte Israels durch Wilhelm Vatke und Julius Wellhausen*, BZAW, Berlin.
Pfeiffer, Robert H.
1930 "A Non-Israelitic Source of the Book of Genesis", *ZAW* 48: 66-73.
Pfeiffer, Rudolph
1976 *History of Classical Scholarship: From 1300 to 1850*, Oxford.
Piø, I.
1971 "Svend Grundtvig (1824-1883)", in D. Strömbäck (ed), 1971: 189-224.

Polzin, R.
1993   *Moses and the Deuteronomist*, Bloomington and Indianapolis.
Pomorska, K.
1971   "Russian Formalism in Retrospect", in L. Matejka and K.
Pomorska (eds), *Readings in Russian Poetics: Formalist and Structuralist Views*, Cambridge, MA: 273-80.
Popkin, R. H.
1987   *Isaac La Peyrère (1596-1676): His Life, Work and Influence*, Leiden.
1996   "Spinoza and Bible Scholarship", in D. Garrett (ed.), 1996: 383-407.
Preminger, A. and Brogan, T. V. F.
1993   *The New Princeton Encyclopedia of Poetry and Poetics*, Princeton.
Procksch, O.
1906   *Das nordhebräischen Sagenbuche. Die Elohimquelle*, Leipzig.

Rad, G. von
1934   *Die Priesterschrift im Hexateuch literarisch untersucht und theologisch gewertet*, BWANT IV, Stuttgart.
1938   "Das formgeschichtliche Problem des Hexateuch", in *Gesammelte Studien zum Alten Testament,* TBAT 8, Munich, 1958 (ET 1966, *The Problem of the Hexateuch and Other Essays*, Edinburgh and London: 1-78).
1972   *Genesis*, London (tr. from 1958, *Das erste Buch Mose, Genesis*, Göttingen.
Rashkow, I. N.
1993   "Intertextuality and Transferance: A Reader in/of Genesis 12:10-20 and 20:1-18", *The Phallacy of Genesis*, Louisville, Kentucky.
Rausmaa, P-L.
1971   "Antti Aarne (1867-1925)", in Strömbäck 1971:35-43.
Reedy, G.
1983   *The Bible and Reason: Anglicans and Scripture in Late Seventeenth Century England*, Philadelphia.
Rendtorff, R.
1990   *The Problem of the Process of Transmission in the Pentateuch*, Sheffield (tr. from 1977, *Das überlieferungsgeschichtliche Problem des Pentateuch*, Berlin).
Rogerson, J. W.
1974   *Myth in the Old Testament Interpretation*, Berlin.
1978   *Anthropology and the Old Testament*, Oxford.
1987   "Introduction" in H. Gunkel 1987: 13-8.

Sandmel, S.
    1961   "The Haggada Within Scripture", *JBL* 80: 105-22.
    1978   *The Hebrew Scriptures*, New York.
Sandys-Wunsch, J.
    1981   "Spinoza – the First Biblical Theologian", *ZAW* 93: 327-41.
Savan, D.
    1983   "Spinoza: Scientist and Theorist of Scientific Method", in M.
    Grene and D. Nails (eds), 1986: 95-123.
Scholtz, G.
    1995   "The Notion of Historicism and 19th Century Theology", in H. G.
    Reventlow and W. Farmer (eds), *Biblical Studies and the Shifting
    Paradigms*, 1850-1914, Sheffield.
Schulz, A.
    1908   *Doppelberichte im Pentateuch. Ein Beitrag zur Einleitung in das
    alte Testament*, Berlin.
Scruton, R.
    1995   *A Short History of Modern Philosophy*, London.
Sebeok, T. A. (ed.)
    1965   *Myth: A Symposium*, London.
Segal, M. H.
    1965   *The Pentateuch. Its Composition and its Authorship, and Other
    Biblical Studies*, Jerusalem.
Smend, R.
    1982   "Julius Wellhausen and His Prolegomena to the History of Israel",
    Semeia 25: 1-20.
Simon, R.
    1678   *Histoire critique du Vieux Testament*, Paris (ET 1682, *A Critical
    History of the Old Testament*, London).
Simpson, C. A.
    1948   *The Early Traditions of Israel: A Critical Analysis of the Pre-
    Deuteronomic Narrative of the Hexateuch*, Oxford.
Sötér, I.
    1970   "The Dilemma of Literary Science", *NLH* 2: 85-100.
Spencer, H.
    1876   *The Principles of Sociology*, vol. I, London.
Spinoza, B.
    1670   *Tractatus Theologico-Politicus, Continens Dissertationes aliquot,
    quibus ostenditur Libertatem Philosophandi non tantum salva Pietate, &
    Reipublicae Pace posse concedi: sed eandem nisi cum Pace Reipublicae,
    ipsaque Pietate tolli non posse*, Hamburg. (ET 1862, *Tractatus
    Theologico-Politicus: A Critical Inquiry into the History, Purpose, and*

Authenticity of the Hebrew Scriptures; with the Right to Free Thought and Free Discussion Asserted, and Shown to be not only Consistent but Necessarily Bound up With True Piety and Good Government, London).
(ET 1883, *Tractatus Theologico-Politicus* etc, London).
Steinthal, H.
1868   "Das Epos", *Zeitschrift für Völkerpsychologie und Sprachwissenschaft* 5:1-57.
1877   "The Legend of Samson", in I. Goldziher 1877: 392-446.
Strauss, L.
1965   *Spinoza's Critique of Religion*, New York.
1973   *Persecution and the Art of Writing*, Westport, Connecticut.
Strömbäck, D.
1971   "Moltke Moe (1859-1913)", in D. Strömbäck (ed), 1971: 339-51.
Strömbäck, D. *et al* (eds.)
1971   *Leading Folklorists of the North*, Oslo.
Sveinsson, E. O.
1958   *Dating the Icelandic Sagas*, London.
1971   *Njals Saga: A Literary Masterpiece*, Lincoln, Nebraska.
Sykes, N.
1976   "The Religion of Protestants", in S. L. Greenslade (ed.), *The Cambridge History of the Bible*, III, Cambridge: 175-98.

Talmon, S.
1960   "Double Readings in the Massoretic Text", *Textus* 1:144-184.
1961   "Synonymous Readings in the Textual Traditions of the Old Testament", *Scripta Hierosolymita* 8:335-385.
1962   "The Three Scrolls of the Law that Were Found in the Temple Court", *Textus* 2:14-27.
1964   "Aspects of the Textual Transmission of the Bible in the Light of Qumran Manuscripts", *Textus* 4:95-132.
1975   "The Textual Study of the Bible—A New Outlook", in F. M. Cross and S. Talmon (eds.), *Qumran and the History of the Biblical Text*, Cambridge and London.
1976   "Conflate Readings", *The Interpreter's Dictionary of the Bible. Supplementary Volume*, 1976: 14-27.
1986   "'In Those Days There was no מלך in Israel' – Judges 18-21", in *King, Cult and Calender in Ancient Israel*, Jerusalem: 39-52.
Thompson, S.
1946   *The Folktale*, London.
Thompson, S. (ed.)
1953   *Four Symposia on Folklore*, London.

Thoms, W., using A. Merton
    1846   "Folk-lore", *Athenaeum* 982: 862-3.
Tigay, J. H. (ed.)
    1985   *Empirical Models for Biblical Criticism*, Philadelphia.
Todorov, T.
    1981   *Introduction to Poetics*, Brighton.
    1990   *Genres in Discourse*, Cambridge.
Tsevat, M.
    1975   "Common Sense and Hypothesis in Old Testament Study", VTS
    28: 217-30.

Utley, F. L.
    1965   "Folk Literature: An Operational Definition", in A. Dundes (ed.)
    1965: 7-24.
    1969   "Oral Genres as Bridge to Written Literature", *Genre* 2: 91-103.

Van Seters, J.
    1975   *Abraham in History and Tradition*, New Haven and London.
    1983   *In Search of History. Historiography in the Ancient World and the
    Origins of Biblical History*, London.
    1992   *Prologue to History. The Yahwist as Historian in Genesis*, Zürich.
    1994   *The Life of Moses. The Yahwist as Historian in Exodus-Numbers*,
    Kampen, The Netherlands.
de Vaux, R.
    1953   "A propos du second centenaire d Astruc: réflexions sur létat
    actuel de la critique du Pentateuque", VTS 1: 182-98.
Voigt, V.
    1974   "Towards a Theory of Theory of Genres in Folklore", in L. Dégh,
    H. Glassie and F. J. Oinas (eds), *Folklore Today A Festschrift for Richard
    M.Dorson*, Bloomington, Indiana.
    1980   "On the Communicative System of Folklore Genres", in L. Honko
    and V. Voigt, *Genre, Structure and Reproduction in Oral Literature*,
    Budapest.
Volz, O.
    1923   "Eissfeldt, Otto: *Hexateuch Synopse*", *Theologische
    Literaturzeitung* 19: 389-91.
Volz, O. and Rudolph, W.
    1933   *Der Elohist als Erzähler. Ein Irrweg der Pentateuchkritik?*,
    BZAW, Berlin.

Warner, S. M.
1979 "Primitive Saga Men", *VT* 29: 325-35.
Weingreen, J.
1982 *Introduction to the Critical Study of the Text of the Hebrew Bible*, Oxford.
Weisinger, H.
1965 "Before Myth", *JFI* 2: 120-31.
Weiss, M.
1984 T*he Bible from Within: The Method of Total Interpretation*, Jerusalem.
Welch, A. C.
1924 *The Code of Deuteronomy*, London.
1932 *Deuteronomy: The Framework of the Code*, Oxford.
Wellek, R. and Warren, A.
1956 *Theory of Literature*, New York.
Wellhausen, J.
1876-7 "Die Composition des Hexateuchs", JDT 21: 392-450, 531-602; 22: 407-79.
1878 *Geschichte Israels, I*, Berlin.
1883 *Prolegomena zur Geschichte Israels*, (2nd edn of *Geschichte Israels, I*, 1978) Berlin (ET 1885, *Prolegomena to the History of Israel*, Edinburgh).
Wenham, G. J.
1978 "The Coherence of the Flood Narrative", *VT* 28: 336-48.
Westermann, C.
1982 *Elements of Old Testament Theology*, Atlanta (tr. from 1978 *Theologie des Alten Testaments in Grundzugen*, Göttingen).
de Wette, W. M. L.
1833 *Lehrbuch der historisch-kritischen Einleitung in die Bibel Alten und Neuen Testamentes*, Berlin (4th, verbesserte u. vermehrte ed.) (ET 1843, *A Critical and Historical Introduction to the Canonical Scriptures of the Old Testament*, 2 vols, tr. and enlarged by Theodor Parker, Boston).
Whybray, R. N.
1987 *The Making of the Pentateuch*, Sheffield.
Widengren, G.
1948 *Literary and Psychological Aspects of the Hebrew Prophets*, UUÅ 1948: 10.
Wilamowitz-Moellendorff, U. von
1982 *History of Classical Scholarship*, Liverpool.

Wild, J.
    1958   "Introduction", in J. Wild (ed.), *Spinoza, Selections*, New York:
    xi-lix.
Winnett, F. V.
    1949   *The Mosaic Tradition*, Toronto.
    1965   "Re-examining the Foundations", *JBL* 84: 1-19.
Witter, H. B.
    1711   *Jura Israelitarum in Palaestinam*, Hildesiae.
Wolf, F. A.
    1795   *Prolegomena ad Homerum*, Halle.
Woodbridge, J. D.
    1988   "German Responses to the Biblical Critic Richard Simon: from
    Leibniz to J. S. Semler", in H. G. Reventlow, W. Sparn and J. D.
    Woodbridge (eds), *Historische Kritik und biblischer Kanon in der
    deutschen   Aufklärung*, Wiesbaden.
    1989   "Richard Simon: Le pére de la critique biblique", in J-R.
    Armogathe (ed.), 1989: 193-206.

Yovel, Y.
    1989   *Spinoza and Other Heretics*. vol. 2: *The Adventures of Immanence*,
    Princeton.

Zac, S.
    1965   *Spinoza et l'interprétation de l'écriture*, Paris.

Index 1: Biblical References

Index 2: Authors

Index 3: Subjects

Folklore studies 3, 5, 24, 41, 47, 75, 76, 115-8, 126, 130-3, 141, 157-61, 167, 177, 194, 195

Genres: origin of 119-20, 122, 124, 130, 136; definition of 120-2, 125-32, 134, 143, 159-60; development of 122-6, 160; debate about orality / literariness 116, 126-7, 133, 143; oral 116, 126, 131; literary 119; spheres of interest 119-20, 130; historical reliability 120; study of 116, 121, 126;

History, as genre 133
Homeric: epics 5, 44, 102, 111, 118; studies 64, 102, 118, 177

Kalevala 118, 142, 144-6, 153
Kalevipoeg 118
Kanteletar 144
King Arthur legend 118
Koran 5, 44

Laws, of composition and transformation: application 149, 152-6; application to both oral and written texts 152, 156; application to now written texts 133;
Aarne, A. 149, 156;
Anderson, W. 149;
Grundtvig, S. 142-3;
Gunkel, H. 134-7, 140-1, 149-51, 160;
Koch, K. 46-9;
Krohn, J. 147-8, 150;
Krohn K. 148;

Moe, M. 142-4;
Nielsen, E. 45-6;
Olrik, A. 137-43, 149-58;
Sydow, W. C. 149;
Van Seters, J. 46, 49, 154-7;
Aristotle's *Poetics* 52; oral laws in general 54, 151, 157-8; universality of 24, 27, 61, 89, 115-6, 126, 134, 136-7, 142, 150-1, 153, 157-8, 194
Legende 120, 129
Literary criticism, *see* source criticism *or* new literary criticism

Märchen-folktale 47, 53-4, 56, 118-133, 138, 143-152, 155-160, 167
Masoretic Text 65, 179, 180, 184
Model, compositional: "archivist-historian" 3, 84, 86, 91-3; "biological" 85; "historian" 2, 84-6, 90, 93-103, 193; "house building" 85; "literary artist" 2, 60, 66, 84-6, 103-8, 114, 193, 196; "midrashic" 2; "nature" 2, 84, 86-95; "theological intention" 2
Myth 20-1, 97, 116-133, 138, 144, 159, 160

Narrative: role of genre in development of 118; oral, now in written form, 133
New literary criticism 3, 55, 63, 64, 67, 71, 85, 98, 103-7

Orality, detectability of 116, 134, 150, 152-7

Oral / written interface 151, 161
Oral performance 150, 153
Oral tradition: inaccessibility 15,
    102, 117; original unit 135;
    reliability: 35-6, 49, 118-20;
    unreliability 23
Oral verbal art 10, 25, 120, 130,
    135-6, 141-4

Poetics 3, 76, 78, 104, 108, 109,
    114, 154, 167, 194, 196

Rig-Veda 118

Saga, Scandinavian 5, 45, 54, 152
Sage-legend 23-5, 28-30, 47, 117-
    142, 150, 152, 160, 188
Sagn 138, 142, 143
Samaritan Pentateuch 49, 179-81
Septuagint 49, 179, 180, 183, 185
Source criticism 3, 12, 14, 16, 30,
    34-6, 39, 46, 49, 50, 55, 64, 73,
    75, 76, 84-6, 94, 98, 103, 108,
    116, 133, 141, 182, 192, 193

Textual criticism 4, 65, 178, 183,
    188
Tenet, critical: "duplication
    indicates literary artistry" 76,
    83, 84, 86, 104, 107;
    "duplication indicates orality"
    3, 75, 85; "duplication indicates
    sources" 4, 75, 76, 83, 84, 86
Tradition-historical criticism 2, 3,
    23, 25, 27, 28, 30-2, 34-7, 41,
    42, 44, 46, 49, 54, 61, 70, 75,
    78, 103, 115, 150, 160, 186,
    192, 194, 196

Variant: textual 4, 46, 163, 177-
    80, 188-91, 195; double reading
    179, 180-91; synonymous
    reading 179-83, 186, 188, 190,
    191; conflate reading 183;
    literary, in technical sense 177;
    see double narratives

Yahwist 18, 20, 23, 29, 31-2, 49

Theology at de Gruyter

John Pairman Brown

Israel und Hellas III

The Legacy of Iranian Imperialism and the Individual

With Cumulative Indexes to Volumes I–III

2001. 23 x 15,5 cm. XXXII, 546 pages. Cloth.
DM 248,– /S 126,80 /öS 1.810,–* /sFr 213,– /approx. US$ 124.00
• ISBN 3-11-016882-0
(Beihefte zur Zeitschrift für die alttestamentliche Wissenschaft 299)

also available:

Israel und Hellas II

Sacred Institutions with Roman Counterparts

2000. 23 x 15,5 cm. XXVIII, 414 pages. Cloth.
DM 198,– /S 101,24 /öS 1.445,–* /sFr 170,– /approx. US$ 99.00
• ISBN 3-11-016434-5
(Beihefte zur Zeitschrift für die alttestamentliche Wissenschaft 276)

Israel und Hellas I

1995. 23 x 15,5 cm. XXII, 407 pages. Cloth.
DM 189,– /S 96,63 /öS 1.380,–* /sFr 163,– /approx US$ 95.00
• ISBN 3-11-014233-3
(Beihefte zur Zeitschrift für die alttestamentliche Wissenschaft 231)

Prices are subject to change / *recommended retail price

WALTER DE GRUYTER GMBH & CO. KG
Genthiner Straße 13 · 10785 Berlin
Telefon +49-(0)30-2 60 05-0
Fax +49-(0)30-2 60 05-251
www.deGruyter.de

W
DE
G

de Gruyter
Berlin · New York

Theology at de Gruyter

Etan Levine
Heaven and Earth, Law and Love
Studies in Biblical Thought

2000. 23 x 15,5 cm. XI, 242 pages. Cloth.
DM 168,– /S 85,90 /öS 1.226,–* /sFr 144,– /approx. US$ 84.00
• ISBN 3-11-016952-5
(Beihefte zur Zeitschrift für die alttestamentliche Wissenschaft 303)

Jacqueline E. Lapsley
Can These Bones Live?
The Problem of the Moral Self in the Book of Ezekiel

2000. 23 x 15,5 cm. XI, 208 pages. Cloth.
DM 158,– /S 80,78 /öS 1.153,–* /sFr 136,– /approx. US$ 79.00
• ISBN 3-11-016997-5
(Beihefte zur Zeitschrift für die alttestamentliche Wissenschaft 301)

Todd A. Gooch
The Numinous and Modernity
An Interpretation of Rudolf Otto's
Philosophy of Religion

2000. 23 x 15,5 cm. VIII, 233 pages. Cloth.
DM 168,– /S 85,90 /öS 1.226,–* /sFr 144,– /approx. US$ 84.00
• ISBN 3-11-016799-9
(Beihefte zur Zeitschrift für die alttestamentliche Wissenschaft 293)

Prices are subject to change / *recommended retail price

WALTER DE GRUYTER GMBH & CO. KG
Genthiner Straße 13 · 10785 Berlin
Telefon +49-(0)30-2 60 05-0
Fax +49-(0)30-2 60 05-251
www.deGruyter.de

W
DE
G

de Gruyter
Berlin · New York